# Religion in secularizing society

# Religion in secularizing society

## The European's religion at the end of the 20th century

edited by

Loek Halman
Ole Riis

*To my friend Jim, the President of the SISR, with all good wishes*

*April 6R, 2000*

Tilburg University Press 1999

The European Values Studies is a series based on a large-scale, cross-national and longitudinal research program. The program was initiated by the European Value Systems Study Group (EVSSG) in the late 1970s, by an informal grouping of academics. These days it is supervised by a foundation, using the (abbreviated) name of the group (EVS). The study group surveyed basic social, cultural, political, moral, and religious values held by the populations of ten Western European countries. The first surveys were conducted in 1981. Researchers from other countries joined the project, which resulted in a 26-nation data set. In 1990, the study was replicated and extended to other countries. The study now encompasses all European countries, including those in Central and Eastern Europe. This series is based on the survey data collected in the project.

Recent volumes include:

*The Individualizing Society* (1993; 1994)
Peter Ester, Loek Halman and Ruud de Moor (eds.)

*Values in Western Societies* (1995)
Ruud de Moor (ed.)

*Political Value Change in Western Democracies* (1996)
Loek Halman and Neil Nevitte (eds.)

*From Cold War to Cold Peace* (1997)
Peter Ester, Loek Halman & Vladimir Rukavishnikov

© 1999 Tilburg University Press

ISBN 90-361-9740-6

# Series editors' preface

This book is the fifth volume in a series on the European Values Project published by Tilburg University Press. The main purpose of this series is to present and distribute the main findings from this large-scale comparative research project on fundamental values in Western societies. The publications are all or partly based on survey data gathered within the framework of what is known as the *European Values Study* (*EVS*). This cross-national European project was an initiative of Professor Jan Kerkhofs of the Catholic University of Louvain (Belgium) and Professor Ruud de Moor of Tilburg University (Netherlands). At the end of the 1970s, they established the *European Value Systems Study Group* (*EVSSG*), a small group of mainly social and political scientists. Their aim was to undertake empirical research on fundamental value patterns in Western Europe. The group succeeded in conducting a large-scale values survey in all countries of the European Community (EC) plus Spain, in 1981. The study aroused interest in many other European and non-European countries, where colleagues and research institutions joined the project and used the original *EVS* questionnaire. In this way, comparable surveys became available outside Western Europe, *i.e.* in the Scandinavian countries, Hungary, Malta, the Soviet Union, the United States, Canada, Chili, Argentina, Japan, South Africa, Australia, and New Zealand. Apart from a large series of books on the findings for individual countries, several cross-national comparative studies were published by, e.g., J. Stoetzel (*Les Valeurs du Temps Présent: Une Enquête Européenne*, Paris: Presses Universitaires de France, 1983), S. Harding, D. Phillips & M. Fogarty (*Contrasting Values in Western Europe: Unity, Diversity & Change*, London: MacMillan, 1986), L. Halman, F. Heunks, R. de Moor & H. Zanders (*Traditie, Secularisatie en Individualisering*, Tilburg: Tilburg University Press, 1987), L. Halman (*Waarden in de Westerse Wereld*, Tilburg: Tilburg University Press, 1991).

In order to investigate changes in values, a replication study was necessary. A second wave of surveys was fielded in 1990 again in all EC countries (minus Greece), as well as in Hungary, the Czech Republic, Slovakia, the Scandinavian countries, South Africa, Japan, the United States, Canada. In Austria, Switzerland, Poland, Bulgaria, the Baltic States, and the former German Democratic Republic the survey was conducted for the first time by associated research teams. Other teams conducted the survey in their own countries on their own initiative, using the *EVS* questionnaire. Professor Ronald Inglehart from the University of Michigan, Ann Arbor, has been very active and successful in getting the survey done in countries other than those participating in the European Values Study (see P. Ester, L. Halman & R. de Moor, 1994: vii-viii). This world-wide project is called the *World Values Survey* (*WVS*) (J. Díez Nicolás & R. Inglehart, *Tendencias Mundiales de Cambio en Los Valores Sociales y Políticos*, Madrid: Fundesco, 1994; R. Inglehart, *Modernization and Postmodernization*, Princeton: Princeton University Press, 1997).

For results and more information on the *EVS* 1990 study, we can refer to many publications, for instance, D. Barker, L. Halman & A. Vloet (*The European Values Study 1981-1990; Summary Report*, London: Gordon Cook Foundation, 1992), S. Ashford & N. Timms (*What Europe thinks; A Study of Western European Values*, Aldershot: Dartmouth, 1992), P. Ester, L. Halman & R. de Moor (eds.) (*The Individualizing Society*, Tilburg: Tilburg University Press, 1994), L. Halman & A. Vloet (*Measuring and Comparing Values in 16 Countries of the Western World*, Tilburg: WORC, 1994), R. de Moor (ed.) (*Values in Western Societies*, Tilburg: Tilburg University Press, 1995). An international source book is available through Michigan University Press (R. Inglehart, M. Basañez & A. Moreno, *Human Values and Beliefs*, Ann Arbor: The University of Michigan Press, 1998). For more information on the European Values project and recent developments, we refer you to EVS on the Internet (http://cwis.kub.nl/~fsw_2/worc/research/evs/evs.htm).

The cross-national analyses of Europe's patterns of religious and moral orientations presented in this book are all based on the 1990 European Values Study survey data and some use both 1981 and 1990 data. Use is also made of more recent data gathered in 1995/1997 within the framework of the World Values Study, directed by Ron Inglehart, as well as data from a recent pilot survey in Japan. The contributions in this book are not written within a common theoretical framework, but from different theoretical perspectives and scientific backgrounds and interests. However, a majority of the chapters focus on the Catholic and Protestant divide in Europe. All in all, the contributions in this book show (parts) of the religious and moral culture in contemporary secularizing societies.

As mentioned above, this is the fifth volume in the Tilburg University Press series on European Values Studies. The first book is *The Individualizing Society; Value Change in Europe and North America* (1993; 1994) edited by Peter Ester, Loek Halman & Ruud de Moor. The second book is *Values in Western Societies* (1995) edited by Ruud de Moor, and the third book is titled *Political Value Change in Western Democracies* (1996) edited by Loek Halman & Neil Nevitte. The fourth volume on a comparison of Russian and European values is written by Peter Ester, Loek Halman and Vladimir Rukavishnikov: *From Cold War to Cold Peace* (1997). This book has also been published in Russian (in 1998).

Loek Halman

# Acknowledgments

This book could not have been written without the help and collaboration of several people. First of all, we would like to thank all those who have accepted our invitation to prepare a chapter for this book. The editors deliberately avoided imposing one single analytic schema on the investigators, and the variation in focus and analytic strategies found in this volume reflects that editorial decision. Instead our editorial goal has been to have a light touch, and to limit ourselves to eliminating repetition and incompatibilities and to stress the commonalities and bridging features. We thank the authors not only for their contributions but also for their patience with the final release of this book.

We would like to express our thanks to the Linguistics Department of Tilburg University for correcting our English. We also thank *WORC*, the Work & Organization Research Centre of the Faculty of Social Sciences of Tilburg University, for facilitating this project in various ways.

Finally, we are grateful to *Tilburg University Press* for being so gracious when we failed to meet several deadlines.

Tilburg/Århus
November 1999

Loek Halman
Ole Riis

# Contents

**Chapter One. Contemporary European Discourse on Religion
and Morality**     1
Loek Halman & Ole Riis

1   Introduction     1
2   Some preliminary observations     5
   2.1   Religiousness     5
   2.2   Morality     10
3   Plan of the book     11
References     16


**Chapter Two. Religion and the Spirit of Capitalism in Modern Europe**     19
Ole Riis

1   Introduction     19
2   The historical background of the European divide     20
3   The Protestant Ethic thesis revisited     21
4   Survey analyses of the Weber thesis     22
5   Hypotheses     23
6   Denominational differences in intrinsic work orientation     25
7   Denominational differences in acquisitiveness     28
8   Denominational differences in individualism     31
9   Modernization and secularization revised     32
10   Conclusions     36
Notes     37
References     39


**Chapter Three. Differential Patterns of Secularization in Europe:
Exploring the Impact of Religion on Social Values**     41
Loek Halman & Thorleif Pettersson

1   Introduction     41
2   Secularization and the impact of religion on social values     43
3   Data, measures and method     50
4   Results     52
5   Discussion     58
Notes     62
References     63

**Chapter Four. Religion and the Family**     67
Karel Dobbelaere, Josette Gevers & Loek Halman

1    Introduction     67
2    Functional differentiation and religion's impact on family issues     68
3    Data, operationalisations and method     71
    3.1    Data     71
    3.2    Operationalisations     71
    3.3    Method     72
4    Results     73
5    Conclusions     78
Notes     80
References     81

**Chapter Five.   Individual Religiosity, Religious Context and Values**
                   **in Europe and North America**     83
Michael Procter & Michael P. Hornsby-Smith

1    Introduction     83
2    Theoretical considerations     85
3    Data sources and measurements     88
    3.1    Data     88
    3.2    Measures of religiosity     89
    3.3    Personal and social values     89
4    Results     90
    4.1    Individual religiosity and religious context     90
    4.2    Church attendance and values     94
5    Discussion and conclusions     97
Notes     99
References     100

**Chapter Six.    Integration into Catholicism and Protestantism in**
                  **Europe: The Impact on Moral and Political Values**     105
Pierre Bréchon

1    Introduction     105
2    Religion, morality, and political attitudes     106
3    Denominational integration     108
4    Religion and ethical attitudes     110
    4.1    Morality of principles     110
    4.2    Moral and civic rigourism     110
    4.3    Family values     112
    4.4    Degree of integration: Does it matter?     112

5    Religious identities and political attitudes                         114
     5.1   Politicisation, political participation, and post-materialism   114
     5.2   Confidence in institutions                                      115
     5.3   Political orientation and economic options                      116
     5.4   Nationalism, national preference, and exclusion of foreigners   119
6    Conclusions                                                          122
Notes                                                                     126
References                                                                130


**Chapter Seven.    Religion and Social Capital Revisited**              131
Loek Halman & Thorleif Pettersson

1    Introduction                                                         131
2    Social capital and religion                                         132
3    Longitudinal changes in the religious and political cultures        136
4    The link between social capital and religion                        138
5    Measurement of social capital and analytic strategy                140
6    Results                                                             144
7    Conclusions                                                         147
References                                                              149


**Chapter Eight.    Globalization and Patterns of Religious Belief
                    Systems**                                           153
Loek Halman & Thorleif Pettersson

1    Introduction                                                        153
2    Globalization and religion: Some theoretical notions               155
3    Measuring structural globalization                                 159
4    Data and measurement of cultural globalization: Cosmopolitism
     and the globalization of religious belief systems                  163
5    Relations between structural globalization and religious cultural
     globalization                                                      166
6    Conclusions                                                        167
References                                                              170


**Chapter Nine.  Japanese Religiosity and Morals**                      173
Robert Kisala

1    Introduction                                                        173
2    Indicators of secularization                                       174
3    Religiosity                                                         175
4    Religious beliefs                                                   177

| | | |
|---|---|---|
| 5 | Confidence in religion | 178 |
| 6 | Religious pluralism and the future of religion | 181 |
| 7 | Public and private morality | 183 |
| 8 | Asian values | 185 |
| 9 | Conclusions | 186 |
| Notes | | 188 |
| References | | 189 |

**Appendix   Tables Chapter Six**                             191

**About the Authors**                             203

# Figures and tables

## Figures

3.1 A comparative schema for the analysis of the differential impact of the religious factor across regions and the public and private sectors    50

5.1 Boxplot of log *Sexual morality*, by country type and respondent's denomination    93

5.2 Boxplot of log *Honesty*, by country type and respondent's denomination    93

5.3 Boxplot of *Collectivism*, by country type and respondent's denomination    94

5.4 Boxplot of log *Sexual morality*, by frequency of church attendance    95

5.5 Boxplot of log *Honesty*, by frequency of church attendance    96

5.6 Boxplot of log *Collectivism*, by frequency of church attendance    96

8.1 Factor model for structural and cultural globalization    163

9.1 Percent of religious affiliation, by age group    175

9.2 Lack of confidence in religion, by age group    180

9.3 Lack of confidence in religion, by level of education    180

9.4 Religious upbringing, by age group    182

9.5 Think about meaning and purpose of life, by age group    183

## Tables

2.1 Intrinsic work orientation in religious and professional groups    26

2.2 A comparison of some basic values of Catholics, Mainline Protestants and members of free churches    34

3.1 Personal religiosity, church attendance and the impact of national context, measures of secularization    53

3.2 Mean scores for four clusters of countries on church attendance and importance of God and degree of secularization based on church attendance and importance of God    54

3.3 The impact of personal religiosity (importance of God) and church attendance on private and public values    57

4.1 Mean scores on family values among frequent and not frequent church attenders (one-way analysis of variance)    73

4.2 Mean scores on family values of Catholics, Protestants and unchurched people (one-way analysis of variance)    74

| 4.3 | Results from one-way analysis of variance with religious affiliation as between-subjects factor | 75 |
|---|---|---|
| 4.4 | Proportion of variance in family values explained by the 2 X 3 between-subjects design with factors religious affiliation (A) and religious involvement (B) | 76 |
| 4.5 | Mean scores on dependent variables by religious affiliation and religious involvement | 77 |
| 5.1 | Average scale scores by country, Catholic density and respondent's denomination | 91 |
| 5.2 | Mean *log* scores on *Sexual morality* and *Honesty* and mean scores on *Collectivism*, by country type and respondent's denomination | 92 |
| 5.3 | Mean *log* scores on *Sexual morality* and *Honesty* and mean scores on *Collectivism*, by frequency of church attendance | 95 |
| 6.1 | Connection between denominational integration and different beliefs | 108 |
| 6.2 | Distribution of the scale of beliefs according to practise | 109 |
| 6.3 | Percentage of individuals in favour of strict ethics, according to religious affiliation and participation in religious organisations | 113 |
| 6.4 | Percentage of right-wing self-placement (positions 6-10) according to religious affiliation and participation in church organisations | 118 |
| 6.5 | Percentage of individuals with a national preference, or xenophobic attitude, according to religious affiliation and participation in church organisations | 121 |
| 7.1 | Responses to the three indicators of social capital and score on the combination of the three items in Sweden, Germany, Spain and the US | 142 |
| 7.2 | The impact of religiosity, postmaterialism, age, education, income, degree of urbanization and gender on the three components of social capital separately and on social capital as a compound variable | 145 |
| 7.3 | Regression analysis results for Catholics and Protestants in the US and Germany | 146 |
| 8.1 | Population, Gross Domestic Product, and trade balance among 16 OECD countries. Data for 1990 | 159 |
| 8.2 | Number of Radio and TV receivers per 1,000 inhabitants, number of telephones per 10,000 inhabitants, and IT market value as percentage of GDP in 16 OECD countries. | 160 |
| 8.3 | International tourism receipts plus expenditures and import of books and newspapers for 14 OECD countries. Entries as share of GDP. Data for 1990 | 162 |
| 8.4 | Cosmopolitism, religious heterogeneity, and internal and external religious differentiation. Data for 1990 | 165 |

| 8.5 | Relationships between structural globalization and cosmopolitan orientation, religious heterogeneity, religious internal differentiation, and religious external differentiation. | 166 |
| 9.1 | Religiosity indicators group 1, by age group (in %) | 176 |
| 9.2 | Religiosity indicators group 2, by age group | 176 |
| 9.3 | Religious beliefs in Japan and Europe (in %) | 177 |
| 9.4 | Adequacy of religion's response to problems (in %) | 181 |
| 9.5 | Private morality, percent saying behaviour never justified | 184 |
| 9.6 | Public morality, percent saying behaviour never justified | 184 |
| 9.7 | Percent of importance placed on Asian values | 185 |

Chapter One

# Contemporary European Discourses on Religion and Morality

**Loek Halman & Ole Riis**

## 1 INTRODUCTION

The Christian religion has exerted a strong influence on Europe for many centuries. Social values, norms, and ethics in Western Europe have been shaped and controlled by the Christian churches. The Christian heritage is often considered the foundation of a common European identity uniting all European countries and their citizens in our own time. At the same time, it has been recognized that such a common identity has not emerged, and that 'this common heritage has [..] been moulded by a great diversity of contextual factors into a number of subtypes or national variations, some (...) very distinct indeed' (Davie, 1992: 230). An important hindrance to the formation of such a common European 'soul' is found in the historical shadows cast by confessional conflicts and the assumed vast differences between the main religious traditions. Catholic and Protestant cultures have shaped national cultures that persist in contemporary Europe (Therborn, 1995).

Western Europe is often considered the first historical example of thoroughly modernized society, and some commentators still utilize the European experience as a general model. The advancement of empirical science and technology, of industrialization and capitalization, of urbanization and social mobility, of legal bureaucracy, democracy and the nation states contributed substantially to a type of society which many Europeans may see as the paradigm of a modern society. Such a society is characterised by a specific constellation of human agents and social institutions: it is based on a principle of associating autonomous individuals through specific rules. The economic system of the market, the political system of democracy, the cognitive system of scientific observations are in principle based on associating free individuals. The citizens of a modern, industrial, bureaucratic, democratic Europe are supposed to relate to society as autonomous, responsible, reflective entities.

In this type of social setting, religion is supposed to have a declining scope and impact. While the churches formerly had a very broad sphere of influence, which touched political, cultural, societal, economic and scientific issues, the religious field has gradually been confined to a limited range of issues, which are peripheral to the debates on the future development of society. The major issues in this debate are generally determined through 'rational' discourses in the political, economic, and scientific fields. The arguments for leaving out religion as irrelevant to these discourses are either based on a political confrontation, or follow a subtle logic about the functional relevance of various institutions. Secularism is the outcome of the former process, as in France, whereas the latter leads to a more covert policy of secularization. Either way, the authority of the churches has been reduced. Moreover, religious freedom is an important part of democracy, granted by all European constitutions, which implies that people are allowed both freedom of religious association and spiritual freedom. The first freedom grants citizens the right to choose to become a member of a religious organization or to leave it. The second implies that people can select and forge their own religious views, free from the interference of clerical or secular authorities. In popular French terms, the first points to 'religion à la carte' whereas the second refers to 'bricolage'.

The emergence of religious pluralism and voluntarism has led to a disestablishment of churches, which formerly held privileges in a close allegiance with the state apparatus. In a society which was formerly dominated by one religion, religious pluralism implies a relativization of the world view. More answers to the ultimate questions about human existence are available and presented as equally plausible. Traditional authorities in all fields of society have been challenged by the logic of autonomy and voluntarism, but it has special consequences in the religious field, where the final source of truth is supposed to remain beyond human comprehension and discourse. Modern reflective citizens are accustomed to taking their own decisions, in all important spheres of life. Therefore, they also take this for granted in the religious field. One of the reactions of religious authorities has been to warn and protest against processes of modernization. Since membership is voluntarily, members who disagree with such a position may protest against the leadership or even leave the organization. Other religious organizations adapt to the conditions of autonomy and voluntarism, which implies, however, an increased dependence on their membership. Whether churches react in a defensive or adaptive manner, they are put in a situation which is critical when seen from the perspective of their former privileges and taken-for-granted authority.

These discussions are often held under the main title of 'secularization'. As a sociological term, this is often criticized since it refers to several processes at different levels of analysis (Dobbelaere, 1981). Secularization thus may refer to a differentiation between institutional spheres at a macro level; it may refer at a meso level to an 'internal secularization' of religious organizations, as they adapt to the conditions of modern society; or it may refer at a micro level to a lessening degree of commitment among modern people, in the forms of declines in church membership or church allegiance, in accepting prescribed beliefs, in participating in rituals, or in accepting the ethical standards prescribed by religious authorities. The contributions in this book focus especially on the individual level. Therefore, the focus is on the last-mentioned range of issues.

Although it is beyond dispute that the authority of the traditional Christian churches has declined throughout this century in Western Europe, this does not imply that secularization is an unavoidable, necessary, functional feature of modernization. Such an argument has ideological undertones, and several objections could be raised. Firstly, the waning status of traditional churches does not define the whole religious field. The very process of privatization opens the way, in principle, for a rather diffuse range of new types of religion, as argued by Thomas Luckmann (1967), and these may even point to the eventual formation of the 'cult of man', prophesied by Emile Durkheim (1965). Secondly, it is dubious whether the historical experience of Western Europe could be regarded as a general model.

Whereas North American society has in many ways developed in parallel with the European experience, religion forms an exception. The constitution of the United States clearly differentiated the religious from the political field. Despite this differentiation or because of it, the religious field has demonstrated a continued vitality in the United States. The churches do not have any direct influence on the major decisions of society, but all indicators of religious commitment indicate stability or even an increase (Greeley, 1989; Finke & Stark, 1992). Some analysts, as Caplow (1985: 103), even talk about a 'sacralization'. The subject of the present study is not to discuss whether the remaining vitality of religion in the US is due to free, internal competition in the religious field, and whether the decline in commitment to the churches in Western Europe is due to their monopolistic positions, as claimed by spokespersons of 'rational choice theory' (Stark & Bainbridge, 1985; Iannaccone, 1997). The American case is referred to here in order to relativize the European experience. This argument could be underlined further by referring to numerous international instances where religion has re-emerged in the political field, despite the predictions of secularization theorists (Riis, 1998). This point could be amplified even further by noticing that the European experience is hardly uniform. As pointed out by David Martin (1978), the secularization processes follow patterns which are so distinct from each other that a common term is misleading. One important aspect of the present study is therefore to make comparisons between European countries in order to point out their similarities and differences regarding religion.

In pre-modern society, the church and its leaders were institutionalized as the final authority on ethical behaviour, values, and principles. It had the prerogative to define obligatory standards for all members of society. People were expected to conform to those standards, and even internalize them. Otherwise, they could be forced to conform to them. In traditional society religion could thus be seen as 'a moral force... and the fear of God was a motive to enforce the laws of society, which were the laws of morality' (Smith, quoted by Yinger, 1970: 52-53). Therefore, pre-modern society is expected to hold a shared, collective set of norms, based on religion. In a modern, democratic society, acceptance of the norms set by the church is voluntary. Furthermore, the scope of authority of the churches has been narrowed due to the process of differentiation. While 'it is assumed that the various social spheres in traditional society were under the presidency of religion...' (Wilson 1996:

17), modern settings are characterized by competition between specialists representing different institutions 'for areas of control that previously were mainly church prerogatives. While religious institutions still proclaim their definitions of deviance and use some measures of social control, their influence is limited in most modern countries' (McGuire 1987: 222). Whether people accept the moral guidance of their vicars, doctors, psychologists, politicians, or other leaders depends on the degree to which people accept their church as an authority and over what issues. The tendency seems to be for modern people to be less prone to accept the churches as moral authorities, though they may still accept them as advisors on a limited range of moral issues. Morality has become a personal concern, and the final authority is the individual (Crittenden, 1992:78). Modern, democratic society is based on autonomous individuals, and this foundation also covers moral issues. Many commentators have regarded this emphasis on individual autonomy, and the corresponding values of self-fulfilment and self-realization, and concern about personal happiness, as threatening any proclamation of collective norms. The opposite of the obligatory, collective standards of pre-modern society seems to be a dissolution of morality with the spreading of egotism, selfishness, narcissism and hedonism. Even sociological commentators, such as Bellah and his associates (1986), have found it necessary to warn against the lurking dangers of dissolving social commitment and consensus through an increased individualism. Other sociological commentators, such as Habermas (1987) and Giddens (1991) see the increased autonomy and freedom of thought as a possible foundation for a voluntary and reflexive setting of normative standards. It is debatable whether the changes in moral standards are related to declining levels of traditional religiosity (Halman & Pettersson, 1996). Even if the moral influence of the churches has declined, this does not necessarily point to a state of anomie. Individualization does not necessarily imply that modern people have become less moral (Bauman, 1995), or that they have become a-moral, embracing the opinion that 'anything goes' (Halman 1995; 1999).

These two topics, religion and morality in contemporary modern European society, are further explored in this book. The main purpose of this book is first of all to explore religious and moral values, attitudes and behaviours among European people and to focus on the main differences and similarities. Is the religious dimension still relevant in Europe? Some have argued that despite the fact that modernization and postmodernization have led to a rise of secular values and an erosion of religious beliefs and behaviours and a decline of the authority of the churches, religion and religious orientations 'have a persisting relevance in advanced industrial societies' (Van Deth, 1995: 11). Is this true in all countries or confined to a small number of countries only? How far has secularization proceeded in Europe? And what empirical evidence can be found for the suggestion that the timing and pace of the religious decline 'differs from one country to the next and from one Church to another' (Dobbelaere, 1995: 1; see also Sigelman, 1977; Campbell & Curtis, 1994). How homogeneous or heterogeneous is Europe as far as religiousness is concerned?

Describing Europe's religious and moral pattern is, of course, one thing, understanding these patterns is quite another. A second aim, therefore, is to understand European varieties in religious values, attitudes, and behaviours. Often these varieties in religious patterns are attributed to the dominant religious traditions, Catholic and Protestant. Catholicism and Protestantism are assumed to have produced different outlooks on life, and are regarded as determining factors for social and individual value orientations (Cécora, 1994: 17). Catholics and Protestants not only differ in religious beliefs, but also in mentality and social and political attitudes. The impact of religion is generally assumed to be stronger in Catholic countries compared with Protestant countries, where the religious involvement is considerably lower, the level of confidence in the churches weaker, etc. (Ester et al., 1994). Many of the contributions in this book dig deeper into the differences between Catholics and Protestants and, generally speaking, the conclusion is that there do indeed appear to be some differences, but that such differences are only modest. Although religious organizations construct images of themselves and their competitors on the religious market, stressing the differences, their adherents either do not perceive such nuances or regard them as unimportant. Even in an age of reflexivity, religious membership and commitment are more often habitual rather than a well-considered choice.

## 2    SOME PRELIMINARY OBSERVATIONS

In a number of publications, the results of the European Values Study have been presented and for a more extensive overview of these results we can refer to this body of literature. Here we will confine the presentation of the results to some of the most striking ones, confirming the idea that Europe's religious and moral pattern is indeed heterogenous.

### 2.1    Religiousness

The European Values Study surveys include a large number of religious indicators tapping mainly traditional institutional properties of (church) religiosity. On the basis of factor analysis, we have made distinctions between 'personal' or 'general religiosity', 'traditional beliefs', 'church adequacy', and 'church involvement' (Halman & de Moor, 1994; Halman & Vloet, 1994). Personal religiosity refers to the more emotional dimension of religiosity rather than to the institutional dimension. As such it is the only dimension which relates not to church religiosity but to an unofficial religiosity. It is determined by questions such as:
– Are you a religious person?
– Which of these statements comes closest to you belief?
  1. there is a personal God; 2. there is some sort of spirit or life force; 3. I don't really know what to think; 4. I don't really think there is any sort of spirit, God or life force;
– How important is God in your life?

- Do you find comfort and strength from religion or not?
- Do you take moments for prayer, meditation or contemplation or something like that?

The answers to these questions seem indicative of a kind of religiosity that may even be applicable to people who do not belong to, or feel (any longer) attracted by, one of the official churches. They reveal a subjective religious disposition or 'a diffuse religiosity' (Riis, 1994: 15) that is 'concerned with religious experiences, those feelings, perceptions, and sensations which are experienced by an actor or defined by a religious group (or a society) as involving some communication, however slight, with a divine essence, that is, with God, with ultimate reality, with transcendental authority' (Stark & Glock, 1968: 15). Scores on this dimension of religiosity are calculated by means of factor analysis (Halman & de Moor, 1994; Halman & Vloet, 1994).

Traditional belief statements in the Europan Values Study include belief in God, life after death, a soul, the devil, heaven, sin, and resurrection. The question simply asked: do you believe in ....? Reincarnation was also part of the list of belief statements which was presented to the respondents, but the analyses showed that this belief is of a different kind than belief in the traditional statements, which, of course, is due to the fact that 'it is not an explicitly Christian belief' (Harding et al., 1986: 48). A simple count of the numbers of belief statements excluding reincarnation thus reveals the degree of traditional faith.

The measures for institutional church religiosity include concrete behaviour and an evaluation or a perception of the church's role. Church adequacy is measured by the question: Generally speaking, do you think that your church is giving in your country adequate answers to: 1. the moral problems and needs of the individual; 2. the problems of family life; 3. people's spiritual needs; 4. the social problems facing our country today? A reliable scale can be constructed from these answers and scores have been calculated by applying factor analysis.

Church involvement is commonly measured by religious practices: church membership and frequency of attending religious services. Church membership is indicated in two steps: Do you belong to a religious denomination, followed by the question, which one? Church attendance is measured by the classic question: Apart from weddings, funerals and christenings, about how often do you attend religious services these days? The answer possibilities are: 1. more than once a week; 2. once a week; 3. once a month; 4. Christmas/Easter day; 5. other specific holy days; 6. once a year; 7. less often; 8. never, practically never.

The figures on church attendance reveal that the Nordic countries are indeed highly secularized; attending religious services is rare, but in terms of church affiliation, the Nordic pattern resembles the Southern European pattern. The high level of church membership in the Nordic countries is often understood from the close links between the church and the state. In the Nordic countries, 'there exists an historically determined connection between church and state, and [...] citizenship implied church membership' (Gustafsson, 1994: 21). Since the level of actual participation is rather low in the Nordic countries, membership in these countries will be less meaningful religiously than in other countries. Most of the people in the Scandinavian countries fall in the category of what is called marginal members: people belong to a church but they hardly go to church. The borderline between marginal church membership and being unchurched is rather vague, as the Scandinavian example demonstrates. In the Netherlands, a large proportion of the people is unchurched: they no longer belong to a denomination. In 1990, this was about half of the Dutch population. The Dutch pluralist situation seems to leave more room for private choices. Apart from a large proportion of unchurched people, a relatively large proportion of the Dutch is strongly engaged in church activities. It seems as if, in the Netherlands, either one is engaged and thus a core or modal member, or one leaves the church and becomes unchurched. Thus, from a religious point of view, there is little difference between the marginal members of the Lutheran church in Scandinavia and the unchurched in the Netherlands. As could have been expected, the highest figures on church involvement are found in Ireland and Poland. Quite remarkable are the differences between Bulgaria and Romania, both mainly Orthodox countries. Bulgarian church involvement resembles the Nordic pattern, but deviates strongly from the Romanian one, where church attendance is modest (30% attend religious services at least once a month).

When it comes to religious orientations, the North-South divide appears again in the sense that Northern Europe is more secular than Southern Europe, an exception to this rule being Iceland. While religiosity and traditional faith are low in Denmark, Norway and Sweden, it is relatively high in Iceland. Icelandic people, more often than other people, believe in reincarnation. About 40% of Icelandic people believe in reincarnation; in most other countries, this belief is limited to less than 30%. The results of our analyses seem to corroborate the idea that secularization has not proceeded at a similar pace all over Europe. However, the analyses also reveal that the Nordic pattern is not similar to the Eastern European pattern, as was predicted by Therborn (1995). Sweden is close to the Czech Republic, Bulgaria, and East Germany, but Norway and Denmark are at a distance from these countries. Secularization and individualization appear to have affected Polish and Irish societies to a much lesser extent than other countries. Religiosity has remained at a high level in these countries, and, above all, it has remained highly traditional. When it comes to the adequacy of church responses to family and moral problems, more people in Eastern Europe than in the West regard the church's replies as adequate. In Denmark and Sweden, the answers the churches provide to such problems are less readily accepted, which confirms the ideas that church-oriented attitudes are less widespread in more modern societies. The churches in present-day society seem to be connected only with spiritual needs rather than with family life and social problems. The Irish case is strange, however. Despite the fact that the Irish are the most religious and highly traditional in their beliefs, only about two-fifths of the population is of the opinion that the churches give adequate answers to social and family problems. Even among Irish people who frequently attend religious services, the pattern is the same. Such proportions are among the lowest in Europe.

It has been noticed that the Irish became less reliant on the churches during the eighties, which may be regarded as a sign that the position of the Catholic church is less strong than before. Perhaps this can be attributed to the 'collapse in the moral monopoly of the church' (Hornsby-Smith & Whelan, 1994: 41). In Spain and in most other countries, this seems to be reflected in the relatively sharp decline in church attendance.

Quite to our surprise, levels of trust in the church increased in Spain, which may be explained by the fact that the Catholic church in this country is no longer closely linked with Franco's dictatorial regime. The Catholic church openly confessed the sinfulness of their role in the Spanish war (Casanova, 1992: 85). In other countries, the perceived adequacy of the church declined. This weakened reliance on the churches during the eighties may be seen in close connection with public debates on moral issues, such as divorce, abortion, and homosexuality. The churches clearly lost authority on such issues of private morality, which, however, not necessarily implies that the churches have lost influence in all other matters.

However, not only church adequacy declined in Europe, also traditional religious beliefs and personal religiosity decreased throughout Europe, Italy being the exception to this general rule of religious change. Italians became not less, but, contrary to all expectations, more religious than they were in 1981. However, Italian society resembles the overall European general decline in traditional institutional religiosity. It is suggested that the increased level of religiosity in Italy can be attributed to the translation of one of the items: belief in a personal God. The formulation of this item changed and the result was a sharp increase in the number of Italians who believed in a personal God: from 28% in 1981 to 67% in 1990. However, at a conference on European Values in Trento organized in 1992 by the Italian research team, the Italian participants assured us that this development of increased religious awareness could indeed be confirmed by other researches in Italy. Apparently, Italians are becoming more and more religious not in the official, traditional, institutional way, but in a personal, unofficial way.

In Iceland, religiosity increased as well, but as has been observed before, this development does not fit into a general Scandinavian pattern of decline. In particular the Danes are the opposites of the Icelanders. In Denmark, a sharp decrease in personal or general religiosity occurred, which is also true in Belgium and the Netherlands. Less dramatic is the decrease in countries such as Ireland and Northern Ireland, which remain the most religious societies in Europe. Apart from a (small) general decline in religiosity, no changes seem to have taken place in the rank ordering of European countries. The Irish remain the most religious people, whereas both in 1981 and in 1990, the French and the Danish, are the least religious people.

In almost all countries, a decline can be noted in the numbers of people who say that the church gives adequate answers to various issues, and it seems as if this, together with the declining levels of church attendance indicate, a decline of the institution of religion, not necessarily a religious decline. Such a suggestion finds even more support in a comparison of various age groups. At a European level, we have followed them in time and the conclusion was that all age groups show increasing levels of general religiosity when they get older, but as soon as institutional aspects are evaluated, all age groups show declining levels of religiosity. So for many people, getting older means an increasing quest for religiosity, but at the same time a decline of institutional church-oriented religiosity. Our interpretation is that there is indeed an institutional crisis, but not necessarily a religious crisis (Halman, 1998).

However, despite the fact that even young people become more religious when they get older, it does not imply that unofficial religiosity grows in society while official religiosity declines. Since young people have been raised and socialized in more secular environments and circumstances, they were expected to reveal lower levels of religiousness. This expectation was corroborated by the data, and not only concern official religiosity but also unofficial religiosity. And although even young generations show increasing levels of this kind of unofficial or personal religiosity when they get older, the starting level of their religiosity is so low that they will never reach the levels of religiosity of the older generations. In other words, even unofficial religiosity is on the wane at macro level, but increases at the individual level as people get older. This seems to indicate that primary religious socialization is more important than the turn to piousness as people get old and frail. The religious decline seems to begin with a lack of primary religious socialization and primary religious role-models. The replacement of generations thus implies that society gradually becomes less and less religious.

The religious decline does not imply that religiosity has disappeared or that people have turned into disbelievers. In most countries, the number of people who do not believe in God or any sort of spirit or life force ranges from around 20% in Denmark and Sweden to less than 1% in Ireland. Large majorities of Western populations thus believe in 'something', although belief in a personal God has decreased, that is the traditional view of God has declined in popularity. In other words, it seems as if the theistic world view is on the decline. A theistic world view may be described as 'an understanding of life that identifies God as the agent who governs life. God is assumed to have a purpose for each person's life' (Wuthnow, 1976: 3-4). This view of a traditional God who is the source of meaning and interpretation has diminished. The question then becomes what comes instead of or next to this traditional way of believing, or to put it in other terms: what alternative meaning systems are arising?

There seem to be an increasing number of people who are attracted by some sort of spirituality or paranormal experiences in order to interpret life and give meaning to it. So, even in a secularized world, the sacred seems to be remarkably alive (Hammond, 1985). Others may have some doubts about the existence of a supernatural power, be it God or something else. They are highly uncertain about the meaning and purpose of human life or they simply reject the idea that we can ever understand the meaning of life. Others simply state that life has no meaning at all. Unfortunately, EVS does not contain information to answer such intriguing questions.

## 2.2 Morality

As far as morality is concerned, the data of the European Values Studies included a long list of behaviours and moral issues, and the respondent was asked to indicate whether or not such issues and behaviours could be justified. A scale was presented ranging from 1 = never to 10 = always. The list included a wide variety of issues and behaviours ranging from cheating on taxes and avoiding paying a fare, to homosexuality, abortion and euthanasia.

Factor analyses revealed two kinds of morality (see also Halman, 1999; Halman & Vloet, 1994): personal or private morality and collective public morality. The first dimension is indicated by the acceptance of behaviours which were, and often still are, regarded as sinful according to traditional Christian doctrine, and such behaviours were severely sanctioned by society in the past (Harding et al., 1986: 11). This moral dimension is indicated by sexual and (bio-) ethical behaviours: adultery, sex under the legal age of consent, homosexuality, prostitution, euthanasia, divorce, suicide. We have tentatively labelled this dimension of private morality 'permissiveness'.

The public morality dimension refers to behaviours which were defined by the law as an offence of crime. It concerns items like: taking free rides on public transport, tax fraud, claiming state benefits illegally, buying stolen goods, joy riding, accepting a bribe etc. This dimension indicates the support of virtues like honesty, integrity, respect for the law, and living a decent life. We have labelled this dimension 'civic morality'.

By means of factor analyses, scores on both dimensions were calculated and the analyses revealed that Dutch people in particular are extraordinarily permissive as far as sexual and bio-ethical behaviours are concerned, whereas Hungarians appear lenient as far as civic morality is concerned. The Danes are the opposites of the Hungarians as far as civic morality is concerned.

Dutch people appear least restrictive towards homosexuality, euthanasia, sex under the legal age of consent, and prostitution. On the opposite side of this permissiveness scale, we find most Central and Eastern European countries, whose people appear far more strict towards such behaviours and issues.

Hungarians appear most tolerant in accepting behaviours such as not paying a fare on public transport, buying something you know was stolen, joy riding, and accepting bribes, whereas, on such issues and behaviours, the people of the Nordic countries appear very reluctant to accept them.

Dutch society was already highly permissive in 1981, but permissiveness has even increased. Rather unexpected was the shift towards greater strictness in Denmark. In 1981, Denmark was among the most lenient countries, but during the eighties permissiveness decreased. Also Swedish society became less permissive. It contradicts the expectations and ideas of ongoing secularization and individualization. The shift occurred in all age groups and the differences between age groups almost vanished in the 1990s. In 1990 there is a much greater consensus on sexual norms, divorce, euthanasia and suicide than there was before. Apparently, Danes and Swedes feel that their society has become too permissive. Also in Sweden, a return to more sexual strictness was observed. Repeat studies in this country in the nineties, revealed that levels of permissiveness were on the increase again. The decline in the eighties has been tentatively attributed to the combined effect of high levels of permissiveness in the beginning of the eighties and extensive mass media campaigns against AIDS at the end of the eighties (Pettersson, 1994).

As far as shifts in civic morality are concerned, it can be noticed that this morality increased slightly in Spain and Ireland. It decreased most in Belgium, Sweden and Italy. Belgium and France became the least strict countries in Western Europe.

Although the European pattern of morality is far from clear and not easy to understand or interpret, it should be noted that 'even for the most justifiable of all these actions, it can only be justified one out of all these actions, it can only be justified one out of every two times. It is not true to say, therefore, that the public is subject to an excess of liberty. Moreover, for the whole of the [...] items listed, the average of the scores given is in the quartile of the scale which indicates the greatest severity' (Stoetzel, 1983: 30-31; translation by Meril James). This conclusion, based on the results of the 1981 EVS surveys, is still valid in 1990. Most countries display rather strict judgments. 'Rarely does a score exceed the halfway point of the scale (i.e., 5.5 out of 10), and most of the scores are considerably lower than this' (Harding et al., 1986: 7). In other words, high proportions of the populations considered most of the behaviours as 'never or hardly justified.' Generally speaking, people in the countries investigated by the European Values Study, are apparently not lenient in their judgements. In an article in the *International Social Science Journal*, we concluded that such results can only be interpreted as a rejection of the idea that an ethic of 'anything goes' is developing (Halman, 1995).

## 3    PLAN OF THE BOOK

All contributions to this book are based on empirical data drawn from the European Values Study, and dig deeply into religious and moral patterns in Europe. A major issue is the Catholic-Protestant divide in Europe. As said before, these differences are assumed to have had far-reaching consequences for people's values, attitudes and behaviours, which is why it makes sense to explore this impact in more detail.

*Ole Riis* starts with a classic theme in sociology in general and the sociology of religion, Religion and the Spirit of Capitalism. In following Weber, Riis argues that the Protestant ethic differed from the Catholic ethic, and that this distinction has been conducive to work ethics and the development of (modern) Capitalism. However, following ideas of modernization in general and rationalization and secularization in particular, one could predict differences between Catholics and Protestants to disappear gradually. The determining force of the religious factor has declined or has already disappeared, and the economic factor has gained importance or is the most important determinant of societal development. Thus one of the aims of his chapter is to examine the differences in work ethics between Catholics and Protestants and to explore if adherents to the two denominations differ with regard to values in other life spheres, e.g., politics.

The impact of religiosity in general and both religious traditions in particular on other values have also been investigated by *Loek Halman* and *Thorleif Pettersson*. They explore levels of religious involvement as well as the relationships between religious involvement and value orientations in other societal spheres in 23 European countries. In theories on modernization, the process of differentiation is regarded as a core process of social change. Due to this and other modernization processes like rationalization and individualization, the traditional functions of the churches have become less important, and the impact of religion on other domains in life is assumed to have decreased. However, a distinction between public and private social spheres seems necessary, for it is often argued that the declining importance of the religious involvement is particularly found in the public sphere, whereas the private sphere is assumed to remain more (strongly) influenced by religion. They empirically test the assumption that religion has a differential impact on the private and public realms. It is also investigated whether the strength of religion's impact on other domains is related to the general level of religious beliefs, e.g., whether one form of secularization (differentiation) is related to another (the declining adherence to religious beliefs). Overall, the results do not support the assumption that lower national levels of religious involvement are related to a weaker impact of the religious involvement on other social attitudes.

Religion and Family are the two topics which *Karel Dobbelaere, Josette Gevers* and *Loek Halman* focus on in their contribution. The central question is to what extent evidence can be found for the idea that religion and family values do indeed have separate domains in contemporary Europe. At aggregate or societal level, functional differentiation has resulted in clear separation between religion and other social spheres, but has this also appeared at the individual level, the level of individual consciousness? Processes of individualization and functional differentiation are assumed to have produced such a separation at the individual level as well. So the question is to what extent religion still has an impact on other social spheres in modern European societies. The analyses presented in their chapter are confined to the relationships between religion and family, and a distinction is made between groups of people with different levels of religious involvement, based not only on church attendance, but also on denominational differences, because it has often been argued that the distinction between Catholics and Protestants produces differential outlooks on people's views on marriage and family life (e.g., Gundelach, 1994). The evidence indicates that secularization of the social system does indeed seem conducive to a separation of religion from family views. The influence of the churches' views on family life appears to be on the decline.

Differences between Catholics and Protestants are also explored in the contribution by *Mike Procter* and *Mike Hornsby Smith*. In their chapter, they examine the impact of religious denomination on moral values not only at the individual level, but also at the aggregate level. In other words, they not only explore if Catholics and Protestants display differential moral patterns, but also if Catholic and Protestant contexts produce different moral outlooks. And, as in the contribution of Karel Dobbelaere, Josette Gevers and Loek Halman, they put forward the idea that differences in actual church involvement are a more important attribute of moral values than denominational differences. This assumption is grounded in rational choice theories, which are confronted with secularization theories. Whereas according to secularization ideas, religion will be of minor importance for moral views, rational choice theories predict a strong impact of religious contexts.

Religious contexts and differences between Catholics and Protestants are also the main topics in the contribution of *Pierre Bréchon*. He explores the existence of what is called Catholic and Protestant identities and the impact both denominations may have on people's behaviours and attitudes. A basic assumption in his chapter is that belonging to Catholicism or Protestantism determines people's behaviours and attitudes to a large extent. Of course, he argues, secularization and modernization may have resulted in a declining impact of these Christian religions, which makes it likely that it is not the differences between Catholics and Protestants that matter, but the differences between Christian religious identities and anti-religious or non-religious identities. Thus, he focusses not only on religion as a (once) important attribute in society, but also on the implications of a non-religious identity.

An issue which has gained prominence lately is social capital. The decline of religion as a moral force, the diminished acceptance of norms set by the churches, together with the increased emphasis on individual autonomy and valuing of self-fulfilment, self-realization and personal happiness, are often regarded as a threat to collective norms, a decline of community, and thus of social capital. Religion is assumed to create social trust, which is considered a major component of social capital. This decline of social capital, in turn, is considered a danger for the maintenance of democracy (e.g., Paxton, 1999). In this discussion, Putnam (1993) claims that religious sentiments and social capital are incompatible, while Coleman (1990) stresses the important differences in social capital between the major religious traditions. Since such expectations concern the aggregate level, it can be questioned whether or not similar results can be found at the individual level as well. *Loek Halman* and *Thorleif Pettersson* elaborate on this intriguing topic, focussing in their contribution in particular on the relationship between religion and social capital at the individual level in four religiously and socio-economically very different Western societies: Sweden, Germany, Spain and the US.

All these contributions on the differences between Catholics and Protestants come to a similar conclusion: although there are differences between the two religious groups, religious context and the degree to which people are involved in their religion appear more important attributes for differences in values, attitudes and behaviours.

Living in modern society means living in a globalized world. Living in such a world means that we are living in 'a global village' (Robertson, 1992: 9). It is assumed that a common social environment is developing which is shared by people all over the world. According to some, it will generate a process of unification or homogenization in the sense that cultures will become more similar and that ultimately a commonly shared culture will arise. Others have argued that it will lead to a loss of a commonly shared model to which societies and people can conform. Each society will create its own distinctive culture, emphasizing its own national culture. In their chapter, *Loek Halman* and *Thorleif Pettersson* address the process of globalization and the ultimate consequences for religious culture in the contemporary global order. The paradox of modernity will have severe repercussions for religion. On the one hand, one might argue that globalization will result in the unification of religious patterns, in the sense of the emergence of one global religious culture. On the other hand, it can be argued that due to the globalized context, traditional religious patterns will erode, and the former homogeneous patterning of religious orientations will gradually disappear. As a result, a highly fragmented religious pattern will arise (Beyer, 1994). Halman and Pettersson test the hypothesis that the more 'globalized' a country is, the more fragmented its religious culture will be. In order to show this, the chapter develops national measures of globalization and compares the levels of globalization with the national predominant patterning of religious orientations and practices.

Such a hypothesis presumes that societal changes follow the same pattern in all countries, and that changes in the various domains of life occur simultaneously, in the same direction, in the same magnitude and the same sequence. The observed varieties in Europe seem to demonstrate the opposite, and also the religious situation in the United States does not support the idea of continual changes in all spheres of life. Despite modernization processes in the US, religion has persisted. Perhaps it is true that Europe is the exception and that secularization is mainly a European concept. The concept of secularization is also 'difficult to apply to the Japanese situation' (Abe, 1998: 11). As Tamaru has argued 'the process of secularization as discussed in the Christian West should not be applied to Japan, because Japanese religion had always been secular' (Tamara referred to by Abe, 1998: 17). Yanagawa (1992) emphasizes that religious rites and services are important even in today's Japanese society but religion's rules and precepts are irrelevant. 'We can say that the ordinary Japanese do not have a basic belief, or a doctrine. Furthermore, they do not have a strong feeling of being members of a particular temple, church or shrine. Nor do they have any feeling that it is wrong to break the precepts [....] many people are what might be called passive believers, not identifying with any religious faith' (Yanagawa, 1992: 11). It seems as if indeed the religious situation in Japan differs in many respects from the European pattern, where a diminishing part of the population is attending religious churches, but where religious beliefs have not vanished. A comparison of the characteristics of Japanese religious beliefs and practices and moral convictions with the European pattern is presented by *Robert Kisala* in his chapter. His conclusion is that despite the different historical-cultural situations of Japan and Europe, similar levels of erosion in religion's influence can be observed in contemporary Japanese society.

# References

Abe, Y. 1998. 'Secularization: Karel Dobbelaere and Japanese Sociology of Religion'. Pp 11-24 in R. Laermans, B. Wilson & J. Billiet (eds.), *Secularization and Social Integration*. Leuven: Leuven University Press.

Bauman, S. 1995. *Life in Fragments. Essays on Postmodern Morality*. Oxford: Blackwell.

Bellah, R.N. *et al.* (1986). *Habits of the Heart. Individualism and Commitment in American Life.* New York: Harper and Row.

Beyer, P. 1994. *Religion and Globalization*. London: Sage.

Campbell, R. & J. Curtis 1994. 'Religious Involvement across Societies: Analyses for Alternative Measures in National Surveys'. *Journal for the Scientific Study of Religion* 33: 215-229.

Caplow, T. 1985. 'Contrasting Trends in European and American Religion'. *Sociological Analysis* 46: 101-108.

Casanova, J. 1994. *Public Religions in the Modern World*. Chicago and London: The University of Chicago Press.

Cécora, J. 1994. 'The Motivational Force of Values and Attitudes on Human Behaviour in the Quest for Happiness, Well-being, and Satisfaction'. Pp. 1-30 in: J. Cécora (ed.), *Changing Values and Attitudes in Family Households with Rural Peer Groups, Social Networks, and Action Spaces*. Bonn: FAA.

Crittenden, J. 1992. *Beyond Individualism. Reconstructing the Liberal Self*. Oxford: Oxford University Press.

Coleman, J. 1990. *Foundations of Social Theory*. Cambridge, Mass: Harvard University Press.

Dobbelaere, K. 1981. 'Secularization: A Multi-dimensional Concept'. *Current Sociology* 29: 1-213.

Dobbelaere, K. 1995. 'Religion in Europe and North America'. Pp. 1-29 in R. de Moor (ed.), *Values in Western Societies*. Tilburg: Tilburg University Press.

Durkheim, E. 1965. *The Elementary Forms of Religious Life*. New York: Free Press.

Ester, P., L. Halman & R. de Moor (eds.) 1994. *The Individualizing Society*. Tilburg: Tilburg University Press.

Finke, R. & R. Stark 1992. *The Churching of America, 1776-1990: Winners and Losers in our Religious Economy*. New Brunswick, NJ: Rutgers University Press.

Giddens, A. 1991. *Modernity and Self-Identity*. Stanford, CA: Stanford University Press.

Greeley, A. 1989. *Religious Change in America*. Cambridge MA: Harvard University Press.

Gundelach, P. 1994. 'National Value Differences. Modernization or Institutionalization?'. *International Journal of Comparative Sociology* XXXV: 37-58.

Gustafsson, G. 1994. 'Religious Change in the Five Scandinavian Countries, 1930-1980'. Pp. 11-58 in T. Pettersson & O. Riis (eds.), *Scandinavian Values*. Uppsala: Acta Universitatis Upsaliensis.

Habermas, J. 1987. *Knowledge and Human Interests*. Cambridge: Polity Press.

Halman, L. 1995. 'Is There a Moral Decline? A Cross-National Inquiry into Morality in Contemporary Society'. *International Social Science Journal* 145: 419-440.

Halman, L. 1998. *Religious Beliefs and Practices in a Secular World*. Tilburg: WORC.

Halman, L. 1999. *Moral Beliefs in Contemporary Europe*. Tilburg: WORC.

Halman, L. & R. de Moor 1994. 'Religion, churches and moral values'. Pp. 37-66 in P. Ester, L. Halman, & R. de Moor (eds.), *The Individualizing Society. Value Change in Europe and North America*. Tilburg: Tilburg University Press.

Halman, L. & T. Pettersson 1996. 'The Shifting Sources of Morality: From Religion to Postmaterialism?'. Pp. 261-284 in L. Halman & N. Nevitte (eds.), *Political Value Change in Western Democracies. Integration, Values, Identification and Participation*. Tilburg: Tilburg University Press.

Halman, L. & A. Vloet 1994. *Measuring and Comparing Values in 16 Countries of the Western World*. Tilburg: WORC.

Hammond, P. (ed.) 1985. *The Sacred in a Secular Age*. Berkeley: University of California Press.

Harding, S., D. Phillips & M. Fogarty 1986. *Contrasting Values in Western Europe*. Houndmills & London: MacMillan.

Hornsby-Smith, M.P. & C.T. Whelan 1994. 'Religious and Moral Values'. Pp. 7-44 in T. Whelan (ed.), *Values and Social Change in Ireland*. Dublin: Gill & Macmillan.

Iannaccone, L. 1997. 'Rational Choice. Framework for the Scientific Study of Religion'. Pp. 25-45 in L.A. Young (ed.), *Rational Choice Theory and Religion*. New York: Routledge.

Luckmann, T. 1967. *The Invisible Religion*. New York: MacMillan.

Martin, D. 1978. *A General Theory of Secularization*. Oxford: Blackwell.

McGuire, M.B. 1987. *Religion: The Social Context*. Belmont: Wadsworth Publishing Company.

Pettersson, T. 1994. 'Culture Shift and Generational Population Replacement: Individualization, Secularization, and Moral Value Change in Contemporary Scandinavia'. Pp. 197-212 in T. Pettersson & O. Riis (eds.), *Scandinavian Values*. Uppsala: Acta Universitatis Upsaliensis.

Putnam, R. 1993. *Making Democracy Work*. Princeton NJ: Princeton University Press.

Riis, O. 1994. 'Patterns of Secularization in Scandinavia'. Pp. 99-128 in T. Pettersson & O. Riis (eds.), *Scandinavian Values*. Uppsala: Acta Universitatis Upsaliensis.

Riis, O. 1998. 'Religion Re-Emerging: The Role of Religion in Legitimating Integration and Power in Modern Societies'. *International Sociology* 13: 249-272.

Robertson, R. 1992. *Globalization. Social Theory and Global Culture*. London: Sage.

Sigelman, L. 1977. 'Review of the Polls: Multi-Nation Survey of Religious Beliefs'. *Journal for the Scientific Study of Religion* 16: 289-294.

Stark, R. & W.S. Bainbridge 1985. *The Future of Religion*. Berkeley: University of

California Press.

Stark, R. & C. Glock 1968. *American Piety: The Nature of Religious Commitment.* Berkeley: University of California Press.

Stark, R. & L. Iannaccone 1994. 'A Supply-Side Reinterpretation of the 'secularization' of Europe'. *Journal for the Scientific Study of Religion* 33: 230-252.

Stoetzel, J. 1983. *Les Valeurs du Temps Présent: Une Enquête Européenne.* Paris: Presses Universitaires de France.

Therborn, G. 1995. *European Modernity and Beyond.* London, Thousand Oaks, New Delhi: Sage.

Van Deth, J.W. 1995. 'Introduction: The Impact of Values'. Pp. 1-18 in J.W. van Deth & E. Scarbrough (eds.), *The Impact of Values.* Oxford: Oxford University Press.

Wilson, B. 1996. 'Religious Toleration, Pluralism and Privatization'. Pp. 11-34 in P. Repstad (ed.), *Religion and Modernity. Modes of Co-existence.* Oslo: Scandinavian University Press.

Wuthnow, R. 1976. *The Consciousness Reformation.* Berkeley: University of California Press.

Yanagawa, K. 1992. 'Religious Views of the Japanese and Their Characteristics'. Pp. 7-12 in K. Yanagawa, K, Morioka, T. Yamaori, S. Oda & Y. Abe, *Religion in Japan Today.* Tokyo: Foreign Press Center.

Yinger, M. 1977. 'A Comparative Study of the Substructures of Religion'. *Journal for the Scientific Study of Religion* 16: 67-86.

Chapter Two

# Religion and the Spirit of Capitalism in Modern Europe

Ole Riis

## 1   INTRODUCTION

Europe is united by a common heritage of Christianity, and divided by the aftermath of the Reformation wars. The contrast between the Protestant regions of Northern Europe and the Catholic regions of Southern Europe has inspired many sociological studies. Troeltsch, Brentano, Weber, Halévy, and Merton have forwarded theories about the consequences of the Protestant Reformation for the modernization of Europe. The most famous is, of course, Max Weber's study of how the Protestant idea of the worldly calling and the ascetic Protestant's quest for signs of salvation paved the way for legitimizing the modern spirit of Capitalism.[1] The closing chapter of *The Protestant Ethic* ends by relegating the difference to the era of early capitalism. Today we are caught in an iron cage of materialism and means-ends-rationality. This passage has inspired numerous theories concerning modernization, secularization and confessional convergence.

In section 2 below, the historical background for the differences between Protestants and Catholics is explored and how religious features are intertwined with societal structures. Section 3 presents Webers' ideal types in order to clarify where later research deviates from his typology. Section 4 presents empirical research on differences in economic ethics between religious groups in a modern, European context. Section 5 argues for three hypotheses about religious differences in economic ethics. Section 6 discusses the first hypothesis which is that there are denominational differences in the orientation toward work. In section 7, the second hypothesis is discussed which assumes that there are denominational differences in the orientation to material goods. Section 8 focusses on the third hypothesis about denominational differences in individualism. In section 9, these three hypotheses are contrasted with a fourth which predicts that religion has become irrelevant for the ethics of modern capitalism. However, this explanation is supplemented by the idea that Catholicism may have aligned its ethics with the social conditions of modern capitalism.

## 2 THE HISTORICAL BACKGROUND OF THE EUROPEAN DIVIDE

In this chapter, Europe is confined to Western-Europe. This subcontinent is a patchwork of nations and ethnic groups, each with their own historical identity and long memories of strife. Religion has been both the great unifier and the great divider in Europe. The Reformation wars cast long shadows in social history. The differences between Catholicism and Protestantism have inspired many scholars (e.g., Weber, Halévy & Thompson, Merton). In their works, Protestantism is ascribed an active role in forwarding modern society, whereas Catholicism implicitly or explicitly is ascribed the role of the traditionalist laggard. All these theses have emerged at the beginning of this century. The main question is whether the split between Protestants and Catholics is still there today in advanced industrial Europe.

Stein Rokkan's (1973, 1980) mapping of the European political cultures pointed at two major lines of division: A north-south axis, where the religious factor is important, in combination with other factors, such as the formation of independent nation states and the establishment of vernacular languages. The east-west axis concerns the split between the coastal regions of commerce, and the inland regions of feudal agrarian production.

The north-south line demarcates where the power of the Roman empire and Latinization waned, and the powers of independent German, Gaul and Celtic chiefs were maintained. Christian religion expanded beyond this zone, aided by the expansion of Carolingian feudalism. However, the north-south line came to demarcate the range of Papal powers. Beyond this line, the real rulers of the local church were the kings and chieftains. The Reformation movement began in the zone of exchange between north and south, but as the North became Protestant strongholds, the denominational cleavages came to coincide with the old historic divide.

Because of the Reformation, local rulers could expand their power and reorganize public services under the crown. Translation of the Bible into vernacular languages helped to establish local cultures, and to diminish the lingua communa of Vulgate. Through the reformation wars, religion became an expression of national loyalties, as well as spiritual aims.

Problems arose in those nations where the secular powers could not monopolize religion. Germany was an instance, and the famous Weber-theses was influenced by the experience of mixing Bavarian-Catholics and Prussian-Lutherans in Bismarck's melting pot.

## 3    THE PROTESTANT ETHIC THESIS REVISITED

The argument of the Protestant Ethic thesis rests on the ideal types: Ascetic Protestantism and the spirit of rationalized Capitalism.[2] Asceticism is characterized as a dual attitude toward the world, where one lives *in* this world, not *for* it. It leads to a state of tension, which may provide a strong motive for committed action. Protestantism transferred Christian Asceticism from the monasteries to common life, through the dogma of the calling. The idea of calling may take a traditional form, which obliges a human being to remain faithfully in the ascribed position, or it may lead to a search for signs that point at one's place in God's providential plan. Succeeding in one's calling may lead to wealth as a sign of God's grace and as means for the benefit of the common weal. The notion about God's providence was stated with the most forceful psychological effect through the dogma of predestination, emphasized by the Calvinists. Religious virtuosi following this dogma were forced into self-disciplined work in their calling, to God's grace and the common well-being of their neighbours. Puritans come quite close to the ideal type, while other varieties of Protestantism and monastic orders may come close to some points, and remain far removed on others.

The 'spirit of capitalism' is illustrated by Franklin's *Necessary hints to whose that would be rich* (1736) and *Advice to a young tradesman* (1748). It is distinguished by its ethical fervor from similar-sounding expressions of greed or utilitarianism. Franklin's views on the moral duty to perform one's deed of a covenant expressed a divine revelation. This differs on the one hand from traditionalism, and on the other from the ancient motive of profiteering, an amoral 'adventurer capitalism'. Thereby, the spirit of capitalism can be specified as seeking accumulation of capital by peaceful trade as an ethical duty.

In the short heroic era of early capitalism, the motive of capital accumulation had to be legitimized by religion, as an inner drive. Today, the motive of accumulation of capital has become an external obligation, induced by the rationale of the capitalist system. 'Weber's thesis' thus demonstrates the transformation from one ideal type (the Protestant Ethic) to another (the modern Spirit of Capitalism), which simultaneously implies a change in the type of rationality, from *Wertrationalität*, where salvation is the focal value which determines the self-disciplined acts, and the calling is regarded as an assignment from God, to *Zweckrationalität*, where acts are determined by calculating means and ends and the calling is an obligation to act prudently and economically for one's own profit and for the common wealth. This transformation simultaneously expresses a process of *Entzauberung*, with the rise of a new world view which depricates the wonders of divine creation by regarding nature and human beings as mere means.

**4    SURVEY ANALYSES OF THE WEBER THESIS**

Several studies have tried to test whether Protestantism still has 'an elective affinity'[3] to the ethos of modern Capitalism. Lenski (1963) found that Jews and white Protestants in Michigan identified with 'the individualistic, competitive patterns of thought and action linked with the middle class and historically associated with the Protestant ethic or its secular counterpart, the spirit of capitalism. By contrast, Catholics and Negro Protestants have more often been associated with collectivist, security-oriented, working class patterns of thought and action...' (Lenski, 1963: 113). Lenski's work has been much criticized. Greeley thus pointed out that the data show no or only minor differences between Protestants and Catholics regarding economic status mobility, ambitions, attitudes to work, status, orientation to savings, or seeing God as endorsing economic efforts (Greeley, 1964: 376-377). The only solid difference demonstrated by Lenski (1963: 387) is that Catholics are more oriented toward trade unions. Lenski admits this but continues by comparisons between persons raised in similar settings. It is certainly necessary to bring intervening factors under control in a causal analysis, but this would imply that conclusions are based on very small samples. Efforts to replicate his results have been unsuccessful, especially outside the US (Lipset & Bendix, 1955; Bouma, 1973). Because of the lack of empirical corroboration and the rather primitive classification of religious positions, Greeley (1964) called for 'a Moratorium'.

Despite this, Listhaug and Lindseth (1994) tried to replicate Lenski's study on the basis of the EVS 90 data.[4] Their analyses[5] indicate that a) the Protestant ethic is not a unidimensional concept, b) different operationalisations of the Protestant Ethic leads to diverging results, c) the pattern seems to be ascribable to national rather than to denominational differences.

The authors do not go into this latter point. Instead they delve into the religiously mixed countries in a multiple regression analysis controling for the impact of sex, age, religious domination, the degree of religious commitment, and social class. The most important factor appears to be social class. No significant impact of religious denomination on work values was found. 'Social class is the only variable that records a consistent impact on work values. The relationship goes in the expected direction with the higher classes having stronger work-directed values' (Listhaug & Lindseth, 1994: 95). Religiosity as such had a positive effect on work values, but only in Great Britain and West Germany. The multivariate analyses could not confirm Lenski's conclusion that the religious factor continues to extert its influence in advanced industrial society.

One could, of course, question the lack of elaboration on the religious dimension in their analysis. Lumping together various types of Protestantism in one common category is problematic if we keep in mind Weber's ideal type of ascetic Protestantism.[6] A distinction should at least be made between membership of Protestant mainline churches, i.e., Lutherans and Anglicans, and free Protestant churches, i.e., Baptists and Jehovah's Witnesses. Besides, Calvinists should be subject to special comparisons whenever possible. That way we still would not have a complete correspondence with Weber's ideal type of Ascetic Protestantism, but it would bring the analyses a step closer.

One further general problem regards the operationalisation of the 'spirit of modern capitalism'. Efforts have been made by Granato et al. (1996) to illuminate the acquisition motive through the EVS material. Their analyses are based on the following question: 'Here is a list of qualities which children can be encouraged to learn at home. Which, if, any, do you consider being especially important?' According to Granato et al., two of the items indicated an achievement motivation according to the ideas of McClelland.[7] These items were 'thrift', specified further as 'saving money and things', and 'determination', specified further as 'perseverance'. Furthermore, two other items seem to contradict achievement motivation by reflecting conformity to traditional social norms, such as 'obedience' and 'religious faith'. The index is therefore based on adding the two former items and deducting the two latter ones. Against the background of the whole discussion of the Weber-thesis, including Inglehart's (1990), further arguments are needed for positioning 'religious faith' on the side of anti-achievement.[8] This combination of items is hardly convincing. Furthermore, national variations on these items seem to depend on associations raised by the wording of these items rather than on comparable value patterns.

Most of the studies inspired by Lenski use a broad set of economic indicators and attitudes which do not pinpoint Weber's specification of the concept. Indicators such as social mobility, self-employment, savings, or entrepreneurship might as well point at what Weber regards as 'adventurer capitalism'. In order to test Weber's thesis, we not only need information about religious membership but we also need to know to what extent people have internalized the economic ethics of their churches, whether they regard themselves as members of an ascetic elite, seeking for signs in their work and their ethical life that indicate whether they are elected to a state of grace. The available data do not fulfill such ideal requirements. As a minimal measure we may look at how committed members of various confessional groups regard work.

## 5    HYPOTHESES

The discussions above led to a set of partially contradictory hypotheses regarding the present-day consequences of Weber's thesis. Lenski's arguments for a continuation of the confessional impact on the economic ethics leads to three hypotheses which relate to Weber's study. The first concerns work as a calling. It states that confessional differences in the view on work are still discernible.

H1)  work is ascribed an intrinsic value as a calling from God among committed members of ascetic Protestant denominations, less so among mainline

Protestant churches, and least among Roman Catholics.[9]

Weber did not present his thesis in an intellectual void. The thesis was influenced by the German Kulturkampf between the industrialized Protestant north and the agrarian Catholic south. The problem of Weber's contemporaries was not to demonstrate that Protestants were more adapted to a capitalist society than Catholics, but to explain this adaption.

Karl Marx indicated an affinity between Protestantism and Capitalism: 'The religious world is but the reflection of the real world. And for a society based upon the production of commodities, .... Christianity with its *cultus* of abstract man, more specifically in its bourgeois developments, Protestantism, Deism etc., is the most fitting form of religion' (Marx, 1954: 83).[10] Georg Simmel argued that money becomes the center of interest of marginalized individuals and classes, such as members of Protestant sects, i.e., the Huguenots, the Quakers, or the Herrnhuter (Simmel, 1978: 221). So there are good theoretical arguments for proposing a hypothesis which links religious conviction to material acquisition, even if we disregard Weber.

One of the characteristics of modern capitalism, according to several scholars, is the importance attached to money and material goods, or covetousness. This point was especially stressed by Werner Sombart (1902, 1913). This motive is not related to a Protestant ethic, but rather to the cynical stance of capitalist tycoons. An entrepreneur who was truly an ascetic Protestant in Weber's sense would seriously doubt whether an acquisitive attitude to wealth is ethically defensible as it may turn a person away from God's cause.[11]

Such arguments show that a distinction should be made between several types of economic motives, and especially between the Weberian orientation toward work as a sacred calling on the one hand and the motive of acquisition of money on the other. One way to circumvent this dilemma is by regarding the Weber-thesis as a special case of a more general motive, which also includes features of the Marx-thesis. McClelland (1961, 1963) for instance, argues for an Achievement-motivation. According to him, some cultures in some periods are especially oriented toward socializing children to regard economic achievement as a positive goal. Such an orientation is often followed by economic dynamism. A hypothesis derived from the Marx-Simmel-McClelland theses states that:
H2) Protestants are more oriented towards accumulation of wealth than Roman Catholics.[12]

Individualization is often referred to as a characteristic feature of a capitalist value system. The theme of individualism was already mentioned by Durkheim, who in his famous study on suicide argued that Protestants were more individualistically oriented than Catholics. Several church historians, such as Ernst Troeltsch, argued that Protestantism enhanced an individualistic orientation by confronting the human being directly with the almighty God, and Weber followed this line by pointing out the inner isolation of especially Calvinists and Puritans. This leads to the hypothesis that:

H3) Protestants are more individualistically oriented than Roman Catholics, especially with respect to morality.

Over these hypotheses we may put one derived from Weber's iron cage thesis. From being a determinant factor in the formation of societal values and ideology, religion has become marginal and dependent on developments of the economic and administrative system.[13] This line of argument can find support in a wide range of modern sociological theories. This argument could be forwarded as a hypothesis:

H4) Denominational differences regarding economic ethical issues, i.e. work, materialism and individualism, are small since these values are mainly determined by economic structures, and because the economic structures have converged in modern, capitalist Europe.

## 6    DENOMINATIONAL DIFFERENCES IN INTRINSIC WORK ORIENTATION

The analysis is based on individual response patterns across Western Europe.[14] Such an approach is closer to Weber's methodological individualism, though it may lump together response patterns which are specific to each nation (Halman & Vloet, 1994).[15] One major result from the EVS study is that work forms a central part of people's identity and value system. In Western Europe, work tops the list of core values, next to the family. Work has, however, several aspects. Understood as labour, work covers physical activities which provide means for consumption and production. Understood as craft, work covers social and creative activities which have developed the means of production to the state of advanced industrialism.

The EVS questionnaire contains a list of fifteen job characteristics and respondents were asked to indicate the importance of each of them. Analyses yielded three clusters of work qualities, and one of these can be interpreted as an intrinsic orientation to work, or work as a craft. Qualities such as 'opportunity to use your initiative', 'responsible', 'you feel you can achieve something', 'meets your abilities', 'interesting', may be combined into a simple, additive index which is related to other attitudes to work,[16] such as whether 'a decrease in the future importance of work is bad'.[17] However, an intrinsic work orientation does not imply an orientation toward hard work.[18]

Preliminary tests support the first hypothesis since the average number of these five qualities mentioned is 2.7 for the whole sample, 2.9 among members of mainline Protestant churches, i.e., Anglicans, Lutherans and Dutch Reformed, and 2.4 among members of the Roman Catholic church. These differences are statistically significant. However, national variations in these indices are noticeable. Among the unchurched, the mean is 2.6, which is quite close to the total mean. However, this empirical distinction is far too rough to grasp the subtle distinction between religious groups and types of members made by Weber.

## Table 2.1 Intrinsic work orientation* in religious and professional groups

|  | Roman Catholics | Mainline Protestants | Free Churches | All including non-members |
|---|---|---|---|---|
| Employer | 2.7 | 3.3 | 3.1 | 2.9 |
| Professional/ Middle-level non-manual | 2.9 | 3.5 | 3.5 | 3.1 |
| Junior level non-manual | 2.6 | 3.2 | 2.9 | 2.7 |
| Foreman/ skilled worker | 2.5 | 2.9 | 3 | 2.6 |
| Semi-skilled / unskilled worker | 1.9 | 2.1 | 2.1 | 2.1 |
| Farmer/ agricultural worker | 1.8 | 2.6 | 1.5 | 2 |
| All | 2.4 | 2.9 | 2.9 | 2.7 |

* Mean index value on five items, Western Europe 1990, weighted

There is a relation between people's work and their tendency to stress intrinsic work-values. People who are employed in jobs characterized by formal training, high status, leadership, responsibility are more likely to mention intrinsic work values than those in low-status jobs. The major religious groups of this study are not evenly composed of job types. The job distribution among Roman Catholics and Protestants is similar, while there is a disproportionate number of members of the free churches that work as Professionals or middle-level non-manual workers. Therefore, comparisons between the religious groups should control for the effects of people's jobs. As national samples are too small for a statistically satisfactory control, all the West-European data available have been combined.

Table 2.1 demonstrates that Roman Catholics are somewhat less oriented toward the intrinsic values of work than both Protestant groups. This difference is not great, though it is statistically significant within all job categories. Weber stressed the differences between the Protestant fractions. Calvinists are assumed to be closer to the ideal type of Ascetic Protestantism than Pietists, Baptists, Methodists, or Lutherans. It is not possible to further distinguish Protestant churches in the combined data set, but we may focus on members of Protestant free churches, such as Baptists, Pentecostals, Dutch Re-reformed, or Mormons. The distinction between mainline Protestants and nonconformist Protestants is admittedly not sharp. Nevertheless, the category of the free church members can be expected to correspond more closely with ascetic Protestantism than mainline Protestantism. Despite this, the findings demonstrate that mainline Protestants and members of free churches are highly similar in their intrinsic work orientation, even when the type of job is controlled for.

Because of the broadness of the category of free churches, this analysis must be followed up by comparative studies of social settings where Roman Catholics and Calvinists are confronted: the Netherlands, Scotland, and Northern Ireland. As for the Netherlands, two major churches are based on Calvinism: the Dutch reformed and the Re-reformed. Both cover a wide range of theological fractions, although the Re-reformed is generally considered more orthodox. The most striking outcome is that differences in work ethic are very small between these three religious communities, despite their different dogmatic traditions. In the few questions where significant differences emerge, members of the Dutch Reformed church seem more work-oriented. These refer to whether one considers work as important in one's life, whether one's children ought to learn to work hard, and whether social utility is an important aspect of work. Members of the Re-reformed church are not more work-oriented than Roman Catholics. These results are not affected by narrowing them down to those who are actually employed. This contradicts H1 on how ascetic Protestantism may inspire a work-orientation. Thus, the Dutch case does not provide any support for the Weber-inspired thesis.

Scotland includes two major religious communities: the Church of Scotland and the Roman Catholic church. The former is inspired by both the Presbyterian-Calvinist tradition of John Knox and the Anglican tradition developed south of the border. The index for the intrinsic valuation of work is 2.0 for Roman Catholics and 2.6 for members of the Church of Scotland.[19] It is especially based on denominational differences on one issue from the scale, namely the importance of using one's initiative in a job. A similar difference can be found in the proportion of people who would find it a good thing if there were less emphasis on work in the future: 42% for Catholics, compared with 26% for Protestants. This difference is highly significant. Therefore, some support can be found for H1 in Scotland.[20]

Northern Ireland is characterized by three major religious communities: The Roman Catholic, the Church of Ireland, and the Presbyterian church. There appear to be no significant differences between these communities regarding their work-orientation. Therefore, despite the existence of clearly diverse denominational groups, the case of Northern Ireland does not support H1.

It must be concluded from these national cases that the Weber-inspired thesis can only be partially supported in the case of Scotland. There is no convincing evidence that members of churches which are historically based on ascetic Protestantism are more oriented toward intrinsic values of work. The conclusion on H1 does not necessarily imply that Protestants and Catholics in modern Europe have similar views on work. An inductive analysis of the work values demonstrates value differences on another dimension than the extrinsic-intrinsic one. In most Protestant countries,[21] the top-ranking quality of work is 'pleasant people to work with', while the top-ranking quality is 'good pay' in most Catholic countries (Riffault, 1995: 36). This juxtaposition does not follow logically from the Weber-thesis. Analyses at an individual level across Western Europe confirm that Protestants tend to stress the ambience of the workplace more than Roman Catholics. Thus, pleasant colleagues are mentioned by 59% of the Roman Catholics, 71% of the mainline Protestants and 75% of the nonconformist Protestants. This finding could lead us to seek for a reformulation of the first hypothesis. However, it is questionable whether this difference can be ascribed to the religious factor. Firstly, intra-national differences between denominations are non-significant. Secondly, it should be noted that the people in the Irish Republic and Northern Ireland are generally similar regarding their views on job qualities, despite denominational differences.

One further step toward testing the first hypothesis is distinguishing between more and less committed members of the religious groups. Here, the hypothesis can not be confirmed. The respondents were asked to indicate the importance of God using a figure from 1 - none - to 10 - very much. The correlation coefficient between the index of intrinsic work values and this index of religious commitment is low for the whole sample (-0.045). The correlations are not statistically significant for either Roman Catholics or for mainline Protestants. In these cases, people's religious commitment does not seem to influence their work ethic. Therefore, the results of our analyses indicate that work values in Northern and Southern Europe are dependent on other social factors than religion, which points in the direction of the alignment-thesis.

## 7    DENOMINATIONAL DIFFERENCES IN ACQUISITIVENESS

The hypothesis refers to a specific denominational orientation toward money and material resources. However, it does not refer to the type of capitalist spirit described by Weber, but rather to the one described by Sombart.

Regrettably, the European Survey Study does not provide issues which illustrate adequate distinctions between various attitudes to money and material rewards. Some issues may be used, however, as a preliminary operationalisation. One of the items is the question whether it would be good if in the near future there would be 'less emphasis on money and material possessions'. This may refer to a materialist orientation and even to some varieties of capitalist orientation. It is possible to follow up the theme of covetousness by regarding those who wanted their children to learn thrift and who simultaneously found it a bad thing if the future development of society put less emphasis on money and material goods.

Actually, the combined Western European data show a slightly stronger materialistic orientation among members of the mainline Protestant churches than among Roman Catholics. Among the Protestants, 61% find such a development a good thing compared with 69% of the Catholics. Among members of Protestant free churches, the proportion is the same as among Catholics. The proportion of mainline Protestants who evaluate such a development as 'bad' is 19%, and thus a little higher than the proportion among the Roman Catholics, 14%, and especially among the nonconformist Protestants, a mere 8%.

A co-variation between materialism and religion could be caused by the respondents' job situation or income. In order to control for this, various employment groups are analysed separately.[22] This analysis indicates that a statistically significant difference remains between Catholics and Protestants in their evaluation of money, though only in a few job categories - among non-manual workers and among skilled and semiskilled workers. Religion thus seems to have an influence on the evaluation of material goods in combination with other factors, such as the standard of living. So religion may be a factor supporting a materialistic orientation, and Roman Catholicism seems to have a closer affinity to materialistic values than Protestantism. This conclusion contradicts the second hypothesis. However, the validity of this item is questionable.

Another adequate item for testing hypothesis 2 occurs in a battery of questions referring to qualities that children ought to develop at home. One of these is 'thrift'. It is mentioned by slightly more Protestants (37%) than Catholics (34%). When the data are split into job categories, statistically significant differences between Protestants and Catholics remain within non-manual workers and unskilled workers. This indicates that religion has some influence in a constellation with other factors.[23] According to hypothesis 2, members of Protestant free-churches should be expected to value thrift more highly than members of mainline Protestant denominations. However, the finding of only 27% refutes this.

A further approach to people's materialistic orientation is whether they regard payment as an important quality of their work. The proportion of all respondents in the combined Western European sample who mention 'good pay' is a little higher among Roman Catholics (69%), than among mainline Protestants (67%), and among nonconformists (60%). This difference is hardly dramatic, although it indicates that ascetic Protestants may be less materialistic in their outlook than members of the mainline churches. This item enables us to retrace the difference between Catholics and Protestants within several of the job categories specified - the employers, the mid-level non-manual workers, the unskilled worker and the farmers.[24]

The three items mentioned above all seem to relate to aspects of materialism, although these items do no combine into a neat scale,[25] and the findings are partially contradictory. In order to clarify the analysis further, we may investigate selected countries in order to contrast Calvinists with Roman Catholics. In Scotland, the data suggest that some confessional differences may exist regarding material values, especially regarding teaching one's children thrift. However, these differences are not statistically significant. As for the Netherlands, Roman Catholics and the Dutch Reformed hardly differ regarding material values. However, none of the Dutch Re-reformed answer that it is a bad thing if there were less emphasis on money and material goods in the future, while relatively many give the ambiguous reply that they 'don't mind'. As for Northern Ireland, no significant differences between the main confessional groups can be traced regarding the view on teaching children thrift or payment as a job incentive. On the third item, however, Presbyterians and nonconformists are less likely than Roman Catholics and members of the Church of Ireland to consider it a good thing if there were less emphasis on money in the future, and are more likely to consider it undesirable.

Such a result indicates a general tendency on the part of nonconformist Protestants to be somewhat less materialistically oriented than both mainline Protestants and Roman Catholics, which contradicts the expectations of the second hypothesis, while it supports Weber's argument on the ambiguity of ascetic Protestants toward material values. However, further data are needed on people's evaluations of economic means, and how these values are influenced by religion. By focussing on hypothesis 2 one may overlook an important supplementary finding: only a minor proportion of today's western Europeans seem to be very focussed on material values. Most people actually consider it a good thing if there were less emphasis on money and material possessions in the future. So, despite Weber's iron cage-thesis, most Western Europeans today express a wish to carry their material worries and wealth as a light, discardable burden.

One may interpret this as an outcome of a shift from material toward post-material values, as indicated by Inglehart (1990, 1997).[26] In a series of publications, he proposes a shift in values from one set oriented toward material and social security to another set oriented toward social influence and self-actualization. Inglehart argues (1990: 54) that Protestantism helped to break the traditionalistic grip of the medieval Christian world view and inspire an economic dynamism in parts of Europe. However, material needs will eventually be saturated with growing prosperity. Throughout their lives, people tend to focus on values which were scarce during their youth. The generations which have grown up in the Western world since 1945 have experienced an unprecedented economic security, which allowed them to focus on nonmaterial needs and values, such as a sense of community and the quality of life. Since the Protestant countries were the first to gain affluence, they are also the first to feel the saturation effect. According to Inglehart, this explains why materialist values seem to be more widespread among Catholic countries in southern Europe while post-materialist values are especially widespread in the Protestant region of northern Europe (1990: 59). This argument is partially based on speculations about value patterns of the past combined with documented short-term fluctuations. However, Inglehart's main argument about the saturation effect of economic growth may explain some of the findings above.

**8**    **DENOMINATIONAL DIFFERENCES IN INDIVIDUALISM**

According to the third hypothesis Protestants are expected to be more individualistic than Catholics. One problem in operationalizing this hypothesis is related to the ambiguity of the concept of 'individualism'. The term covers a wide range of meanings, from autonomy to selfishness. Empirical studies of the EVS data have demonstrated that items which point at individualism in different social fields do not form an unidimensional pattern (Halman, 1996) and moreover, the degree of individualization in different fields is not related to the economic level of the society. It is necessary to specify sub-hypotheses regarding different types of individualism, ethical, cultural and economic individualism.

As far as ethical individualism is concerned one of the morality dimensions relating to the private life can be used (Harding et al., 1986). There is a slight tendency for Roman Catholics to be more restrictive than Protestants in issues relating to private morality, such as divorce, infidelity, abortion, suicide, euthanasia. This result, however, is dependent on differences in religious commitment between the two denominations. Members of the Protestant churches in general tend to be less religiously committed than members of the Roman Catholic church. If comparisons are restricted to the most religiously committed members, differences in moral attitudes are almost evened out. Therefore, ethical individualism depends on the general religious commitment rather than on religious affiliation.

Economic individualism is a value-orientation which is close to Conservative or Liberal ideologies, though not necessarily identical to these. The 1990 EVS study contains a series of questions which illustrate people's attitudes toward a number of economic issues, namely more differentiated incomes, private ownership and free competition. Since answers to these questions do not form a scale, it is necessary to analyse them one by one. The general tendency is for mainline Protestants to be slightly more individualistic regarding economic issues than Roman Catholics on all the questions asked. Thus, mainline Protestants more often state that competition is a good thing, that there should be greater incentives for individual effort, that private ownership of business and industry should be increased. These results support the hypothesis, although the differences are not large. As for the nonconformist Protestants, the answers do not point at a higher degree of economic individualism than among mainline Protestants. They are on a par with Catholics regarding the view on competition and private ownership. If religion is an influential factor, then differences between more and less religiously committed persons should emerge. We may again utilize the importance of God as an indicator of religious commitment. However, this analysis does not render noticeable differences regarding economic individualism within the religious groups.[27]

One way to operationalize cultural individualism is by presenting a hypothetical choice between freedom and equality. Given such a choice, 52% of the Roman Catholics[28] preferred liberty compared to 66% of the mainline Protestants and 56%

of the nonconformist Protestants. This seems to pinpoint a profound divergence in views between the major denominations. However, the Protestant minorities seem less culturally individualistic than members of the major Protestant churches, which contradicts the expectation. Also in this instance, a control for the degree of religious commitment is called for. This does not reveal any internal variation among nonconformist Protestants. Preference for freedom is slightly lower among the highly committed members of the mainline Protestant churches than among members with a lower commitment, 63% and 67% respectively. The clearest contrast can be found among the Catholics, where 56% of the least committed Catholics prefer freedom, while the proportion is only 49% among the most committed ones. This indicates that religious commitment tends to counteract tendencies of cultural individualism prevailing in a capitalist society.

Cultural individualism may also be illustrated through its opposite, authoritarianism. In the questionnaire the respondents were asked to evaluate a series of changes that might take place in the near future, one of which was 'greater respect for authority'. This is one of the few items where the denominational divergence was noticeable. 76% of the free-church members found such a development a good thing, compared to 61% among the Roman Catholics, and only 37% among the members of mainline Protestant churches. It is furthermore remarkable that the appreciation of authority increases with religious commitment in all three communities which seems to indicate that cultural individualism among Protestants is not due to religion, but more to the cultural setting in which their church is embedded. Furthermore, cultural individualism seems to be hindered rather than enhanced by non-conformist Protestantism.

## 9    MODERNIZATION AND SECULARIZATION REVISED

The three hypotheses were not unambiguously supported by the data. On a few indicators, mainline Protestants seemed slightly more work-oriented, materialistic and individualistic than Roman Catholics. However, the indicators used did not demonstrate a consistent pattern, and the differences between Protestants and Catholics could not be explained by their religious commitment. Furthermore, nonconformist Protestants were generally less accommodating to a capitalist spirit than mainline Protestants. Efforts to actualize the Weber thesis for modern Europe seem to rest on false assumptions.

This could imply that society has become secularized and that religion has thus become irrelevant for the work ethics in modern capitalist society (H4). The basic hypothesis derived from modernization theory states that 'the more economically advanced a country is, the more progress both secularization and individualization will have made' (Ester et al., 1994: 41).[29] Ester et al., classified the countries according to the real gross domestic product per equivalent adult in 1988 in US-dollars in three categories, and they related this to the proportion of unchurched, marginal, modal, and core membership of churches. Their conclusion was that 'the stage of economic development is, at least in the short term, not as decisive in explaining church attendance as the (first) hypothesis assumes' (Ester et al., 1994: 46). The countries with the highest proportion of core members include the most and the least advanced countries in economic terms. They furthermore correlated measurements of orthodox beliefs with the stage of economic development, which also refuted the hypotheses. Ester et al concluded that even 'if the hypothesis that the individualization and secularization processes are economically based is restricted to Western Europe, differences between countries at the same level of wealth were too large to accept a kind of economic determinism' (Ester et al., 1994: 52). Similar results emerge when more sophisticated measurements of religiosity are used. The modernization theory needs to be revised - at least for its implications about secularization.

The vital question here is not whether people are becoming more or less religious, but whether their economic ethics and values are influenced by religious teachings. Studies of the EVS90-data show that even though core members are generally orthodox, they do not accept all the tenets, and many core members combine a belief in resurrection with a belief in reincarnation.

For the discussion of how religious views may influence people's ethics, particularly in the economic field, it is especially important to look at the types of answers they seek in the church, and which questions the churches are allowed to take up. Following up on the discussion on the relevance of the denominations in economic values and ethics, it is worth noting that less than a third (31%) of the mainline Protestants think that their church answers moral problems *adequately*, that less than a half of the Catholics have a similar opinion (44%). There are probably very few who associate the question with economic ethics. The major churches are mostly seen as providing spiritual answers, and they may take up great ethical themes such as racial discrimination, euthanasia, abortion, or the ecological balance, although they are not supposed to raise political questions. The members are split on whether their church may speak on unemployment, with 49% among the Catholics and 41% among the mainline Protestants. This does not seem to indicate that the members of the major churches welcome guidance regarding economic ethics. The free churches - which are generally closer to the ideal type of Ascetic Protestantism - are allowed by their members to take up a wider range of themes.

Another possible explanation is that the churches may still have some indirect impact on the ethical views of their adherents, though their ethical positions have changed with the establishment of modern capitalist society. The history of Europe points to the great denominational divide between North and South, and most of the studies of the EVS90 data focus upon value differences, within and between nations and groups, rather than value consensus. The final point here is to underline the basic consensus about social values among Protestants and Catholics in Western Europe today.

It is often overlooked that significant but small differences in mean indices express a considerable degree of overlapping values. A rough comparison between members of the Roman Catholic church, members of the mainline Protestant churches, and members of Non-Conformist Protestant churches[30] demonstrates that there is considerable consensus regarding the basic values: Most West Europeans agree that there should be more emphasis on family life, on individual development, on a simple and more natural lifestyle, and a considerable majority agree that there should be less emphasis on money, and more on technology. There is less agreement about whether it would be a good thing if there were greater respect for authority in the future and less emphasis on work.

**Table 2.2 A comparison of some basic values of Catholics, Mainline Protestants and members of free churches**

| % who find it a good thing if there would be: | Catholics | Mainline Protestants | Free Churches | All West Europeans |
|---|---|---|---|---|
| Less emphasis on money | 69 | 61 | 69 | 67 |
| Decreasing importance of work | 34 | 30 | 34 | 34 |
| More emphasis on family life | 92 | 90 | 88 | 88 |
| A simple and more natural lifestyle | 86 | 74 | 81 | 83 |
| More emphasis on technological development | 63 | 58 | 57 | 61 |
| More emphasis on individual development | 89 | 85 | 81 | 86 |
| More respect for authority | 57 | 46 | 78 | 53 |

It is very difficult to organize value patterns under headlines which make sense. However, Erik Allardt's (1975, 1978) suggestion that values can be put into three basic types, having, being and loving seems to offer a sensible distinction for the present task. The responses indicate that loving and being are the most important values, whereas having seems to have an instrumental status, as a condition for a good life rather than being a value in itself. This pattern of values seems to correspond to basic Christian teachings. It is a classical theme to stress loving and being as valid values and to reject the importance of having or Mammon. Nevertheless, it is questionable whether this pattern of values is directly derived from the Christian teachings.

In order to elucidate the alignment thesis, we must take a closer look at the changing economic conditions of North and South from Weber's time till the present day, and at the changing ideologies. At the turn of the century, the dynamic centers of the European economy were situated in the North, and the spokesmen of the Protestant churches were mostly allied with the bourgeoisie. Since the sociological literature has focussed rather narrowly on the economic ethics of Protestantism, it would be of interest here to outline the economic ethics of modern Catholicism.

The Catholic regions industrialized slowly, and the Catholic church found it difficult to cope with the modernization of society. *Rerum Novarum* (1891) tried to steer a middle course between Socialism and Capitalism, by stressing the dual obligations between masters and workers. This type of thinking was elaborated in *Quadragesimo Anno* (1931), which could be read as legitimizing a corporativist ideology. Mussolini's own attitude was secularistic, and Italian Fascism originally rested on its own vitalistic world-view. However, the *Concordate* paved the way for mutual respect if not understanding. It also established the principle of subsidiarity, which ensured that children could still attend Catholic schools, workers could join Catholic unions, consumers could join Catholic cooperatives, that sick persons could go to Catholic hospitals, and so forth. The corporative line of Catholicism became dominant in Austria before the Nazi takeover, in Spain under Franco, in Portugal under Salazar, and in several Latin-American countries. The fall of Fascism led to a problem of legitimization. However, the church found a new role as a bulwark against Communism. The democratic character of the third way between capitalism and Socialism was stressed by Catholic leaders in Western Europe.

Simultaneously, an economic expansion took place in Southern Europe. During the 20th century, Northern and Southern Europe have converged in their economies. Inglehart (1990: 57-61) thus points out that, whereas a high economic growth was once and almost uniquely a Protestant phenomenon, since 1965, the Catholic countries of Europe were likely to have experienced a higher economic growth rate than the Protestant countries.[31] This may help to explain why Catholics and Protestants differ so little on economic ethics today. Inglehart argues that the entrepreneurial outlook emerged in Catholic Europe during this century, while it receded in the Protestant regions (1997, 219). Inglehart has a point, since the new centres of capitalist dynamism are Munich, Torino, Milano, Madrid, Brussels, all of these cities where Catholicism continues to be strong. Furthermore, in the latest social encyclical, *Centesimus Annus* (1991), the Catholic church has revised its position slightly, be it conspicuously, toward an accommodation with private ownership of capital, while warning against cynical capitalism. In relation to the Weber thesis, it is worth noting that it also contains a full-fledged acceptance of the ethics of work. The Pope often advocates a third way between Capitalism and

Socialism. However, his attitude toward Capitalism does not differ much from the critique of Luther against cynical merchants and the warnings of Calvinist preachers against worshiping Mammon. So it seems that the Catholic church has aligned itself with the economic ethics of Protestantism.

## 10   CONCLUSIONS

Weber's thesis has inspired a series of studies on the relationship between religion and economic values in modern society. It is therefore appropriate to investigate whether such a relationship can be demonstrated in survey data from modern Western Europe. The relationship was specified in hypotheses about the differences between Catholics and Protestants in their work ethos, their attitude to wealth, and their individualism. Our analyses do not provide much evidence for these hypotheses. In modern Europe, the two main religious groups do not differ much in their work ethics, economic individualism, or emphasis on wealth, though there is some indication of differences with respect to cultural individualism. These results point at an alternative argument which stresses that economic modernization leads to secularization, implying that religion is generally regarded as irrelevant for the functioning of the economic field. The findings seem supportive to such a conclusion. However, although religion is less important for setting explicit social goals for Western Europe, it may be influential in forming implicit ideologies about human nature and human rights, the nature of society, and social justice. Whereas religion may not be seen as a legitimate and appropriate foundation for economic ethics which either legitimizes or criticizes modern capitalism, religion may still form a template of basic social values, which indirectly influences people's views on the economic system. Even today, religion may form the starting point for a critique of the capitalist economic system, since religion can from its very source underline that this system is a human creation, which necessitates some degree of loyal support in order to function and be reproduced.

**Notes**

1 The main argument of this famous essay rests on distinctions between Catholic and Protestant ethics, and between the spirit of adventure-capitalism, exemplified by the Fuggers, and the spirit of modern capitalism, exemplified by Franklin. The latter spirit is tempered and legitimized by the ideals forwarded by Ascetic Protestantism.

2 The discussion at hand does not aim at discussing the relation between the capitalist spirit and capitalism as an economic system.

3 Using Parsons' misleading translation of Goethe's term '*Wahlverwandschaft*'.

4 The units of the analysis were nations and religiously mixed countries (Great Britain, Northern Ireland, the Netherlands, West Germany) were split into a Protestant and a Catholic population. Members of other denominations were excluded. The analysis was thus rather crude with respect to the religious indicator, and Bouma's suggestion to define the type of religious belief, i.e., belief in predestination, was not followed here.

5 They operationalised the Protestant work ethic with four indices. The first one was based on Lenski's items. The second added some further items to the list. A third index on motivation for work was added. The fourth index combined preference for competition and hard work.

6 Also, Catholicism can hardly be regarded as a unified creed with respect to its economic ethics.

7 Though hardly according to the ideas of Weber.

8 Inglehart (1990: 184) has pointed out that Judaeo-Christian norms tend to be most firmly espoused by the Materialist value type, i.e., by persons who give highest priority to economic and physical security. The national variation of the Achievement Motivation Index seems rather odd. For instance, the US is on a par with Turkey, Brazil, Ireland, Spain, and India (Inglehart, 1997: 223). Furthermore, its correlation with the rate of capital economic growth depends mainly on contrasting Africa and East Asia. As for Europe, the correlation is very low.

9 It is not at all clear that a job-orientation may be regarded as a type of calling. It is entirely possible that the Protestant Ethic has become dissipated and secularized in modern times. That is, in fact, the essence of Weber's final remarks in his essay.

10 Marx also argued that the monetary system is essentially Catholic while the credit system is essentially Protestant (MEW 25. 3: 606).

11 Weber emphatically stressed that covetousness or profit-seeking had no relation in itself with capitalism in the introduction which he added for the *Gesammelte Aufsätze zur Religionssoziologie*: 'Erwerbstrieb, "Streben nach Gewinn", nach Geldgewinn, nach möglichst hohem Geldgewinn hat an sich mit Kapitalismus gar nichts zu schaffen' (Weber, 1975 :12).

12 Following Sombart, it is not necessary to stress ascetic Protestantism here. Weber would probably add that wealth is also seen by truly ascetic Protestants as a temptation for pleasure and leisure which must be castigated in order to

use it prudently according to God's will as a tool for investment and production.

13    Material goods were regarded by Baxter as a light mantle on the shoulders of the pious, but they have turned into a steel cage. 'Indem die Askese in die Welt umzubauen und in der Welt sich auszuwirken unternahm, gewannen die äusseren Güter dieser Welt zunehmende und schliesslich unentrinnbare Mach über den Menschen, wie niemals zuvor in der Geschichte' (Weber, 1975: 188).

14    Comparisons of overall figures for nations are not the best way to investigate religion as an individual motive for economic ethics. Such cross national comparisons may lead to conclusions which rest on an ecological fallacy.

15    France, UK, Western Germany, Italy, Spain, the Netherlands, Belgium, Denmark, Norway, Sweden, Ireland, Iceland. Mean index values are weighed according to population size.

16    A high degree of intrinsic work-orientation is empirically correlated with job satisfaction and freedom to take decisions in one's job. However, since the coefficients are rather weak, these issues are not identical.

17    Respective averages for those who agree and disagree are 2.38 and 2.73.

18    Those who mention hard work as a desirable quality for their children tend to score lower on the index of intrinsic work than those who do not, the respective averages being 2.43 and 2.59.

19    Which is significant at 5% level.

20    As differences between these communities with respect to job satisfaction are non-significant, the difference in attitudes to work can be interpreted as expressing an ethical view.

21    This is not easily observable in Riffault's study, since she only includes one Scandinavian country. The countries where most people mention 'pleasant people to work with' are in Riffault's study: Western Germany, Denmark, the Netherlands, Portugal. We can add Iceland, Norway, and Sweden to the list, and thus underline the regional pattern.

22    With simplified categories for the free church members.

23    Same as above.

24    Same as above.

25    As demonstrated by both factor analysis and reliability analysis.

26    Inglehart's theoretical assumptions and his operationalisations have been subject to much debate. This is not the proper place for thorough comment. Notwithstanding this critique, Inglehart has presented an inspiring new theme in the study of value changes.

27    Which points to the alternative hypothesis that economic individualism of the mainline Protestants can mostly be ascribed to their socioeconomic situation.

28    Excluding don't know answers.

29    They add 'at least in Western democracies' as a condition against the effects of secular politics in the former Socialist countries.

30    Catholics tend to give positive answers on all the value questions referred to.

31    Inglehart's conclusion is beyond dispute, though historical data on economic growth are notoriously problematic.

# References

Allardt, E. 1975. *Att ha, att älska, att vara*. Om välfärd i Norden. Lund: Aros.

Allardt, E. 1978. 'Objective and Subjective Social Indicators of Well-Being'. *Comparative Studies in Sociology* 1: 42-73.

Alwyn, D. F. 1986. 'Religion and Parental Child-Rearing Orientations: Evidence of a Catholic-Protestant Convergence'. *American Journal of Sociology* 92: 412-440.

Bouma, G.D.1970. 'Assessing the Impact of Religion: A Critical Review'. *Sociological Analysis* 31: 172-179.

Bouma, G.D.1973. 'Beyond Lenski: A Critical Review of Recent 'Protestant Ethic' Research'. *Journal for the Scientific Study of Religion* 12: 141-155.

Durkheim, E. 1969. *Le Suicide*. Paris: PUF.

Ester, P., L. Halman & R. de Moor 1994. *The Individualizing Society. Value Change in Europe and North America*. Tilburg: Tilburg University Press.

Furnham, A.1984. 'The Protestant Work Ethic: A Review of the Psychological Literature'. *European Journal of Social Psychology* 14: 87-104.

Furnham, A.1990. 'A Content, Correlational and Factor Analytic Study of Seven Measurements of the Protestant Work Ethic'. *Human Relations* 43: 383-399.

Granato, J. et al. 1996. 'The Effect of Cultural Values on Economic Development: Theory, Hypotheses, and Some Empirical Tests'. *American Journal of Political Science* 40: 607-630.

Greeley, A.M. 1964. 'The Protestant Ethic: Time for a Moratorium'. *Sociological Analysis* 25: 20-33.

Greeley, A. M.1967. 'The Influence of the 'Religious Factor' on Career Plans and Occupational Values of College Graduates'. *American Journal of Sociology* 68: 658-671.

Greeley, A.1989. 'Protestant and Catholic - Is the Imagination Extinct'. *American Sociological Review* 54: 485-502 .

Halman, L. et al. 1987. *Traditie, secularisatie en individualisering*. Tilburg: Tilburg University Press.

Halman, L. & A. Vloet 1994. *Measuring and Comparing Values in 16 Countries of the Western World*. Tilburg: WORC.

Harding, S., D. Phillips with M. Fogarty 1986. *Contrasting Values in Western Europe: Unity, Diversity and Change*. London: MacMillan.

Inglehart, R. 1990. *Culture Shift in Advanced Industrial Society*. Princeton: Princeton University Press.

Inglehart, R. 1997. *Modernization and Postmodernization. Cultural, Economic and Political Change in 43 Societies*. Princeton: Princeton University Press.

Jones, H. B. Jr. 1997. 'The Protestant Ethic: Weber's Model and the Empirical Literature'. *Human Relations* 50: 757-778.

Lenski, G.1963. *The Religious Factor*. New York: Anchor-Doubleday.

Lindseth, O. H. & O. Listhaug 1994. 'Religion and Work Values in the 1990s: A Comparative Study of Western Europe and North America'. Pp. 85-98 in T. Pettersson & O. Riis (eds.), *Scandinavian Values*. Uppsala: Uppsala University Press.

Marx, K. 1954. *Capital. A Critical Analysis of Capitalist Production*. Vol. 1. Moscow (reprint of 4th ed. 1890)

Marx, K. 1973. Theorien über den Mehrwert, MEW 26.1-3. Berlin: Dietz.

McClelland, D. 1961. *The Achievement Motive*, Princeton, N.J.: Princeton University Press.

McClelland, D. 1963. 'The Achievement Motive and Economic Growth'. Pp. in: B.F. Hoselitz & W.E.Moore (eds.), *Industrialization and Society*. The Hague: Mouton/ UNESCO.

Mirels, H. L. & J.B. Garrett.1971. 'Protestant ethic as a personality variable'. *Journal of Consulting and Clinical Psychology*, vol. 36: 40-44.

Riffault, H.1995. 'Les Européens et la valeur travail'. *Futuribles*, no. 200, Jul-Aug.: 25-46.

Rokkan, S. 1973. 'Cities, States and Nations: A Dimensional Model for the Study of Contrasts in Development'. Pp. 73-98 in S.N. Eisenstadt & S. Rokkan (eds.), *Building States and Nations*. London: Sage.

Rokkan, S. & D. Unwin 1980. *Economy, Territory, Identity*. London: Sage.

Simmel, G. 1978. *The Philosophy of Money*. London: RKP.

Scarborough, E. 1995. 'Materialist-Postmaterialist Value Orientations'. Pp. 123-150 in J. van Deth & E. Scarborough (eds.), *The Impact of Values*. Oxford: Oxford University Press.

Sombart, W. 1902. *Der moderne Kapitalismus* 1 + 2. Leipzig: Duncker & Humblot.

Sombart, W. 1913. *Der Bourgeois. Zur Geistesgeschichte des modernen Kapitalismus*. München: Duncker & Humblot.

Tang, T. L. 1993. 'A Factor Analytic Study of the Protestant Work Ethic'. *The Journal of Social Psychology* 133: 109-111.

Weber, M.1975. *Die protestantische Ethik I*. Hamburg: Siebenstern.

Weber, M. 1987. *Die protestantische Ethik II, Kritiken und Antikritiken*. Hamburg: Siebenstern.

Chapter Three

# Differential Patterns of Secularization in Europe: Exploring the Impact of Religion on Social Values

**Loek Halman & Thorleif Pettersson**

## 1    INTRODUCTION

The trajectory of modernization in the religious domain is usually described by social scientists in terms of secularization. Although this phenomenon is heavily debated and often contested, a major theme in contemporary theories on secularization is religious decline. Most often, and especially in Europe, evidence of this decline is found in decreasing levels of church attendance and adherence to traditional religious beliefs. In the United States, the religious decline is less pronounced. Trends in church attendance in the US indicate that religion is not on the wane but has persisted, which, according to some observers, is a clear refutation of the ideas of modern societies being or becoming secularized (Stark, 1997: 18; Stark & Iannaconne, 1994; Finke & Stark, 1992; Greeley, 1989).

However, since secularization is not a one-dimensional phenomenon, but a multi-dimensional concept, it would be 'inadequate to declare secularization false only by reference to individual-level belief and practice' (Chaves, 1998: 4). Indeed, the long-term trend of declining levels of church adherence and practice in Europe is just one manifestation of this process. Secularization also refers to the process in which religion gradually loses its once strong and encompassing determining impact on human life. Religion is assumed to have lost substantial parts of its role as a 'sacred canopy' influencing all segments of social life, which it has been able to do for such a long time in history (Berger, 1969). 'Secularization occurs when religious authority structures decline in their ability to control societal-level institutions, meso-level organizations, and individual level beliefs and behaviours' (Yamane, 1997: 15). Most advocates of the ideas of secularization make such a distinction in macro-, meso-, and micro-level. At the societal level, secularization refers to the declining capacity of religion 'to exercise authority over other institutional spheres. Secularization at the organizational level may be understood as the religious authority's declining control over organizational resources within the religious sphere. And secularization at the individual level may be understood as the decrease in the extent to which individual actions are subject to religious control' (Chaves, 1994: 757).

The diminishing impact of religion on social behaviour is assumed to be related to other modernization processes like specialization and structural differentiation, which have resulted in a functionally differentiated society in which religion has become one 'subsystem alongside other subsystems, and religion's overarching claims are losing their relevance' (Dobbelaere, 1993: 24). Such a decline of the importance of the religious factor is further assumed to be related to the processes of individualization and de-institutionalization. Increasingly, 'individuals claim a sort of *do it yourself* in religious matters' (Willaime, 1998b: 266), and people no longer automatically accept the prescriptions and rules from traditional institutions like the church. It has been argued that in modern settings, cultural factors have become increasingly independent of religion, political values have become less associated to religion, and social morality has become less dominated by a religious orientation (Holm, 1996: 1). In this chapter, we focus on the impact of religious orientations on orientations in other societal spheres. Is there empirical evidence for the secularization thesis that people's religious values have become largely irrelevant to their attitudes in the other domains of life?

This question needs to be fine-tuned in at least two respects. First, as with other processes of societal change, secularization processes may well differ in different social and cultural contexts. As Wilson has argued, 'the specificity of cultural conditions and historical circumstances ensure that the process by which religion loses social influence follows a distinctive, perhaps even unique, course in each separate social setting' (Wilson, 1998: 49). In other words, differences between various cultural regions must not be overlooked. For instance, even five centuries after the Reformation, obvious differences between Northern and Southern Europe with regard to the importance of the religious factor seem to remain. In Europe, secularization is considered 'an uneven process. It has affected the major Protestant churches more strongly than the Catholic Church' (Therborn 1995: 274). The explanation for this uneven process is partly found in the theological differences between Catholicism and Protestantism. The extensive, dogmatic, collective creed of the Catholic church is assumed to impose a stronger collective identity upon its members (Jagodzinski & Dobbelaere, 1995a: 81). And, as Willaime has argued, a religious culture like Protestant and Catholic cultures 'which has pervaded for centuries the mentalities, land and history of a whole nation, cannot disappear overnight' (Willaime, 1998a: 160). Thus, secularization theory must allow for variation and differences between different social and cultural regions.

The secularization thesis that in contemporary Europe, religious values are no longer linked with people's attitudes in other societal domains, must also be fine-tuned with regard to the distinction between private and public areas. In spite of counter-arguments (cf., Casanova, 1994), it is often argued that the declining impact of religious beliefs is found particularly in the public sphere, whereas the decrease of the religious influence is assumed to be less evident in matters relating to the private. 'Religious norms are no longer applicable in secular institutions, the economy and the polity, to wit the so-called public, objective world, but are rather restricted to the 'private sphere', the so-called secondary institutions or the subjective world'

(Dobbelaere, 1985: 380). Thus, this chapter focuses on whether religion has indeed a differential impact on the public and private social spheres and whether this impact does vary across the different European regions in a manner which is consistent with secularization theory.

In section 2 we will briefly discuss the differential patterns of the religious factor in Europe in general and the differential impact of religion on different social values in particular. Two hypotheses will be formulated to be empirically investigated in the subsequent sections of the paper. In section 3, we present our data, measurements and analytical strategies, and in section 4, we present the results of our analyses. The chapter concludes with a short discussion of our findings.

## 2 SECULARIZATION AND THE IMPACT OF RELIGION ON SOCIAL VALUES

Although most often evidence for or against the occurrence of secularization is found in levels of church attendance and adherence, this is just part of the evidence for or against secularization. Such figures do not indicate the significance religion may have for people living in modern society, and it is this aspect of religion's role in contemporary society which is at the core of secularization theories. As Wilson has argued, 'the secularization thesis focuses not on the decline of religions practice and belief *per se*, but on their diminishing *significance* for the social system. Clearly, decline in practice and belief might be part of such lost significance, but the decline which matters is decline in their importance, not necessarily, even if usually, decline in their appearance' (Wilson, 1998: 63).

According to the secularization thesis, religion has gradually lost substantial parts of its former impact on social life. This process is regarded as an intrinsic part of the much broader concept of modernization. The 'secularization thesis asserts that modernization (in itself no simple concept) brings in its wake (and may itself be accelerated by) 'the diminution of the social significance of religion'' (Wallis & Bruce, 1992: 11). There is more or less consensus among sociologists of religion to attribute this diminution to, or at least to consider it related to, other features of modernization, like social differentiation and specialization, rationalization, economic development, and individualization.

Social differentiation refers to the process 'by which specialized roles and institutions are developed or arise to handle specific features or functions previously embodied in, or carried out by, one role or institution' (Wallis & Bruce, 1992: 12). In traditional societies, all life spheres as well as the values within these spheres were assumed to be closely connected. Religion in particular restricted the individual's freedom and governed and shaped the values in the various domains of social life. The process of differentiation made each social sphere in life increasingly autonomous and a specialized unit in society with its own set of values and rules (Münch, 1990: 443). People in contemporary society take part in different universes of meaning which are no longer guided by a single authority. The values governing the various spheres of life are 'no longer sanctioned directly by religious beliefs, but by an autonomous rationality' (Smelser, 1973: 275). The churches have lost several of their traditional functions such as schools, hospices, social welfare, registry of births, marriages and deaths, culture, and organization of leisure (Dogan, 1995: 416). Institutional domains have become segmented in the sense that within each institutional sphere, norms and values have become functional, rational, and above all autonomous. Arguing along such lines, secularization can be regarded as 'the repercussion of these changes on the religious subsystem. It denotes a societal process in which an overarching and transcendent religious system is reduced to a subsystem of society alongside other subsystems, the overarching claims of which have a shrinking relevance' (Dobbelaere, 1995: 1). In other words, religion has lost its societal and public functions, and religion has become privatized and marginalized within its own differentiated sphere (Casanova, 1994: 19).

Among others, Weber attributed the weakened impact of religion on social life also to the rationalization and de-enchantment of the world. The decreasing importance of religion is seen as a more or less 'natural' consequence of societies becoming increasingly rational. Norms and rules in the various life spheres are increasingly legitimized by functional rationality. 'The traditional legitimation from 'above' [...] is replaced by legitimation from 'within'' (Luckmann, 1967: 101). According to Weber, modernity can be described in terms of the transformation of traditional religious authority to secular rational authority. Inglehart uses similar arguments: according to him religion has lost its encompassing influence over other spheres of life because of rapid economic growth and the development and further advancement of modern welfare states, resulting in an increasing sense of security. This is assumed to diminish the need for absolute rules as imposed by the churches and to reduce the crucial functions of the religious views, for example, the maintenance of the family unit. Further, people are said to experience inconsistencies between their daily experiences and the religious traditions: 'the daily life experience of people today is basically different from the kind of life experience that shaped the Judaeo-Christian tradition. (.....) today we live in an advanced industrial society, in which computers are far likelier than sheep to be part of one's daily experience. Consequently, not only the social norms, but also the symbols and world view of the established religions, are not as persuasive or compelling as they were in their original setting' (Inglehart, 1990: 179).

The religious decline might thus be seen as a result of increasing levels of security, produced by the modern welfare state. The increased sense of security leads to a gradual value shift 'from emphasis on economic and physical security above all, toward greater emphasis on belonging, self-expression, and the quality of life' (Inglehart, 1990: 11). The value shift from a predominantly materialistic orientation towards a post-materialistic one is expected to be 'accompanied by declining emphasis on traditional political, religious, moral, and social norms' (Inglehart, 1990: 66). In other words, in highly developed countries, the growth of postmaterialism will be accompanied by a declining impact of traditional, church-influenced social values and morality. In such societies, a decreasing number of people are inclined to accept all of the traditional religious dogmas. Economic growth, the spread of affluence, rising levels of education, increased mobilization, increased technological knowledge and its many applications, have reduced the previously dominant role of religion in human society. Due to individualization, people have become increasingly free and autonomous in selecting their own personal convictions, beliefs, and practices. Such decisions are no longer based on what the religious institutions prescribe, but on individual wants and needs. And as a result of increasing levels of international communication, not least that provided by the ever-growing mass media and the rapid spread of modern communication means, people encounter a great variety of cultural habits, values, norms, and become familiar with a large number of alternative world views. Since the cultural environment has become internationally oriented, and people's freedom to choose from an enlarged pool of religious and moral alternatives, the homogeneity in peoples' religious-moral value systems will almost by statistical necessity decrease. An increasing number of people will demonstrate their own, private religious and moral patchwork, and reject the 'menu' of the churches (Jagodzinski & Dobbelaere, 1995b). The increase in alternatives to select from and the individual's freedom to decide for themselves make it unlikely that a more or less uniform religion will remain a basic source for people's ideas and opinions in other life spheres. In fact, as has been argued before, the lives of people have become compartmentalized according to the various subsystems of society (Dobbelaere, 1995: 3), and religion is just one of these subsystems.

Although secularization may not be a global process but rather confined to Europe (cf., American theorists like Stark, Finke, and Iannaconne), the weakened social significance of religion does not occur in the same way or the same speed in all parts of Europe. Secularization, 'is observable to a variable extent in the different countries and religious cultures ... of occidental Europe' (Willaime, 1998b: 265). It has, for example, been demonstrated that the religious decline is less noticeable in the Southern countries as compared with the Nordic. In the former, the religious involvement is considerably higher, the confidence in the churches is stronger, and people are more inclined to believe in a traditional Christian way (Ester et al., 1994). It can be argued that although the two dimensions of secularization that we have discussed (the levels of religious involvement, and the impact of religious involvement on other kinds of social attitudes, respectively), do indeed concern two different aspects of social change, they should nevertheless be related. Of course, one could argue that a comparatively high degree of religious involvement is by and large facilitated by a kind of religious involvement which is unrelated to contested and debated social issues. The more religious involvement is associated with social issues which divide a people, the less it would be capable to attract all people. However, we disregard such arguments and rather assume that low levels of church attendance and adherence to traditional religious beliefs are counterbalanced by a weaker impact of religion on other domains of life.

As indicated above, Europe is not homogeneous in religious matters, and Northern Protestant Europe is most often found to be more secularized than Southern Catholic. Such differences may be interpreted from two different perspectives. The first refers to differences in theological traditions (the Catholic-Protestant divide), and the second to differences in economic development. Among others, Grace Davie (1992) attributed the different patterns of religious decline in Europe to the differences between Protestant and Catholic cultures. Due to, among other things, the greater incentives for religious individualism among Protestants, Protestant culture is assumed to be more affected by the process of secularization than Catholic culture, both in terms of a lower level of religiosity and a weaker impact of religion on other social domains. These differences have at least partly been explained by the *theological* differences between Catholicism and Protestantism. The 'seeds of individualism were manifest much earlier in Protestantism. In contrast to Catholics, Protestants are personally responsible before God in religious matters, and the church has a lesser role as mediator between the believer and God. The Catholic church, with its extensive, dogmatic, collective creed imposes a more collective identity upon its faithful' (Jagodzinski & Dobbelaere, 1995a: 81).

In his analysis of the post-modernization dimension, Inglehart found empirical evidence for the Catholic-Protestant divide in Europe. The fact that people belong to a certain religious tradition appeared more important for similarities in basic value orientations than their geographic proximity (Inglehart, 1997: 95). His 'cultural geography of the world' substantiates the assumption of a Catholic cultural profile that can be distinguished from a Protestant one. Furthermore, his analysis suggests that the cultural profile of Catholics is a global phenomenon and that all Catholic cultures are close to each other in the cultural space, irrespective of their geographical belonging. That the denomination of a country plays a crucial role in the differential European decline in 'familism' (Gundelach, 1994) is yet another sign of the importance of the differences between Catholicism and Protestantism.

In other words, there appears to be a cultural-economic syndrome of Protestantism: 'The wealthier countries and those with highly developed tertiary sectors are most likely to be long-established democracies, and the publics of these nations tend to show relatively high rates of political discussion, have less Materialist value priorities, and tend to be Protestant in religion' (Inglehart, 1990: 57). If, following Casanova, secularization is seen as a modern historical process and if it is accepted that 'the Protestant Reformation, the rise of the modern state, the rise of modern capitalism, and the rise of modern science set in motion the dynamics of the process by undermining the medieval system and themselves became at the same time the carriers of the process of differentiation, of which secularization is one aspect, then it follows that one should expect different historical patterns of secularization. As each of these carriers developed different dynamics in different places and at different times, the patterns and the outcomes of the historical process of secularization should vary accordingly' (Casanova, 1994: 24-25). Thus, the modernization, secularization, individualization processes have taken a specific form in the Northern Protestant parts of Europe, whereas in Southern European Catholic countries, the same kinds of processes have developed in a different way. Thus, the impact of religion is generally assumed to be stronger in the Catholic countries compared with Protestant countries.

Needless to say, other explanations for the differences in levels of religious involvement between Catholic and Protestant countries are also afforded. Some of these focus on economic factors. In general, countries in Northern Europe score higher on wealth and prosperity than countries in the Southern part of Europe. Since it has been assumed that 'economic development goes hand in hand with a decline in religious sentiment' (Wald quoted by Lipset, 1996: 62), the north-south cultural divide might also be explained by such economic differences. That the North-South differences in economic development can, in turn, be explained from the differences in religious traditions is a classical and disputed theory that we will not discuss in this paper. But the impact of economic factors on the degree of secularization can be understood, at least partly, from the ideas which have been put forward in deprivation-compensation theory. Among others, Charles Glock has argued that the acceptance of religion as a prime source of reference in daily life is rooted in experiences of deprivation. According to the theory, the most deprived groups in society 'are more involved religiously because they find 'alternative' gratification in this way' (Roof, 1978: 61). In other words, 'those with the strongest sense of deprivation [..] were the most likely [..] to embrace religion [...] to compensate them for the specific sort of deprivation which they suffered' (Wilson, 1982: 8). If one argues along such lines, it is most likely that people in less wealthy countries in the Southern and Eastern parts of Europe will be more inclined to be in search for compensation than people in the Northern parts of Europe, where, in general, social security provisions are well advanced, offering people more opportunities. Thus, within Europe, a North-South-East divide is likely to be found. Rokkan's conceptual map of Europe is also based on such economic and cultural parameters. The North-South divide in Europe is particularly based on the distinction Catholic-Protestant and the different conditions for integration these religious cultures provide. The East-West divide is mainly based on economic development (Rokkan, 1973).

However, 'the East' is far from homogeneous, even in terms of economic development. Countries like Poland, Czech Republic and Hungary are 'top performers' as far as economic development is concerned. The Baltic states and Slovenia are considered followers, while Bulgaria and Romania are lagging far behind (Nagle & Mahr, 1999: 53). According to Nagle and Nahr, this differential pattern of economic performance in Eastern Europe can be ascribed to a number of cultural and historical factors of which religious tradition is an important one. 'One factor often cited as advantageous is the Western Christian orientation of the northern states versus the Eastern Orthodox tradition (which is viewed as morally passive) of the southern ones [...] The key element of the religious tradition, [...], is the greater emphasis on collectivity in Eastern Orthodoxy, versus emphasis on the individual in Western Christianity' (Nagle & Mahr, 1999: 53 referring to Lewis). As we have argued before, an emphasis on the collectivity is generally regarded a strong hindrance of secularization. Therefore, one can assume that the impact of religion will be strong in these Orthodox countries.

However, such a conclusion disregards the large differences between these countries in the degree to which the churches were allowed to play a role in social and economical life. For instance, in Poland, the church played an important role in Polish struggle against communism, while in Hungary the church did not resist the party. In Czechoslovakia the Catholic church was persecuted, and controlled by the state. 'Due to the effective persecution of the Church and the more secular nature of Czechoslovak society, churches did not play a collective role in the struggle for human rights, although individual clergymen did sign Charter 77' (Nagle & Mahr, 1999: 73). Such differential patterns of religion's role in society make it hard, if not impossible, to define clear expectations as to the impact of religion on other spheres of life at the individual level.

However, apart from this regional division of Europe, another division is also likely to influence the degree to which religion is still affecting people's attitudes in other spheres of life. This division refers to the differentiation between the public and private spheres. It has been argued that religion's generally weakened impact on social life is especially noticeable in the public, economic-political realm in contrast to matters concerning the private, familial life (Berger, 1969: 129-134; Luckmann, 1967: 85f). Due to social differentiation and increasing religious diversity, religion with its overarching claims was more or less 'forced' to withdraw from the public domain, while it remained influential for matters concerning family life and personal growth (Fenn, 1972: 31), for matters 'relevant to interpersonal relations, for face-to-face contacts, for the intimacies of the family, courtship, friendship, and neighborliness' (Wilson, 1976: 6). Thus, it has been noted that a 'large and growing body of theory and research indicates that religious communities and belief systems help to shape a variety of attitudes and behaviours germane to family life: the selection of marital partners, marital quality, desired and actual family size, the timing of family formation, attitudes towards gender roles, and sexual attitudes and conduct, to name but a few areas of inquiry' (Ellison & Sherkat, 1993: 313). Apparently, religion continues to demonstrate a stronger impact on family life, the core of the private sphere, in contrast to matters in the public one. The latter domain is more separated from the churches, and institutional areas like education, welfare, medicine and law 'operate as public arenas under the general surveillance of secular government. The churches as specialized institutions have been relegated to the periphery of social life in providing certain optional rituals for baptism, marriage and death' (Turner, 1991: 199).

Thus, in comparison with private family life, religion's impact on public, social life is assumed to be weaker. 'Religion may continue within the private space of the body of individuals, but the public space of the body of populations is now subordinated, not to the *conscience collective*, the sacred canopy or the civil religion, but to secular disciplines, economic constraints and political coercion. The public realm is desacralized in Western industrial societies' (Turner, 1991: 9). Such a conclusion might also be substantiated from the political sciences, where the contemporary state of the arts seems to suggest that the religious cleavage is of less importance for political involvement and voting behaviour. Needless to say, this does of course not imply that all links between religion and politics have dissolved, but rather that they are generally weaker than the links with various dimensions of the private sphere (see, for example, Casanova, 1994; Heath et al., 1993; Jagodzinski, 1996). That religion's impact on the public sphere is weaker compared to the private, might also find support from yet another group of studies, i.e., those which concern the relation between religion and work values, another classical area of research in the social sciences of religion. In this field, 'most research suggests that religion is largely irrelevant to the work experience' (Davidson & Caddell, 1994: 135; cf., Lindseth & Listhaug, 1994). It has even been suggested that 'in the absence of other institutions capable of providing a coherent, overarching values system, it also seems likely that companies will increasingly serve that role, filling needs for personal (and material) development' (Harding & Hikspoors, 1995: 453). Thus, in the area of work, the direction of causation might be reversed from religion's impact on work u (the Weber thesis) to work experience as the provider of 'religion' (overarching meaning systems).

To summarize, then, the levels of religious involvement and the impact of religion are assumed to be of different magnitudes across two sorts of divisions, one regional and one societal. The regional division concerns the differences between Northern and Southern Europe, a division that coincides with the division between Protestantism and Catholicism. The Protestant countries are assumed to be more affected by secularization than the Catholic countries. Thus, in Catholic Europe, the impact of religion on both the private and the public sector, is assumed to be stronger than in Protestant Europe, and the levels of religious involvement are assumed to be higher.

The societal division concerns the difference between the private and public sectors. It has been argued that the impact of religion is generally stronger on values in the private domain as compared to the public. In 'the modern context, religion influences more the private than the public realm' (Tamney & Johnson, 1985: 361). As the public sectors of economy and politics developed their own rationalities and value hierarchies, traditional religion became increasingly dysfunctional when applied to these spheres. And hence, religion's impact remained stronger in the private sector than in the public.

A schema for the analysis of the differential impact of religion across the societal and regional divisions is shown in Figure 3.1.

|                | Protestant | Catholic |
|----------------|:----------:|:--------:|
| **Public sphere**  | a | b |
| **Private sphere** | c | d |

**Figure 3.1 A comparative schema for the analysis of the differential impact of the religious factor across regions and the public and private sectors**

In Figure 3.1, the cells (a through d) indicate the 'impact of religion'. As mentioned above, the impact is expected to be stronger in the Catholic than in the Protestant (a < b; c < d), and stronger on the private sphere than on the public sphere (a < c; b < d).

Thus, in this chapter we try to find empirical evidence for the general assumption that the impact of religiosity on both the public and private spheres is stronger in Catholic Europe compared to Protestant Europe. Further, we hypothesize that both in Catholic as well as in Protestant Europe, the impact of religion will be stronger on values in the private sphere than on values in the public sphere.

As we have argued, the Catholic-Protestant divide certainly disregards the Eastern European countries. In these countries, a distinction between Orthodox and Catholic countries has been suggested, but it has also been argued that Catholicism in Poland is of a different kind than, for instance, in Hungary or Czechoslovakia. Therefore, we refrain from formulating a clear-cut and general hypothesis on the impact of religion in the Eastern European countries, although we have for explorative purposes included these countries in our analyses.

## 3 DATA, MEASURES AND METHOD

Our empirical analyses are based on the survey data from the 1990 European Values Study in France, Great Britain, West Germany, Austria, Italy, Spain, Portugal, the Netherlands, Belgium, Denmark, Norway, Sweden, Northern Ireland, Ireland, Poland, East Germany, Bulgaria, Hungary, the Czech Republic, the Slovak Republic, Romania, Estonia, Latvia, Lithuania (for more information, we refer to Halman & Vloet, 1994).

One may argue that in order to establish the impact of religion, one should focus on institutional religion, that is investigate whether or not churches are (still) an important voice in contemporary society, whether or not churches have any influence on national politics or on the running of a business, whether or not it matters what religious leaders say about modern family life, etc. However, we have argued that secularization refers to individual religious values and behaviours as well. Consequently, we focus on people's religious convictions and their religious practices: personal religiosity and church attendance.

As indicators of individual religious involvement, we included one measure of traditional institutional religiosity (church attendance) and one of religious beliefs (importance of God). The latter does not necessarily refer to traditional, Christian, institutional religiosity. Church attendance is measured by the question: 'Apart from weddings, funerals and christenings, about how often do you attend religious services these days?'. The answer possibilities ranged between 1 ( = More than once a week) and 8 ( = Never, practically never). *Importance of God* is measured by the question: 'And how important is God in your life? As answer categories, a 10-point scale was used (1 = not important at all; 10 = very important).

As a value measure relevant to the private sphere, we selected four variables referring to family life and the relationships between (nuclear) family members.[1] These items tap what might be labeled as '*Non-traditional family values*', e.g., whether or not children need both father and mother to grow up happily, whether or not one approves of a woman who wants to have a child without having a stable relationship with a man, and whether or not parent-child relations are to be based on strict hierarchical relations and obligations. The internal consistency of the scale is rather limited ($\alpha$ = .31). Nevertheless, by applying factor analysis to these four items, a score was calculated indicative of the (non-)preference for a traditional family view.

As measures relevant to the public domain, a large number of orientations are available from the EVS-data. We understand the public sphere as primarily linked to 'the area of race, politics, economics, and national life' (Tamney & Johnson 1985: 360), i.e., to the organization of society. Three questions in the EVS questionnaire relate to this dimension. In each of the three questions, the respondents were asked to choose between two opposite statements: A) 'incomes should be made more equal' versus 'there should be greater incentives for individual effort'; B) 'private ownership of business and industry should be increased' versus 'government ownership of business and industry should be increased'; and C) 'individuals should take more responsibility for providing for themselves' versus 'the state should take more responsibility to ensure that everyone is provided for'. These items tap people's views on politics and economy, i.e., they indicate if people are in favour of equality, individual freedom and responsibility. These *political views* have a high internal consistency ($\alpha$ = .68). As was the case for private values, we applied factor analyses to calculate a mean score on the public dimension.

A first step in our empirical investigations is to assess the levels of religious involvement in each of the 23 countries. To this end, we will combine two kinds of analyses. First, we will rank the countries according to the levels of church attendance and the importance of God, respectively. Next, we will apply regression analyses, regressing church attendance and importance of God, respectively, on age, gender, level of education, together with a set of country dummy variables, where

Northern Ireland is the reference category. The obtained unstandardized regression coefficient for the country dummy variables are then used as measures of the national impact on the level of church attendance and importance of God, respectively. The lower the regression coefficient, the lesser the impact (cf., Dobbelaere & Jagodzinski, 1995: 210-212). Thus, by these two kinds of analyses, we will obtain 4 orderings of the levels of religious involvement in the 23 countries: two orderings from the national means of church attendance and the importance of God, respectively, and two from the regression analyses of the country dummies.

As a next step, we will explore the impact of religion on the private (family values) and public (political values) sectors. For each country, 'traditional family values' and 'political views' will be regressed on importance of God, church attendance, age, education, and gender. The unstandardized regression coefficients of the variables 'importance of God' and 'church attendance' can then be used as measures of the impact of each of the indicators of religious involvement on the private and public spheres.

In order to investigate the relationships between the two forms of religious decline (the national levels of religious involvement, and the national degrees of the impact of the religious involvement on family values and political view), the ordering of the countries with regard to 1) the levels of religious involvement, and 2) the impact of the religious factors on the private and public factors, will then be compared, both vis-à-vis each other as well as vis-à-vis structural socio-economic dimensions, such as GDP per capita.

## 4    RESULTS

In Table 3.1, the 23 countries are ranked according to each of the two analyses of church attendance and the importance of God, respectively. It is obvious that the four measures we use, rank the countries in a very similar way. Thus, the Spearman rank correlation coefficients range between .92 and .99. The orderings of the national means for church-attendance and the countries' regression coefficients for church attendance are almost identical ($r_s$ = .99; p < .001). A similar result is obtained for the rankings of the national means for the importance of God and the countries' regression coefficients for the importance of God, respectively ($r_s$ =.97, p < .001). The rank correlation between the national means for church attendance and importance of God is somewhat lower but still highly significant ($r_s$ .92; p < .001). The rankings of the two measures of the national impact on church attendance and the importance of God, respectively, are also significantly similar ($r_s$ .92; p < .001). Since the four different rankings of the countries with regard to the levels of religious involvement yield such similar results, we calculated a mean ranking for the 23 countries. The mean rankings are presented in the last column of Table 3.1.

**Table 3.1 Personal religiosity, church attendance and the impact of national context, measures of secularization**

| | Importance of God | | | | Church attendance | | | | Rank | |
|---|---|---|---|---|---|---|---|---|---|---|
| | B | rank | mean | rank | B | rank | mean | rank | mean | rank |
| Czech Rep | -4.25 | 1 | 3.54 | 1 | -2.83 | 3 | 2.59 | 3 | 2.00 | 1 |
| Bulgaria | -4.12 | 3 | 3.56 | 2 | -2.84 | 2 | 2.58 | 2 | 2.25 | 2 |
| Sweden | -3.64 | 5 | 3.75 | 4 | -2.87 | 1 | 2.40 | 1 | 2.75 | 3 |
| E. Germany | -4.19 | 2 | 3.65 | 3 | -2.62 | 55 | 2.82 | 6 | 4.25 | 4.5 |
| Denmark | -3.66 | 4 | 3.92 | 5 | -2.72 | 4 | 2.65 | 4 | 4.25 | 4.5 |
| France | -3.23 | 6 | 4.43 | 6 | -2.62 | 55 | 2.75 | 5 | 5.50 | 6 |
| Norway | -3.05 | 7 | 4.55 | 8 | -2.48 | 7 | 2.91 | 7 | 7.25 | 7 |
| Great Britain | -2.60 | 10 | 5.25 | 11 | -2.42 | 8 | 3.05 | 8 | 9.25 | 8 |
| Latvia | -2.99 | 8 | 4.46 | 7 | -1.60 | 13 | 3.74 | 13 | 10.25 | 9 |
| Netherlands | -2.75 | 9 | 4.90 | 9 | -1.88 | 12 | 3.51 | 12 | 10.50 | 10 |
| Belgium | -2.49 | 12 | 5.22 | 10 | -1.99 | 11 | 3.42 | 11 | 11 | 11.5 |
| Hungary | -2.51 | 11 | 5.41 | 13 | -2.09 | 10 | 3.41 | 10 | 11 | 11.5 |
| Iceland | -1.28 | 17 | 6.11 | 15 | -2.21 | 9 | 3.06 | 9 | 12.50 | 13 |
| W. Germany | -2.49 | 13 | 5.36 | 12 | -1.52 | 14 | 3.94 | 14 | 13.25 | 14 |
| Slovak Rep. | -1.81 | 14 | 5.97 | 14 | -1.12 | 17 | 4.28 | 17 | 15.50 | 15 |
| Spain | -1.56 | 15 | 6.25 | 16 | -1.17 | 16 | 4.24 | 16 | 15.75 | 16 |
| Portugal | -0.99 | 18 | 6.72 | 18 | -1.23 | 15 | 4.10 | 15 | 16.50 | 17 |
| Austria | -1.54 | 16 | 6.26 | 17 | -1.06 | 18 | 4.38 | 18 | 17.25 | 18 |
| Romania | -2.36 | 20 | 7.45 | 20 | -.74 | 19 | 4.66 | 19 | 19.50 | 19.5 |
| Italy | -.65 | 19 | 7.15 | 19 | -.27 | 20 | 5.15 | 20 | 19.50 | 19.5 |
| N. Ireland | .00 | 21 | 7.82 | 21 | .00 | 20 | 5.45 | 21 | 21 | 21 |
| Ireland | .16 | 22 | 7.93 | 22 | 1.27 | 23 | 6.69 | 23 | 22.50 | 22.5 |
| Poland | .68 | 23 | 8.43 | 23 | .88 | 22 | 6.31 | 22 | 22.50 | 22.5 |

In order to find regional patterns with regard to the national levels of religious involvement, we performed cluster analyses[2] of the four measures of the levels of religious involvement. The results are presented in Table 3.2. The Czech Republic appears most secular together with Bulgaria, Sweden, East Germany, Denmark, France, and Norway. A second cluster of countries consists of somewhat less secular societies: Great Britain, Latvia, the Netherlands, Belgium, Hungary, Iceland, and West Germany. A third cluster contains Spain, the Slovak Republic, Portugal, Austria, whereas Romania, Italy, and Northern Ireland appear in a fourth cluster. Finally, the countries with the highest degrees of religious involvement are Ireland and Poland. Table 3.2 presents the mean scores on church attendance and the importance of God for these five groups of countries.

**Table 3.2  Mean scores for four clusters of countries on church attendance and importance of God and degree of secularization based on church attendance and importance of God**

|  | Church attendance | Importance of God | Secularization (church) | Secularization (imp God) |
|---|---|---|---|---|
| 1 most secular (CZ, Bu, Sw, EG, De, No, Fr) | 2.67 | 3.91 | -2.71 | -3.73 |
| 2 (GB, La, Nl, Be, Hu, Ic, WG) | 3.51 | 5.09 | -1.92 | -2.47 |
| 3 (Sp, Sl, Por, Au) | 4.01 | 6.26 | -1.36 | -1.44 |
| 4 (Ro, It, NI) | 5.09 | 7.47 | -.34 | -.30 |
| 5 most religious (Ir, Pl) | 6.50 | 8.18 | 1.06 | .43 |

Some interesting results from the cluster analysis deserve attention. For instance, although the Czech and the Slovak Republics were still united at the time when the 1990 EVS data were collected, they appear very different with regard to the levels of religious involvement. The Czech Republic appears as the most secular country, while the Slovak belongs to the more religious parts of Europe. Furthermore, Italy appears more religious than Spain and Portugal, two countries that are *less* modernized compared to Italy when economic parameters are investigated. Particularly Portugal is less developed economically. Thus, this country is expected to display lower levels of secularization than the likewise Catholic Spain and Italy. However, the opposite appears to be the case.

Further, the results do not indicate a clear difference between Eastern and Western Europe. Poland is among the most religious countries in Europe, while the Czech Republic, Bulgaria and Eastern Germany display high levels of secularization similar to these obtained for Sweden, Denmark, and Norway. Romania resembles the Italian religious pattern, while Hungary and Latvia are closer to Great Britain, the Netherlands and Belgium than to other Eastern European countries. Thus, as expected, the countries of Eastern Europe do not appear as a distinct and homogenous region with regard to the religious dimensions we have investigated.

As seen from Table 3.2, a certain division between Catholic and Protestant countries seems to exist with regard to the two religious dimensions we investigated, with indeed lower levels of religious involvement in the Protestant Nordic countries, and higher levels in the Southern Catholic ones. However, Iceland is mainly Protestant, but in terms of the level of religious involvement, it evidently demonstrates higher levels than the other Nordic countries. France belongs to the cluster of most secular countries, although about 60% of its population is Catholic. A similar remark can be made with respect to Belgium. This is clearly a Catholic country, but it belongs to the cluster of the more secularized countries. So, although the Catholic-Protestant divide can be traced by the cluster analysis, there are obvious exceptions to the general assumption that the religious involvement is lower in the Protestant countries as compared to the Catholic. In this regard, it should also be mentioned that a cluster analysis of only the Western European countries does not demonstrate the expected Catholic-Protestant divide. In a similar sense, it should be noticed that the orthodox countries are not homogenous either in terms of church attendance and the importance of people's beliefs in God. The Bulgarian orthodox culture appears comparative secularized, while the Romanian orthodox culture appears to score comparatively high on religious involvement.

Thus, as a concluding remark, it should be emphasized that a clear-cut and easily interpretable regionalisation does not emerge with regard to the levels of religious involvement among the 23 European countries. The patterns that emerge only partly relate to the differences between the main Christian traditions. Therefore, besides the differences between the theological traditions, the national levels of religious involvement must depend on other factors as well. As we have argued, the degree of economic development should be one of these. As expected, the mean ranking of the levels of religious involvement is fairly similar to the national levels of economic development (GDP per capita) ($r_s$ -.38; $p < .05$; one-sided test; a low rank on the scale means a low level of religious involvement). The corresponding rankorder correlation including only the Western European countries is -.77 ($p < .01$). The corresponding coefficient for the Easter European countries is -.60 ($p < .06$). Thus, among the 23 countries, there is a significant relationship between the national levels of economic development and religious involvement. However, from the magnitude of the rank correlations, it can be concluded that the degree of economic development is far from being the only factor determining the national levels of religious involvement. With regard to the national levels of economic development, it should also be noted that there is a significant relationship between GDP per capita and the percentage of Protestants among the 23 countries ($r = .67$; $p < .000$; $r_s = .64$; $p < .000$). At the same time, the proportion of Protestants in a country is indecisive for the degree to which a society is secularized. More important, however, is the proportion of Catholics. The more Catholics in a country, the less secular the country ($r=.68$; $p < .000$; $r_s = .71$; $p < .000$). The same applies to the importance of God ($r = .59$; $p < .000$; $r_s = .57$; $p < .000$). Thus, with regard to the *levels* of religious involvement, there seems to be some evidence for the existence of a Catholic-Protestant divide in Europe.

Our hypotheses that the impact of religious involvement would be stronger on values pertaining to the private sphere as compared to the public, and that the impact would be stronger in Catholic countries as compared to Protestant ones was tested empirically by means of regression analyses. In Table 3.3, the relevant unstandardized regression coefficients are displayed. The higher the regression coefficients, the stronger the relationship between church attendance on the one hand and the importance attributed to God, family values and political views on the other. First, it should be noted that the results do not reveal any systematic relationship whatsoever between the magnitude of the unstandardized regression coefficients and the national levels of religious involvement, either among the 23 countries as a group or among any of the subgroups of countries (Western vs non-Western; Catholic vs Protestant).

The attitude towards the family is least influenced by the importance of God in Hungary, Bulgaria, the Czech Republic, Slovakia, and East Germany, and most influenced in Northern Ireland and Ireland. Church attendance appears to be least important for the attitude towards the family in Bulgaria and Latvia, and most important in West Germany, Sweden, and the Netherlands. Although Poland and Romania demonstrated high levels of religious involvement, the impact of the importance of God on attitudes towards the family is hardly noticeable. The same can be said about Ireland, with regard to the impact of church attendance on family values. In Nordic countries like Sweden, religious involvement is low, yet church attendance in this country appears to affect the family orientation. The effect is even stronger than in Poland and Ireland, two societies with considerably higher levels of religious involvement. Thus, although the countries differ as to the impact of the religious involvement, we cannot find any clear regionalisation of the countries with regard to the magnitude of this impact.

With regard to the political values, the magnitude of the regression coefficients in Table 3.3 is indeed weak. However, when we attempt to cluster the countries according to this dimension, it is suggested that religious involvement seems to have a stronger impact on people's political views in Eastern as compared to Western Europe, although East Germany is an exception as far as the importance of God is concerned. The rankings of the regression coefficients indicating the impact of religious involvement on family values and political views appear highly similar to the rankings of the countries according to economic prosperity. The more wealthy a country is, the stronger the impact of church attendance of family attitudes, but the lower its impact on political views. A similar conclusion can be drawn as far as the effect of importance of God on both value orientations is concerned. The different levels of impact do not seem to be related to the proportions of Catholics, Protestants and/or unchurched people in a country.

Thus, our hypothesis that the impact of religious involvement would be stronger in Catholic countries as compared to the Protestant ones is not substantiated by our results. With regard to the Catholic-Protestant divide, we have only found it to be related to the *levels* of religious involvement, and not to the *degree* to which it is related to family values and political views.

**Table 3.3  The impact of personal religiosity (importance of God) and church attendance on private and public values**

| PRIVATE SPHERE | | | | PUBLIC SPHERE | | | |
|---|---|---|---|---|---|---|---|
| Importance God | | Church attendance | | Importance God | | Church attendance | |
| Country | B | Country | B | Country | B | Country | B |
| HU | .036*** | BU | .023 | AU | .000 | BE | .000 |
| BU | .042*** | LA | .026* | EG | .000 | SP | .000 |
| CZ | .043*** | IC | .034*** | FR | .000 | FR | .000 |
| SL | .046*** | CZ | .042*** | WG | .001 | SW | .001 |
| EG | .047*** | RO | .047*** | DE | .001 | IC | .001 |
| RO | .051*** | SL | .058*** | NO | .001 | NL | .001 |
| LA | .052*** | HU | .066*** | SW | .001 | GB | .001 |
| PT | .056*** | PL | .073*** | PT | .001 | IT | .002 |
| FR | .058*** | BE | .074*** | NL | .002 | NO | .002 |
| AU | .060*** | EG | .078*** | SP | .002 | NIR | .003 |
| PL | .061*** | PT | .081*** | BE | .002 | IR | .003 |
| NO | .071*** | SP | .082*** | IT | .002 | PT | .004 |
| DE | .076*** | GB | .085*** | IC | .002 | DE | .004 |
| BE | .080*** | AU | .091*** | CZ | .002 | WG | .005* |
| SW | .085*** | IR | .094*** | RO | .003 | AU | .006 |
| GB | .087*** | FR | .097*** | GB | .003* | SL | .008 |
| SP | .089*** | NIR | .101*** | NIR | .003 | CZ | .010 |
| IT | .090*** | DE | .103*** | IR | .005* | PL | .013 |
| NL | .110*** | NO | .104*** | PL | .010 | EG | .013 |
| IC | .113*** | IT | .104*** | HU | .012 | HU | .029 |
| WG | .118*** | NL | .118*** | SL | .044* | BU | .030 |
| NIR | .131*** | SW | .121*** | LA | .053 | RO | .035 |
| IR | .143*** | WG | .149*** | BU | .054** | LA | .057 |

Note: unstandardized regression coefficients; * P < .05; ** P < .01; *** P < .001

According to our second hypothesis, the impact of religious involvement should be stronger on values pertaining to the private sphere (family values) as compared to values relating to the public sphere (political values). In general, this hypotheses seems to be in accordance with the results (mean of the unstandardized regression coefficient for religious involvement and family values is .08, as compared to .009

with regard to religious involvement and political views). Disregarding whether the relationships are significant or not, and only considering the numeric values of the regression coefficients in Table 3.3, we see that the relationship between the importance of God and family values in no less than 21 of the all in all 23 instances are higher than the corresponding coefficients for the relationship between the importance of God and political views. The corresponding relation for church attendance is 20 out of 23 instances. Such results in favour of our hypothesis would hardly occur by chance. Furthermore, if we look only at the regression coefficients which are statistically significant, the importance of God is significantly related to family values in all 23 countries, while it is only significantly related to political views in 4 countries. Church attendance has a significant relationship to family values in 22 of the 23 countries, while it has a significant effect on political views in only 1 country. In summary, it can therefore be concluded that by and large the impact of religious involvement seems to be stronger on values pertaining to the private than on values pertaining to the public sphere.

## 5    DISCUSSION

In this Chapter, we have investigated patterns of secularization among 23 European countries. First, we touched upon the relation between the two dimensions of secularization which concern the levels of religious involvement, and the impact of religious involvement on other dimensions of social life, respectively. Our cross-sectional analyses of the 23 countries suggested, contrary to our expectations, that the national levels of religious involvement were by and large unrelated to the relationships between the religious involvement and family values and political views.

In a certain sense, this result can be related to studies which have found the impact of religion on other domains, for example, moral beliefs, to be *unrelated* to the secularization process (Jagodzinski & Dobbelaere, 1995b: 230). According to such a view, declining individual church attendance does not imply a decreasing impact of church attendance on, for example, individual moral values. However, in such matters, one should be careful in making inferences about social processes from cross-sectional analyses. Therefore, we can only conclude that in our analyses the levels of religious involvement, and the impact of religious involvement on private and public issues, respectively, seem to be unrelated. Whether this also indicates that the changes in one of them are unrelated to the changes in the other is quite another issue.

Of course, this does not exclude the possibility that the two dimensions are also unrelated in a longitudinal sense. In this regard, we assume that people's moral values depend on several factors, of which their religious involvement is one. When the religious factor 'disappears' (declines), the degree to which their moral values will be influenced by the remaining factors will be greater. And hence, the lower the national levels of religious involvement, the lower the impact of religious involvement on the moral values.

Of course, there is the possibility that among the decreasing flock of the religiously involved, religious involvement may become of *increasing* importance to their moral values. For those who remain religiously involved, their religious involvement may become the sole determinant of their moral beliefs. If this should be the case, then declining national levels of religious involvement would not necessarily be accompanied by a decreasing impact of the religious involvement on other social domains. However, the analyses we have performed do not allow of any definitive conclusions in these matters. We can only conclude that we have not found convincing evidence that people who differ in the degree to which they attend religious services adhere to different family values or political views. Church attendance does matter, but in a majority of the countries only to a very limited extent.

The explanation for this finding might, among other things, be found in our suggestion that comparatively high degrees of religious or church involvement are by and large facilitated when the involvement is unrelated to contested and debated social issues. To the degree to which the social issues we have investigated (family values, and political views, respectively) are contested and disputed, they should be unrelated to religious involvement in countries where the religious involvement is comparatively high. On the other hand, in countries where the religious involvement is comparatively low, the situation might be reversed. In such a case, the religious involvement might be more easily related to a specific view on contested social issues.

But whatever the explanation, and whatever the consequences for secularization theory, we conclude that in our cross-sectional analyses, the national levels of religious involvement seem to be largely unrelated to the strength of the relationship between the religious involvement and views on family values and political views, respectively.

With regard to the impact of religious involvement on different social issues, we have investigated two hypotheses. As for the regional differences, we assumed the impact of the religious involvement to be stronger in Catholic countries as compared to Protestant ones. With regard to substantial or social issues, we assumed that irrespective of the dominant religious tradition, the impact of the religious involvement would be stronger on issues pertaining to the private sphere than on issues more relevant to the public sphere.

We performed several multivariate analyses to test these hypotheses. Overall, the results were not very supportive of our assumptions. With regard to the regional differences and the assumed Catholic-Protestant divide, we found only positive results with regard to the levels of religious involvement, but not with regard to the impact of religious involvement on other domains of social life. The impact of religious involvement on family values and political views did not vary systematically across countries with different levels of religious involvement, and we found no clear-cut Catholic-Protestant divide with respect to the dimensions we have analysed. Likewise, we did not find any obvious East-West divide, neither with regard to the levels of religious involvement, nor in terms of the impact of religion on public and private issues.

As for the suggestion about the differential impact of religion on private and public issues, our results were more in accordance with our theoretical expectations. The relationship between the religious involvement and the family values seemed to be generally stronger as compared to the relationship between religious involvement and political views. However, in most countries, the differential impact of religion on the private and public sectors appeared fairly modest and the positive results in this regard should not be exaggerated.

Nevertheless, we have found some evidence in favour of the hypothesis that religious involvement is differently related to family values and political views, i.e., to what we assumed to be indicators of the private and public sectors. At the same time, it should be noted that the distinction between the private and public sectors has been questioned. It has been argued that people's decisions and choices in both the public and the private domain are decisions of the individual, and that in this sense they are privatized. In this sense, it seems artificial to divide the social structure into two different parts, one private and one public (Dobbelaere 1985: 381). We agree that most kinds of social behavior are becoming increasingly privatized, i.e., that the individual has increasing freedom of choice in all social domains. We have argued that modernization has liberated the individual from traditional constraining institutions and that in the contemporary social order, people are increasingly autonomous and free to decide for themselves. According to Inglehart, the contemporary cultural and social developments indicate a fundamental shift in which people increasingly reject all kinds of authority and mainly focus on their own well-being (Inglehart, 1997).

However, at the same time, the freedom for individual choices is greater in some sectors than in others. In the economic and political sectors, individual freedom and personal choice are more restricted. In these sectors, norms and behaviours are legitimized by functional rationality, and the options to choose from are determined and constrained by politics and laws. As far as private life is concerned, greater freedom is allowed. The traditional nuclear family is no longer the only accepted type of family. Increasing numbers of non-traditional families and forms of households have become acceptable. In contrast to the economic and political sectors no new boundaries or limitations are imposed on people's choices. As has been reported elsewhere, individualization has resulted in a great variety of relationships and family types people can opt for, although their actual preferences for the traditional patterns remain remarkably alive (Halman, 1998: 29; see also

Inglehart, 1997).

In summary, then, we have found some evidence that the impact of the religious involvement is stronger in the private sector than in the public, although the impact of the religious involvement proved to be weak. Even if the countries differed in the degree to which religious involvement had an effect, the magnitude of this effect was rather limited. Furthermore, the differences between the countries in this regard could hardly be attributed to the fact that they were part of a specific cultural and/or political system. The level of economic development appeared more important. Thus, the differences we have found between the countries with regard to the two dimensions of secularization should also be explained by other, more specifically, economic factors, than the ones we have investigated. To find these factors, one might, for example, explore in more detail the different institutional settings and/or historical antecedents in the various countries. The former option would provide some kind of a general, nomothetic understanding of the differences between the countries, the latter some kind of a detailed and ideographic understanding. Of course, a third option might be to conclude that national differences with respect to the dimensions of religious involvement which we have investigated are small. Thus, the countries we have investigated are astonishingly similar with respect to both the levels of religious involvement and the impact of the religious involvement on attitudes in the private and public sectors. In this sense, our analyses of the 23 European countries suggest that Europe is fairly homogenous with regard to dimensions of religious involvement.

**Notes**

1 The four items address the question whether or not children need both a father and a mother to grow up happily (yes, no); whether or not one approves of a woman who wants to have a child without having a stable relationship with the father (approve, disapprove, neither). Both items tap views on family patterns. Two additional items tap the relationships between parents and their children. The first item is 'Which of these two statements do you tend to agree with? A. Regardless of what the qualities and faults of one's parents are, one must always love and respect them; B. One does not have the duty to respect and love parents who have not earned it by their behaviour and attitudes'; and the second 'Which of the following statements best describes your views about parents' responsibilities to their children? 1. Parents' duty is to do their best for their children even at the expense of their own well-being; 2. Parents have a life of their own and should not be asked to sacrifice their own well-being for the sake of their children'.

2 Ward's method was used.

# References

Berger, P.L. 1969. *The Sacred Canopy. Elements of a Sociological Theory of Religion*. Garden City: Doubleday & Company.

Casanova, J. 1994. *Public Religions in the Modern World*. Chicago and London: The University of Chicago Press.

Castles, F. 1994. 'On Religion and Public Policy. Does Catholicism Make a Difference?'. Paper presented at the *Swedish Collegium for Advanced Study in the Social Sciences*, Uppsala: SCASSS, Uppsala University.

Chaves, M. 1994. 'Secularization as Declining Religious Authority'. *Social Forces* 72: 749-774.

Chaves, M. 1998. 'In Appreciation of Karel Dobbelaere on Secularization'. Pp. 3-5 in R. Laermans, B. Wilson & J. Billiet (eds.), *Secularization and Social Integration*. Leuven: Leuven University Press.

Davidson, J.C. & D.P. Caddell (1994). 'Religion and the Meaning of Work'. *Journal for the Scientific Study of Religion* 33: 135-147

Davie, G. 1992. 'God and Ceasar: Religion in a Rapidly Changing Europe'. Pp. 216-238 in J. Bailey (ed.), *Social Europe*. London and New York: Longman.

Dobbelaere, K. 1985. 'Secularization Theories and Sociological Paradigms: A Reformulation of the Private-Public Dichotomy and the Problem of Societal Integration'. *Sociological Analysis* 46: 377-387.

Dobbelaere, K. 1993. 'Church Involvement and Secularization: Making Sense of the European Case'. Pp. 19-36 in E. Barker, J.A. Beckford & K. Dobbelaere (eds.), *Secularization, Rationalism and Sectarism*. Oxford: Clarendon Press.

Dobbelaere, K. 1995. 'Religion in Europe and North America'. Pp. 1-30 in R. de Moor (ed.), *Values in Western Societies*. Tilburg: Tilburg University Press.

Dobbelaere, K. & W. Jagodzinski 1995. 'Religious Cognitions and Beliefs'. Pp. 197-217 in: J.W. van Deth and E. Scarbrough (eds.), *The Impact of Values*. Oxford: Oxford University Press.

Dogan, M. 1995. 'The Decline of Religious Beliefs in Western Europe'. *International Social Science Journal* XLVII: 405-418.

Ellison, C. & D. Sherkat 1993. 'Obedience and Autonomy: Religion and Parental Values Reconsidered'. *Journal for the Scientific Study of Religion* 32: 313-329.

Ester, P., L. Halman & R. De Moor (eds.) 1994. *The Individualizing Society*. Tilburg: Tilburg University Press.

Fenn, R.K. 1972. 'Toward a New Sociology of Religion'. *Journal for the Scientific Study of Religion* 11: 16-32.

Finke, R. & R. Stark 1992. *The Churching of America, 1776-1990: Winners and Losers in our Religious Economy*. New Brunswick, NJ: Rutgers University Press.

Greeley, A. 1989. *Religious Change in America*. Cambridge MA: Harvard University Press.

Gundelach, P. 1994. 'National Value Differences. Modernization or Institutionalization?'. *International Journal of Comparative Sociology* XXXV: 37-58.

Halman, L. 1998. *European Images and Discourses on the Family*. Tilburg: WORC.

Halman, L. & R. de Moor 1994. 'Comparative Research on values'. Pp. 21-36 in P. Ester, L. Halman & R. de Moor (eds.), *The Individualizing Society*. Tilburg: Tilburg University Press.

Halman, L. & A. Vloet. 1994. *Measuring and Comparing Values in 16 Countries of the Western World*. WORC Report. Tilburg: WORC.

Harding, S. & F. Hikspoors. 1995. 'New Work Values: In Theory and in Practice'. *International Social Science Journal* XLVII: 441-456.

Heath, A., B. Taylor & G. Toka. 1993. 'Religion, Morality and Politics'. Pp. 49-80 in R. Jowell, L. Brook & L. Dowds (eds.), *International Social Attitudes. The 10th BSA report*. Aldershot: Dartmouth.

Holm, N.G. 1997. 'The Study of World Views'. Pp. 1-12 in N.G. Holm & K. Björkqvist (eds.), *World Views in Modern Society*. Åbo: Åbo Akademi University.

Inglehart, R. 1990. *Culture Shift in Advanced Industrial Society*. Princeton: Princeton University Press.

Inglehart, R. 1997. *Modernization and Postmodernization*. Princeton: Princeton University Press.

Jagodzinski, W. 1996. 'The Transformation of the Religious Cleavage in West European Party Systems'. Paper presented at the 13th Nordic Conference in Sociology of Religion *Religion and Politics*, Lund, August 15-18.

Jagodzinski, W. & K. Dobbelaere 1995a. 'Secularization and Church Religiosity'. Pp. 76-119 in J. van Deth & E. Scarbrough (eds.), *The Impact of Values*. Oxford: Oxford University Press.

Jagodzinski, W. & K. Dobbelaere 1995b. 'Religious and Ethical Pluralism'. Pp. 218-249 in J. van Deth & E. Scarbrough (eds.), *The Impact of Values*. Oxford: Oxford University Press.

Lindseth, O.H. & O. Listhaug. 1994. 'Religion and Work Values in the 1990s: A Comparative Study of Western Europe and North America'. Pp. 85-98 in T. Pettersson and O. Riis (eds.), *Scandinavian Values. Religion and Morality in the Nordic Countries*. Upssala: Acta Universitatis Upsaliensis.

Lipset, S.M. 1996. *American Exceptionalism*. New York/London: W.W. Norton & Company.

Luckmann, T. 1967. *The Invisible Religion*. New York: MacMillan.

MacIntyre, A. 1981. *After Virtue*. Notre Dame, IN: University of Notre Dame Press.

Münch, R. 1990. 'Differentiation, Rationalization, Interpretation: the Emergence of Modern Society'. Pp. 441-464 in J.F. Alexander & P. Colomby (eds.), *Differentiation Theory and Social Change*. New York: Columbia University Press.

Nagle, J.D. & A. Mahr 1999. *Democracy and Democratization*. London: Sage.

Rokkan, S. 1973. 'Cities, States, and Nations: A dimensional model for the study of contrasts in development'. Pp. 73-97 in S.N. Eisenstadt & S. Rokkan (eds.), *Building States and Nations*. Beverly Hills: Sage.

Roof, W.C. 1978. 'Social Correlates of Religious Involvement: Review of Recent Survey Research in the United States'. Pp. 53-70 in J. Matthes, B. Wilson, L. Laeyendecker & J. Séguy (eds.), *The Anuual Review of the Social Sciences of*

*Religion*. The Hague: Mouton.

Smelser, N.J. 1973. 'Toward a Theory of Modernization'. Pp. 268-284 in E. Etzioni-Halevy & A. Etzioni (eds.), *Social Change*. New York: Basic Books.

Stark, R. 1997. 'Bringing Theory Back in'. Pp. 3-24 in L. Young (ed.), *Rational Choice Theories of Religion*. London: Routledge.

Stark, R. & L. Iannacone, 1994. 'A Supply-Side Reinterpretation of the 'Secularization' of Europe'. *Journal for the Scientific Study of Religion* 33: 230-252.

Spybey, T. 1996. *Globalization and World Society*. Cambridge: Polity Press.

Tamney, J.B. & S.D. Johnson 1985. 'Consequential Religiosity in Modern Society'. *Review of Religious Research* 26: 360-378.

Therborn, G. 1995. *European Modernity and Beyond*. London, Thousand Oaks, New Delhi: Sage.

Turner, B. 1991. *Religion and Social Theory*. London: Sage.

Wallis, R. & S. Bruce 1992. 'Secularization: The Orthodox Model'. Pp. 8-30 in S. Bruce (ed.), *Religion and Modernization*. Oxford: Clarendon Press.

Willaime, J.-P. 1998a. 'Religion and secular France between Northern and Southern Europe'. *Social Compass* 45(1): 155-174.

Willaime, J.-P. 1998b. 'Religion, Individualization of Meaning, and the Social Bond'. Pp. 261-75 in R. Laermans, B. Wilson & J. Billiet (eds.), *Secularization and Social Integration*. Leuven: Leuven University Press.

Wilson, B. 1976. *Contemporary Transformations of Religion*. Londen: Oxford University Press.

Wilson, B. 1982. *Religion in Sociological Perspective*. Oxford: Oxford University Press.

Wilson, B. 1998. 'The Secularization Thesis: Criticisms and Rebuttals'. Pp. 45-65 in R. Laermans, B. Wilson & J. Billiet (eds.), *Secularization and Social Integration*. Leuven: Leuven University Press.

Yamane, D. 1997. 'Secularization on Trial'. *Journal for the Scientific Study of Religion* 36: 109-122.

**Chapter Four**

# Religion and the Family

Karel Dobbelaere, Josette Gevers & Loek Halman

## 1    INTRODUCTION

In 1961, Lenski published *The Religious Factor*[1] a study in which he demonstrated the impact of the degree of the individual's involvement in religious communities on his economical, political, educational and familial behaviour. This study was undertaken in the immediate post-war period and before the processes of rationalisation and functional differentiation were to have their full impact on the perspectives of people living in the Western hemisphere. It was, for example, only in the mid-sixties that in Western Europe, the Christian and Socialist pillars - the organisational complexes which were active, on a religious or ideological basis, in areas that are primarily defined as secular[2] - started tottering as a consequence of the processes of rationalisation and professionalization. Furthermore, under the impact of the process of functional differentiation, the pillars were unable to secure the cohesion of their organisational complexes under a strict religious canopy. Expressive or cultural integration on the basis of a specific collective consciousness was rapidly replaced by instrumental integration, which functioned according to the logic of the respective sub-subsystems to which the participating organisations belonged, e.g., schools were organised according to educational values and norms, and mass media according to the logic of communication, and no longer according to religious values and norms.

In this chapter, we address the following question: even if one witnesses a functional differentiation on the *societal* level, does this result on the micro level, i.e., in the *individual* consciousness, in a compartmentalisation on the one hand, of a religious outlook and, on the other hand, the vision of politics, education, economy or the family? In other terms, does religion still have an impact, and if so to what extent, on the economical, political, and educational motivations, options and behaviour of individuals. In this chapter, however, we will reduce this general question to the effect of the religious involvement of individuals on their conceptions of the family. This question is related to Luhmann's statement: 'die Sozialstruktur ist säkulariziert - nicht aber das Individuum' (Luhmann, 1977: 172). We will investigate if this is, according to the data of the European Values Study (EVS) of 1990, still a correct evaluation more than ten years later, to wit, after a more extensive and intensive institutionalisation of functional differentiation on the societal level?

We start in section 2 exploring the links between religion and family issues. According to the idea of functional differentiation, it can be expected that this relationship has decreased and that nowadays this relationship is only modest or has vanished. This hypothesis is succeeded by an introduction of the data, the measures used and methods applied to test this assumption. The results are presented in section 4 while the main conclusions are drawn in section 5.

## 2    FUNCTIONAL DIFFERENTIATION AND RELIGION'S IMPACT ON FAMILY ISSUES

In the family, the influence of the processes of functional differentiation, rationalisation, and specialisation were also felt. Domestic technological devices gradually promoted the rationalisation of the behaviour of housewives, and so did the newly promoted birth control techniques - even taking the pill required some planning: one had to take it daily, at the same moment of the day, for a set number of days. Indeed, the rationalisation of lifestyles was as much the result of technological developments, especially for the older generations, as for the younger generations, the promotion of science in the school curricula. Even the Catholic church promoted rational behaviour with its recommendation of the so-called natural birth control method. Indeed, to be able to determine their infertile period, women had to take their basal temperature in the morning, plot it on a graph, and calculate the time of ovulation. Life became more and more rational, i.e., structured according to the basic values and norms of the respective sub-systems. Human action was increasingly based on observations, calculation and planning, i.e., directed by what Weber called functional rationality, and such rationality is radically different from value rationality, which is typical of the religious field.

The theory of secularisation specifies that religion, and consequently the churches and other religious organisations which occupy this sub-system, has lost authority over other sub-systems of the social system as a consequence of functional differentiation and rationalisation. Each sub-system, in its internal and external communications, uses its own medium: economical communication is based on money; politics is about power, education about valid truth, and the family about love. Sub-systems develop their own structures: the economy develops enterprises, which promote a systematic and rational-cost benefit calculation, the polity developed a rational bureaucracy, and the educational system has elaborated a school system socialising the students on the basis of *validated* truth. What about the family?

Religion has always been a 'major source of moral proscriptions and normative expectations for many individuals [...]. For example, religious teachings form many of the basic marital expectations toward child rearing, sexual behaviour, friendship networks, and other aspects of marital relationships' (Call & Heaton, 1997: 383). And in general, religious teachings were traditional and conservative. Marriage has been long considered 'a sacrament, that had, as its central purpose, procreation. That being the case, certain things followed: divorce, adultery, and polygamy were wrong because they violated the sacred status of conjugal union, and abortion and infanticide were wrong because they were inconsistent with the principle that sex exists for the production of children' (Wilson, 1993: 202). The churches always have taken a strong position against the legalisation and practice of abortion, birth control, non-marital cohabitation and divorce, and they strongly emphasise and preach traditional morality and family life (e.g., *Veritatis Splendor* which appeared in 1993). According to the Christian tradition, abortion is regarded a violation of God's rights. Abortion is seen as manslaughter and thus abortion is rejected (Spruit, 1991): 187). Birth control is regarded a violation of God's command to procreate and thus a rejection of divine authority (Ellison & Goodson, 1997: 514). Sexual relationships are strictly reserved for the married couple. The acceptance of 'biblical teachings about the sanctity of marriage and prohibitions against fornication and adultery may act as a barrier against divorce by reducing the likelihood of non marital sex' (Call & Heaton, 1997: 383).

Today, in the family sub-system, we are witnessing the development of different types of cohabitation, but the Catholic church, for example through the bishops in Belgium and France, has voiced its opposition to the legal recognition of these different types of unions as equivalent to legal marriage. The intervention of the Catholic church in matters of the family is not new. In 1968, in the encyclical *Humanae Vitae*, the Pope decreed which family planning practices were permitted for Catholics. The negative reactions of the great majority of church members is well documented. They rejected the papal prescriptions, and claimed that husband and wife had the right to decide for themselves about the goals of their union and the techniques they might use to achieve them. This indicates the evidence for the functional differentiation of religion and family. Before the Second World War, some Protestant churches had already accepted this view, which indicates that these churches more readily accepted the process of secularisation than did the Catholic church.

We will, however, not discuss the impact of religious involvement on the attitude of people towards abortion and the number of children in the family, nor on the individual's attitude to sex. Many studies, including some based on the EVS-data, have reported extensively on these issues (e.g., Lambert, 1998), and the results of such studies are well known. They confirm the idea that, generally speaking, religion is a conservative traditional force in human society. The discussion of the family in this chapter is confined to questions concerning the effect of religion and religious involvement on the following aspects of family life - considered as dependent variables:
– the significance in marriage of *cultural homogeneity*;
– the attitude towards the *traditional family pattern* and the *parent - child relationship*;

– the importance attached to *qualities* a child should be encouraged to learn at home.

Why are these aspects of family life considered to be potentially influenced by religion? The stress on cultural homogeneity is a feature of church policies. Indeed, the Catholic church discourages inter-religious marriages by imposing a promise on mixed couples that their children be baptised and brought up in the Catholic faith. And by establishing pillars, Protestant churches in the Netherlands and the Catholic church in many European countries, promoted an in-group mentality which ultimately expressed itself in Christian political parties. According to several studies, a patriarchal view on the family might be the result of a fundamentalist interpretation of the bible; other studies, to the contrary, have stressed the impact of religious involvement, across denominations, on traditional values and beliefs concerning the family, gender roles, and the education of children (e.g., Grasmick, Wilcox & Bird, 1990; Peek & Brown, 1980).

A first issue to deal with in this chapter is the distinction between those who are involved in religion and those who are not. Those who frequently attend religious services are not only more frequently exposed to the rules and prescriptions of the church, they are also more likely to act in accordance with these prescriptions. Church attendance 'affect the amount of indoctrination a person receives in a particular theology' (Call & Heaton, 1997: 383). Since religion is conducive to conservative and traditional views, the expectation is, of course, that those who are involved will display more traditional views than people who are not religiously involved.

A second issue deals with denominational differences. According to Therborn 'secularisation has affected the major Protestant churches more strongly than the Catholic churches' (Therborn, 1995: 274). Gundelach has found empirical evidence that the differential decline in familism in Europe could be explained from denominational differences. 'Family values are determined by religious denomination and not by either economic factors or internal structure of the family' (Gundelach, 1994: 47). As we have argued before, the Catholic stances towards family life are different from Protestant views, and the Catholic view is more traditional than the Protestant. The Pope in particular emphasises the traditional family and conventional family values, while Protestants views appear more secularised and more individualistic, less conventional. Such differences will be elaborated more extensively in this chapter.

# 3    DATA, OPERATIONALISATIONS AND METHOD

## 3.1    Data

Data for this study are taken from the European Values Survey 1990. EVS is an international comparative, longitudinal survey research project that covers a wide variety of orientations in various spheres of life, including values on family life. Our analysis are limited to the data from the following 14 Western European countries (number of respondents enclosed in brackets): France (1002), United Kingdom (1484), West-Germany (2101), Italy (2018), Spain (2637), Portugal (1185), the Netherlands (1017), Belgium (2792), Denmark (1030), Norway (1239), Sweden (1047), Northern Ireland (304), Ireland (1000) and Iceland (702).

## 3.2    Operationalisations

The present study discusses the effect of religion and religious involvement on three particular aspects of family life, namely: the significance in marriage of *cultural homogeneity*; the attitude towards the *traditional family pattern* and the *parent-child relationship*; the importance attached to the *qualities* a child should be encouraged to learn at home.

These aspects of family life are measured by means of seven scales, elaborated by Halman and Vloet (1994: 67-82; see also Ester, Halman & de Moor, 1994: 97-127) which will be described here only briefly. The significance in marriage of *cultural homogeneity* is operationalised by means of three items indicating that being of the same social background, sharing religious beliefs and agreeing on politics is considered important for a successful marriage. A positive attitude towards the *traditional family pattern* is reflected in agreement with the statement that a child needs a home with both a father and a mother, and in the disapproval of a woman being a single parent. The operationalisation of the conceptions of individuals about gender roles involves two scales: the *rejection of traditional women's roles* and a preference for *equal roles for men and women*. Rejection of traditional women's roles is expressed in agreeing that a working mother can have a good relationship with her child, and in disagreement with the statements that what most women really want is a home and children, that a pre-school child is likely to suffer if the mother works and that being a housewife is as fulfilling as working. The preference for equal roles for men and women is based on agreement with the statements that having a job is the best way for a woman to be independent and that both husband and wife should contribute to the household income. Agreement with the statements that a child should love it's parents regardless of their qualities and faults, and that parents have to do their best for their children even at the expense of their own well-being provides a measure of the preference for a *democratic parent-child relationship*. Finally, two distinct attitudes towards the education of children emerged from a factor analysis: an *achievement orientation* (based on the following qualities which children should be encouraged to learn at home: hard work, thrift selfishness and intolerance) and an attitude of *conformity* (expressed by the qualities good manners, religious faith, and obedience; and the rejection of independence, imagination and determination). Thus, we use seven dependent variables to measure attitudes toward the family life, i.e., cultural homogeneity, traditional family pattern, rejection of traditional women's roles, equal roles for men and women, democratic parent-child relationship, achievement orientation and conformity orientation. The scores on these variables are transformed into z-scores to enable comparison across the different aspects of family life under study.

Our analysis employs two independent variables: religious affiliation and religious involvement. Religious affiliation is operationalised in three categories: Catholics, Protestants and the unchurched. With respect to religious involvement, which is only applicable to Catholics and Protestants, we distinguish core members, modal members and marginal members. The core members category encompasses people who regularly go to church on weekends and are involved in church related organisations. Modal members are identified as people who go to church once in a while. Marginal church members are those people who define themselves as members but who are not involved in church life. In order to control for the effect of demographic characteristics on the dependent variables, gender (1 = male; 2 = female), age and educational attainment (measured by means of one's age at completion of full time education) are included in the analyses.

## 3.3   Method

We start with some bi-variate analyses. It will be explored if family values differ between groups with varying degrees of church involvement (church attendance) and among different denominations. This can be achieved by comparing the mean scores of these different groups in the distinctive family values. In the next step church involvement and church membership will be combined in order to explore if and how strong family values are affected by these two values.

To examine the effects of religious affiliation on attitudes towards family life, first, a multivariate one-way between-subjects design was employed, with religious affiliation (Catholic, Protestant, unchurched) as a single factor and age, gender and educational attainment included as covariates. A second analysis assessed the effect of religious involvement on the attitudes towards family life and on the relationship between religious affiliation and the dependent variables. This analysis involved a multi-variate 2 X 3 factorial between-subjects design with the factors religious affiliation (Catholic, Protestant) and religious involvement (core members, modal members, marginal members). The unchurched were excluded from the analysis as religious involvement is not applicable to this group. Once again, age, gender and educational attainment were defined as co-variates. In the analyses we have eliminated the effects of differences in sample sizes by setting the number of cases in each country at 1000.

# 4    RESULTS

A first indication of the differential outlooks on family values among frequent and less frequent church attending people can be found in Table 4.1 where the mean scores on the selected family values are presented for those who attend religious services at least once a month and those who attend religious services less frequently.

## Table 4.1 Mean scores on family values among frequent and not frequent church attenders (one-way analysis of variance)

| | Mean score by church attendance | |
|---|---|---|
| Dependent variables: | Frequent | Non-frequent |
| Cultural homogeneity[*] | 1.13 | 0.93 |
| Traditional family pattern[*] | 4.17 | 3.50 |
| Democratic parent-child relationship[*] | 1.78 | 2.50 |
| Rejection of traditional women's roles[*] | 1.43 | 1.49 |
| Equal roles for men and women[*] | 4.70 | 5.00 |
| Socialize children towards achievement | 1.51 | 1.50 |
| Socialize children towards conformity[*] | 3.97 | 2.98 |

Note: [*] Means in the same row differ at $p = .001$

As expected, regular church-goers display more traditional, more conservative values towards family life. However, as can be seen, although the differences may be statistically significant, they are too modest to draw firm conclusions from it.

In Table 4.2 we have displayed the means cores on the dimensions we have selected for Catholics, Protestants and unchurched people, revealing that religious affiliation has virtually no effect on the dependent variables. The minor differences shown here seem to suggest that Catholics are, indeed, slightly more conservative than Protestants and the unchurched.

**Table 4.2 Mean scores on family values of Catholics, Protestants and unchurched people (one-way analysis of variance)**

| | Mean score by religious affiliation | | |
|---|---|---|---|
| Dependent variables: | Catholics | Protestants | Unchurched |
| Cultural homogeneity* | 1.05 | .96 | .90 |
| Traditional family pattern* | 3.96 | 3.55 | 3.42 |
| Democratic parent-child relationship* | 1.88 | 2.58 | 2.58 |
| Rejection of traditional women's roles* | 1.41 | 1.50 | 1.55 |
| Equal roles for men and women* | 4.94 | 4.83 | 5.02 |
| Socialize children towards achievement* | 1.64 | 1.42 | 1.42 |
| Socialize children towards conformity* | 3.73 | 2.96 | 2.86 |

Note: * Means in the same row differ at $p = .001$

The results show that Catholics are slightly more inclined to favour cultural homogeneity in a marriage, the traditional roles of women, a traditional family pattern, undemocratic parent-child relationship, and they emphasise more strongly that children should learn to conform. It seems that if religion has an impact it is among Catholics. However, before such a conclusion can be drawn we will dig deeper into the relationships described here. The two religious denominational groups we have distinguished here are far from homogeneous and both contain a wide variety of more or less religiously involved people. For instance, church attendance is more frequent among Catholics than among Protestants. Core membership is more common among Catholics while the large majority of the Protestants belong to what can be called marginal members: people who say to belong to a denomination, but who hardly go to church. Such a practice is common in the Scandinavian countries. Thus, the differences between Catholics and Protestants may very well reflect the differential patterns of church attendance. Therefore, we have explored the impact of both phenomena together.

A number of analyses have been performed in which both religious involvement and church membership were combined. The results of the one-way analysis of variance are shown in Table 4.3. The results provide evidence of a significant though limited influence of religious affiliation on attitudes towards family life, when controlling for age, gender and level of educational attainment. In total, the model as specified explains 13% of the variance in attitudes towards cultural equality in marriage, 11% in attitudes towards both democratic parent-child relations and traditional family pattern, a mere 1% in attitudes towards equal roles of men and women, 15% in the rejection of the traditional role of women, 18% in the preference for conformity qualities and 6% in the preference for achievement qualities.

**Table 4.3 Results from one-way analysis of variance with religious affiliation as between-subjects factor**

| Dependent variables (z-scores): | % variance explained | | Mean score by religious affiliation | | |
|---|---|---|---|---|---|
| | Total model | Religious affiliation | Catholics $n=3364$ | Protestants $n=2606$ | Unchurched $n=1641$ |
| Cultural homogeneity | 13.3 | 2.7 | $0.21_a$ | $-0.05_b$ | $-0.25_c$ |
| Traditional family pattern | 11.1 | 2.9 | $0.20_a$ | $-0.19_b$ | $-0.32_b$ |
| Democratic parent-child relationship | 10.7 | 3.6 | $-0.23_a$ | $0.26_b$ | $0.23_b$ |
| Rejection of tradit-ional women's roles | 14.8 | 1.3 | $-0.15_a$ | $0.18_b$ | $0.25_b$ |
| Equal roles for men and women | 1.1 | 0.4 | $-0.04_a$ | $-0.14_b$ | $0.03_a$ |
| Socialize children towards achievement | 5.7 | 0.5 | $0.06_a$ | $-0.18_b$ | $-0.13_b$ |
| Socialize children towards conformity | 18.0 | 7.0 | $0.38_a$ | $-0.21_b$ | $-0.27_b$ |

Note: Means in the same row that do not share subscripts differ at $p = .001$

However, looking at the effect sizes of religion on these value orientations, we see that religious affiliation alone explains only a fraction of the variances (ranging from 0,4 % to 7 % of explained variance). Thus, as we now focus on the differences in attitudes between Catholics, Protestants and the unchurched in more detail, one should keep in mind that the effects are very small. For a start, we will only acknowledge differences at .001 level of significance. Simple contrasts show that it is predominantly the Catholics that differ in their value orientations towards family life from both the Protestants and the unchurched. The minor differences suggest that Catholics are slightly more conservative than Protestants and unchurched as they attach more importance to cultural homogeneity in marriage, highly value the traditional family pattern, favour an undemocratic parent-child relationship and show a stronger preference to socialise children towards conformity.

Moreover, Catholics are less inclined to reject the traditional women's roles than the Protestants and unchurched are. The unchurched are most likely to reject the traditional women's roles and are also more supportive of equal roles for men and women than the Protestants are. Protestants attach more importance to cultural homogeneity than the unchurched do. Thus, Protestants and unchurched primarily diverge in their attitudes towards cultural homogeneity in marriage and gender roles, whereas they converge in their views on the relationship with, and the socialization of the child.

The results of our second multivariate analysis of variance, which involved the factors religious affiliation and religious involvement, are reported in Table 4.4.

**Table 4.4    Proportion of variance in family values explained by the 2 X 3 between-subjects design with factors religious affiliation (A) and religious involvement (B)**

| Dependent variables: | Total model | % variance explained Religious affiliation (A) | Religious involvement (B) | A x B |
|---|---|---|---|---|
| Cultural homogeneity | 15.0 | 0.0 | 2.0 | 0.1 |
| Traditional family pattern | 13.1 | 0.3 | 3.2 | 0.1 |
| Democratic parent-child relationship | 12.5 | 0.8 | 1.2 | 0.5 |
| Rejection of traditional women's roles | 15.0 | 0.3 | 0.2 | 0.7 |
| Equal roles for men and women | 2.8 | 0.3 | 2.2 | 0.0 |
| Socialize children towards achievement | 6.6 | 0.3 | 0.5 | 0.4 |
| Socialize children towards conformity | 19.6 | 0.9 | 3.1 | 0.1 |

Although the second model is not entirely comparable to the first because the unchurched had to be deleted, the results suggest that including religious involvement improves our model somewhat as the total model now explains 2% to 20% of the variance in the dependent variables. Moreover, religious involvement appears to be more important in shaping attitudes towards family life than religious affiliation is. Still, its effects prove to be very small, explaining no more than 3 % of the variance at the most.

The results suggest that, with the exception of the rejection of traditional women's roles on which it has no effect, stronger religious involvement coincides with a more conservative approach towards the family life. The more people are more involved in religion, the more they stress the need for cultural homogeneity in marriage; the more they value traditional family patterns and the less they are opposed to the traditional division of labour between the sexes.

The largest differences are noted between marginal members on the one hand, and modal and core members of the church on the other hand. Marginal members are more in favour of a democratic relationship with their children and are less inclined to socialise their children towards conformity than modal and core members are. The results thus make clear that involvement in the churches promotes a more traditional view of the aspects of family life under study. This finding applies to Protestants as well as to Catholics, as is revealed in Table 4.5.

**Table 4.5 Mean scores on dependent variables by religious affiliation and religious involvement**

|  | Religious involvement by religious affiliation | | | | | |
|  | Catholics | | | Protestants | | |
| Dependent variables: | core | modal | marginal | core | modal | marginal |
| Cultural homogeneity | 0.44 | 0.31 | 0.02 | 0.50 | 0.30 | -0.17 |
| Traditional family pattern | 0.45 | 0.31 | -0.04 | 0.41 | 0.16 | -0.31 |
| Democratic parent-child relationship | -0.27 | -0.30 | -0.14 | -0.16 | -0.09 | 0.36 |
| Rejection of traditional women's roles | -0.10 | -0.07 | -0.27 | 0.04 | -0.04 | 0.22 |
| Equal roles for men and women | -0.35 | 0.08 | 0.11 | -0.57 | -0.15 | -0.08 |
| Socialize children towards achievement | -0.04 | 0.04 | 0.22 | -0.11 | -0.14 | -0.20 |
| Socialize children towards conformity | 0.48 | 0.54 | 0.14 | 0.29 | 0.21 | -0.32 |

Their response patterns are fairly similar, except with respect to the parent-child relationship, the rejection of traditional women's roles and the encouragement of achievement qualities in children.

Protestants are more in favour of democratic parent-child relations than Catholics, but whereas the marginal members of the Catholic church are only slightly more positive about democratic parent-child relations than the modal or core church members, within the Protestant church the marginal members are far more positive about such a democratic relation than the modal members, who are in turn also more positive than the core members. With respect to children's socialisation towards achievement qualities, these are especially encouraged by marginal members of the Catholic church, whereas the scores for marginal, modal and core members of the Protestant church are fairly equal. Similarly, with respect to traditional women's roles it is also the marginal members of the Catholic church that show a different attitude. Whereas the score of the members of Protestant church are fairly equal, the marginal members within the Catholic church show a stronger rejection of the traditional women's roles.

## 5 CONCLUSIONS

Among others, Niklas Luhmann, has argued that although society may be secularized, this does not imply that its citizens are also secular (Luhmann, 1977: 172). This statement reflects his idea that at societal level we may be witnessing a functional differentiation, but not at the individual level. In this chapter we have investigated this idea by exploring the linkages between a person's religious involvement and his/her views on family life. We are particularly interested in this linkage because in the past religion has always been an influential source of people's views and behaviours concerning marriage and family. In their teachings, the churches have always displayed conservative, traditional stances. Nowadays a great variety of family types exist and people's behaviour has become more rational and as it seems less dependent upon what the churches prescribe and preach. As such it can be predicted that religion and family views are not very likely to go together, and thus that religion and family views are no longer closely linked .

We have investigated this assumption by exploring family values among groups of people with different levels of religious involvement. We not only distinguish between groups of people according to the frequency of church attendance, but also according to what denomination they belong: Catholic and Protestant. According to many observers, the distinction between Catholics and Protestants are still major sources for differential outlooks on people's views on marriage and family life (e.g., Gundelach, 1994).

Core church members appear to have indeed in general a more integrated view of religion and family than less involved church members. Since, according to the European Values Study of 1990, the Catholic church has a larger number of core members than the Protestant churches, we may conclude that the differences between Catholics and Protestants must be explained by this different distribution. The differences between Catholics and Protestants, while existing in general, largely arise from a difference in degree of involvement of the members. The two waves of the EVS study (in 1981 and 1990) furthermore revealed that the involvement of members in their respective churches was declining (Ester, Halman & de Moor, 1994: 44). Consequently, we may conclude that the secularisation of the social system is promoting a compartmentalisation in the consciousness of the people between religion and views of the family, which goes parallel with a decline of involvement of people in the churches. The influence of the churches' views on family life is rapidly dwindling. They still hold for only a very limited number of church members, especially core members. Our particular conclusions concerning people's views of the family confirm the analysis of Lambert, who has found that 'religion has little ascendancy over life in general, except for the core members' (1998: 231).

**Notes**

1  The study was carried out in the Detroit Area in 1958.
2  For example, in Belgium, the Catholic pillar provided almost all possible services to its members from the cradle to the grave. Its organisational complex consisted of, among other agencies, schools (from kindergarten to university), hospitals, old people's homes, youth movements, cultural and professional associations, sports clubs, travel agencies, mass media (newspapers, magazines, book clubs, and libraries), banks, health insurance funds, a trade union, and a political party.

# References

Call, V.R.A. & T.B. Heaton 1997. 'Religious Influence on Marital Stability'. *Journal for the Scientific Study of Religion* 36: 382-392.

Ellison, C.G. & P. Goodson 1997. 'Conservative Protestantism and Attitudes toward Family Planning in a Sample of Seminarians'. *Journal for the Scientific Study of Religion* 36: 512-529.

Ester, P., L. Halman & R. de Moor 1994. *The Individualizing Society: Value Change in Europe and North America.* Tilburg: Tilburg University Press.

Grasmick, H.G., L.P. Wilcox & S.R. Bird 1990. 'The Effects of Religious Fundamentalism and Religiosity on Preference for Traditional Family Norms'. *Sociological Inquiry* 60: 352-369.

Gundelach, P. 1994. 'National Value Differences'. *International Journal of Comparative Sociology* 35: 37-58.

Halman, L., & A. Vloet 1994. *Measuring and Comparing Values in 16 Countries of the Western World: Documentation of the European Values Study 1981 - 1990 in Europe and North America.* Tilburg: WORC.

Lambert, Y. 1998. 'The Scope and Limits of Religious Functions According to the European Value and ISSP Surveys'. Pp. 211-232 in R. Laermans, B. Wilson & J. Billiet (eds.), *Secularization and Social Integration.* Leuven: Leuven University Press.

Lenski, G. 1961. *The Religious Factor.* Garden City, NY: Doubleday.

Luhmann, N. 1977. *Funktion der Religion.* Frankfurt am Main: Suhrkamp Verlag.

Peek, C.W. & S. Brown 1980. 'Sex Prejudice among White Protestants: Like or Unlike Ethnic Prejudice'. *Social Forces* 59: p. 169-185.

Spruit, L. 1991. *Religie en abortus.* Nijmegen: ITS.

Therborn, G. 1995. *European Modernity and Beyond.* London: Sage.

Wilson, J.Q. 1993. *The Moral Sense.* New York: Free Press.

Chapter Five

# Individual Religiosity, Religious Context and Values in Europe and North America[1]

### Michael Procter & Michael P. Hornsby-Smith

## 1    INTRODUCTION

What difference does religion make to the way people live their lives? Are differences in individual religiosity reflected in different personal and social values, and especially political values and activity? In particular, what differences are there between Catholics and Protestants, and are these differences more or less important than differences in strength of adherence within a denomination? What difference does the religious complexion of a country make? Does a high density of fellow adherents reinforce the influence of religion or on the contrary lead to its dilution? Are there indications of similar value patterns which might be attributed to similar modernizing processes or are there distinct differences which require explanation?

In this chapter we explore the impact of religion on personal and social morality. In other words, we consider religion as an *independent* variable. Our analysis represents both an extension to a larger group of countries and a departure from recent analyses from the European Values Systems Study Group (Ester et al., 1994) which treat a variety of religious variables as *dependent* upon the social and economic transformations associated with the notion of modernization.

The general theoretical orientation of the European Values Systems Study Group is that, as a result of modernization processes in society, there are associated processes of secularization and individualization which are, in turn, reflected in the various value domains such as religion, politics, morality, family and work. A secondary concern of the Tilburg team of analysts is to identify the extent to which there is value convergence between western societies as a result of the globalization of culture and the internationalization of political, economic and technological domains, and the areas where nation-specific interpretations and explanations are still necessary (Ester et al., 1994: 1-20). Inevitably, therefore, recent EVS studies have investigated changes between the two sets of data from the surveys of 1981 and 1990.

In contrast, this chapter will investigate the moral consequences of religion and in particular sexual morality, honesty in financial matters, and a collectivist orientation to social responsibility, using the 1990 World Values Surveys. In order to explore the relationship between religion and morality, we have confined our analysis to 27 countries in Europe and North America where the dominant religious cleavage is between Catholicism and Protestantism. Countries where Orthodox forms of Christianity have been dominant have been excluded for present purposes.

There is a sense in which the Judeo-Christian religious tradition, which is what chiefly concerns the EVS group, inevitably presupposes a moral dimension such as is enshrined in the ten commandments. This was seen to be a *social fact* by Durkheim for whom a unified system of beliefs and practices welded adherents into a moral community (Durkheim, 1915: 47). Our research problem was to investigate the extent to which social control of moral decisions continues to be exercised by religion when, as a result of extensive social differentiation and socio-economic transformations, the nature of social solidarity shifts from the 'mechanical' to the 'organic' (Ester et al., 1994). Inglehart (1977; 1990), for example, has suggested that there have been significant cultural shifts in values among the peoples of western industrialized societies in recent years. He has characterized this shift, found disproportionately among the younger cohorts, as one from materialist to post-materialist values.

Previous research has shown that religious affiliation has been closely related to political party preferences and attitudes, ethnocentrism and racial prejudice, and social attitudes generally, in both Britain and the United States (Argyle & Beit-Hallahmi, 1975: 101-123). Various studies have also shown a close association between conservative religion and conservative politics (e.g., Bruce, 1990; Swatos et al., 1994). Recent cross-national studies have shown that religious 'independents' (individuals reporting no religious identification) were less likely than religious affiliates to hold traditional family values (Hayes & Hornsby-Smith, 1994) and more likely to oppose the role of religion in politics (Hayes, 1995).

While a number of studies have shown that Catholics differ significantly from Protestants in their attitudes to abortion and, to a lesser extent, sexual and marital morality, contraception and divorce, it is also clear that with the post-war dissolution of the distinctive Catholic subcultures in Britain (Hornsby-Smith, 1987) and the United States (e.g., Greeley, 1977; Wuthnow, 1989), there has been a substantial convergence of values (e.g., Johnson, 1994; Kellstedt et al., 1994).

There is some evidence that for Catholics, at least, there may be a significant disjunction between personal and social values. For example, a study of Catholic elites in England and Wales showed that many of those who were 'progressive' in the sense of having a strong social justice orientation were 'traditional' in terms of sexual and marital morality (Hornsby-Smith et al., 1987).

For analysis purposes it is also important to note significant variations between mainline Protestants and conservative (Johnson, 1994) and evangelical (Kellstedt et al., 1994) Protestants. Interpretations of biblical literalism are particularly salient.

Eckberg and Blocker (1989) showed that a literal interpretation of the Bible was significantly related to a lower concern with environmental issues though Greeley (1993) suggested that it was not biblical literalism as such which was related to environmental concern, but rather a rigid political and religious orientation.

In our own work we have considered religion as an independent variable with consequences for personal, social and political values and behaviour. Our longer-term purpose was to explore the controversial relationship between religion and politics. For example, an analysis of the 1990 EVS data from fourteen European nations led to the conclusion that in the aggregate, and in spite of the efforts of religiously inspired activists, religion has little or no discernible impact on the emergent forms of the environmentalist politics that are increasingly found in advanced industrial societies today. We suggested that this may be due to the marginalization of justice and peace activists within Roman Catholicism and to serious conflicts over the proper relationship between religion and politics within Protestantism (Hornsby-Smith & Procter, 1995).

Among recent contributions to the analysis of value patterns and shifts over time, the European Values Surveys are noteworthy for having surveyed populations cross-nationally in the fields of religion, politics, morality, family, and work. Among the hypotheses which have been tested with the longitudinal data (1981-1990) are those of increasing secularization and individualism (Ester et al., 1994). Both processes are thought to explain a weakening in the overarching importance of traditional Christian beliefs and a 'disengagement from the institutional church' and also an increasing stress on individual achievement, choice and decision-making. There is evidence of 'greater moral permissivity' and that 'religious people tend to be less tolerant than non-religious people'. Regular church attendees and those for whom God is important in their lives are less likely to approve of abortion or euthanasia. Those who express altruistic motives for voluntary work are more likely to have strong religious beliefs. It seems that matters of personal and sexual morality are determined less by the traditional prescriptions of the churches and more by personal choice in pluralist societies.

For our present purposes, the EVS data enable us to explore relationships between religion and both personal and social morality. They are also relevant to the current debate about the relevance of rational choice theory and the claim that there has been a major paradigm shift in the Sociology of Religion which suggests that pluralism, far from indicating a decline in the salience of the sacred canopy, is in fact a sign of religious vitality.

## 2    THEORETICAL CONSIDERATIONS

Stark and Bainbridge (1980; 1985; 1987) have proposed an exchange theory of religion in terms of the rewards and costs of religious commitment. They suggest that religious organizations provide 'compensators' based on supernatural assumptions and that these offer answers to questions of ultimate meaning such as innocent suffering and the purpose of life. Over the past two decades a considerable body of research has sought to offer empirical support for the rational choice model of religion.

These have included historical analyses of secularization in England and Wales (Stark et al., 1995), Denmark (Buckser, 1995), Europe (Stark & Iannaccone, 1994), and the United States (Finke & Stark, 1992), the study of the religious market in contemporary Sweden (Hamberg & Pettersson, 1994), the testing of hypotheses about religious monopolies and pluralism in such matters as Catholic commitment (Stark & McCann, 1993), religious practice and financial giving (Iannaccone, 1990; 1997), and even the attempt to interpret Mother Teresa's religious behaviour (Kwilecki & Wilson, 1998). All have claimed that hypotheses derived from the religious economies model are substantially supported. Iannaccone (1995) has reviewed the rational choice paradigm and urged that it has unified a wide range of empirical findings and stimulated the generation of new research questions.

The religious market model has come under fierce empirical and conceptual attack from a number of writers. Wallis and Bruce (1984) criticized the Stark-Bainbridge theory of religion for reducing religious belief to this-worldly considerations. Later Bruce (1992; 1995) challenged the Stark and Iannaccone interpretation of the religious statistics of Britain in the nineteenth century. Elsewhere (1993) he has argued specifically that *economic* forms of rationality are inappropriate for understanding religious belief and behaviour because they fail to take account of the perceptions of the actors and because salvation is not simply another consumer good which can be chosen rationally. Chaves (1995) has argued that the meta-claims of the approach are misleading overstatements and largely incorrect. Carroll (1996) criticized the theory for its Eurocentric (but mainly American Protestant) and androcentric biases which have resulted in a misperception of the nature of religious experience in Catholic countries.

A number of researchers have employed multivariate cross-national comparisons in the investigation of a variety of measures of religious involvement. The importance of national context has been demonstrated by Campbell and Curtis (1994) using World Values Survey data from 22 countries in 1981-1983. Jelen et al. (1993) used a subset of the same surveys in Western Europe to offer a contextual analysis of abortion attitudes and reported that while at the individual level, a Catholic socialization was quite successful, the reverse was found in the case of national religious context. Socialization was most effective where Catholics were in a minority while pro-choice counter-mobilization was strongest where the Catholic church was perceived to be part of the 'establishment'. In subsequent work, Jelen and Wilcox (1998) have reported similar results in the case of religious observance and the role of women in politics and participation in the labour market. They interpret their findings as supporting the new 'pluralist' paradigm which, following notions of free-market competition, argues that religious vitality is likely to be greater in situations of religious pluralism .

However, using data from the 1990 European Values Survey for 16 countries and various measures of modernization and culture, researchers from Tilburg University concluded that the religious market theory did not offer the best explanation for the observed cross-national differences but that 'modernization and culture, both representing value differences, are the most important predictors of religious mentality' (Verweij et al., 1997: 321).

The relevance of the rational economic model of religion for secularization theory has also generated debate. Warner (1993) has suggested that the rational choice model of Stark, Finke, Iannaccone and their co-workers, which predicts religious vitality where there is intense competition for market share in situations of religious pluralism, constitutes a new paradigm in the Kuhnian sense. This is said to have replaced the old paradigm articulated by theorists such as Berger (1973), Martin (1978), Wilson (1982), and Tschannen (1991), which predicted that secularization resulted from the breakdown of the overarching 'sacred canopy' found in situations of religious monopoly. Lechner (1991) has offered a defence of secularization theory and Chaves (1994) suggests that it is best interpreted as declining religious authority. Yamane (1997) develops this and considers the area of religion and politics.

In this present study we examine, using simple methods of statistical and graphical analysis, the influence of three components of religiosity on a range of personal and social values. We consider:
*individual* Roman Catholic or Protestant identity;
Roman Catholic or Protestant national *context* (in terms of the proportion of respondents who were ever Catholics; and
*level* of religious adherence, as indicated by a simple measure of frequency of church attendance.

Secularization theory would lead us to anticipate that individual religiosity has little effect on social and political values. The new paradigm would lead us to expect that in the countries of Europe and North America, Catholic or Protestant religious context is of greater significance. Two conflicting hypotheses corresponding to the old and new theoretical paradigms might be considered. There might be:
a *reinforcement* effect with a co-cultural, monopolistic context supporting an individual religiosity.
Alternatively, the reverse might be the case in a pluralistic context with strong *cultural defence* (Wallis & Bruce, 1992) on the part of a minority culture being reflected in an inverse relationship between individual religious identity and context.
Finally, on the basis of secularization theory, we would anticipate that level of adherence or commitment is more important than theological details of that adherence in terms of denominational adherence.

## 3    DATA SOURCES AND MEASUREMENTS

### 3.1    Data

While the main concern of the Tilburg researchers (Ester et al., 1994) has been the analysis of value change between the two sets of surveys in 1981 and 1990, our concern in this chapter is to explicate the nature of the relationships between the various measures of religiosity (identity, context and involvement), on the one hand, and both personal and social morality, on the other hand, using the cross-sectional data from the 1990 surveys only. These were carried out on nationally representative samples of those aged 18 or over. A total of 38,231 respondents in 27 countries in Europe and North America were surveyed in 1990-91. Other countries were surveyed as well. From these we selected a sub-sample of 30,191 ever-Christian (Catholic or Protestant) identifying respondents.

The WVS sample,[2] unweighted because the published weights appear to be of varying reliability, for the 27 countries included in the analysis consisted of 30,304 identifying Christians. 48 per cent of the sample were male, 39 per cent aged 35 or under, and 56 per cent continued their full-time education over the age of sixteen. According to conventional survey criteria, 42 per cent were in the upper or middle class status group and 57 per cent were working class.

An outline of the various problems to be faced when undertaking comparative research has been comprehensively reviewed by Halman and de Moor (1994a: 25-31; see also Hantrais, 1996; Ragin, 1989; 1991). While noting the dangers of culture-specific interpretations of questions or response styles and whether or not latent constructs detected by statistical analysis are comparable, we take the pragmatic view that the data are the best available for present purposes and that the interpretation of our results are inevitably provisional and open to scientific challenge and revision (see also Halman & de Moor, 1994a: 29).

Perhaps the biggest problem in the secondary analysis of data collected for somewhat different purposes (Dale et al., 1988; Procter, 1993b) is the identification of indicators that will correspond sufficiently well to the concepts and theories under investigation. In the present case we hoped to find measures of personal and social values and of various aspects of religiosity. Our data sources were the 370 or so variables of the 1990 WVS, many of which were indeed intended to measure constructs in these domains. Considerable efforts have been devoted, both by others (e.g., Halman & de Moor, 1991; 1994b) and by ourselves to the identification and construction of scales with substantive and formal properties suitable to our analytical purposes. The results are not entirely satisfactory but this is intrinsic to the secondary analysis of large data sets.

## 3.2   Measures of religiosity

We included three measures of religiosity. First, we needed a measure of strength of religious adherence. The WVS includes a number of questions concerning details of belief, and we would ideally have liked to base our measures on these. To this end in previous investigations we carried out a number of factor analyses (Procter, 1993a). We were disappointed to find that none of the factor scales which resulted performed well as an independent variable, the essence of *construct validity* (Cronbach & Meehl, 1955). In subsequent work we have for the most part simply used a seven-point scale of frequency of religious attendance, with the mnemonic name FREQ. In the present analysis we collapsed the categories of FREQ into 'attend a service once a month or oftener', 'attend less than once a month', and 'never attend'.

Secondly, we had a measure of Christian denominational identity, and simply dichotomised between those who identified themselves, either at the time of the interview or in the past, as Roman Catholic or as some kind of Protestant (RCPROT). Our primary concern was to explore the extent to which the major post-Reformation dichotomy between Catholics and Protestants continued to have salience at the end of the twentieth century. We also wished to minimise the loss of data which would have resulted had we excluded those with no current religious identification. We argued that this would have introduced considerable between-country variations (particularly in the Netherlands where over half the population have no current religious identification; see Hayes, 1995), and that it might reasonably be supposed that it was early religious socialization which was likely to have most significance in the determination of current expressions of morality. Respondents with no present or past Christian identification were excluded from subsequent analyses. According to the 1991 *International Social Survey Programme* data for the United States and seven countries in Western Europe, current non-affiliates account for over one quarter of the population and have significantly less traditional moral attitudes than those with a religious identity (Hayes & Hornsby-Smith, 1994; Hayes, 1995).

Third, we included a *religious context variable*, based on RCPROT: it was defined simply as the number of self-identifying Roman Catholics in each country's *sample* divided by the number of Catholics and Protestants. This proportion ranged from under one per cent in the case of the Scandinavian countries to nearly 100 per cent in the Latin countries and fully 100% in Slovenia. For the most part we used this variable to classify countries as predominantly Catholic, predominantly Protestant, or 'mixed' The details of this are presented in Table 5.1.

## 3.3   Personal and social values

The WVS interview included a set of items in which the respondent was asked to indicate whether each of twenty-four behaviours was always, sometimes or never justified, using a ten-point scale. (This set has come to be referred to by WVS analysts as the justifiability items.) In order to measure personal morality we constructed two scales: a scale of sexual morality (SEXMORAL) based on the justifiability of homosexuality, prostitution, abortion, divorce, extramarital affairs, and sex under the legal age of consent ($n = 6$; $r = .42$; $\alpha = .82$), and a scale (HONESTY) based on the justifiability of claiming state benefits which you are not entitled to, avoiding a fare on public transport, cheating on tax if you have the chance, buying something you knew was stolen, keeping money that you have found, and lying in your own interest ($n = 6$; $r = .38$; $\alpha = .78$ ). For the purposes of this present analysis, both scales were scored so that high values indicated a less restrictive and more permissive morality.

In the same way we constructed a scale of social morality. This scale of collectivism (COLLECT) indicates a preference for collective rather than individual responsibility measured views on private or government ownership of business or industry, individuals or the state taking more responsibility for providing for people, whether or not unemployed people should be required to take any available job, whether competition is good or harmful, and whether hard work or luck brings a better life ($n = 5$; $r = .26$; $\alpha = .63$).

## 4    RESULTS

### 4.1    Individual religiosity and religious context

A summary of the average scale scores and the Catholic densities for each of the 17 countries from Western Europe, seven from Central/Eastern Europe and three from North America have been given separately for Catholics and Protestants in Table 5.1. Countries have been grouped in order of their Catholic density. Eleven countries have Catholic densities of 88 per cent or more; seven have Protestant densities of 84% or more; the remaining nine countries are religiously 'mixed'. The standard deviations within the entire sample are: sexual morality: 2.0; honesty: 1.71; collectivism: 8.51.

For ease of interpretation, the main part of our analysis will be presented graphically in the form of boxplots (Tukey, 1977; Marsh, 1988) which are centred on the median scale value and show the upper and lower quartiles for each of the three groups of countries. Preliminary analysis showed that both the sexual morality and honesty scales of permissiveness were strongly skewed. (This reflected the fact that most respondents regarded the listed behaviours as generally unacceptable). Following common practice in such cases, the raw data were subjected to a transformation using the common logarithm, producing roughly symmetric distributions.

**Table 5.1 Average scale scores by country, Catholic density and respondent's denomination (n = 30,304)**

| Country | Catholic density | Sexual morality[1] | | | Honesty[1] | | | Collectivism[2] | | |
|---|---|---|---|---|---|---|---|---|---|---|
| | | RC | Prot. | All | RC | Prot. | All | RC | Prot. | All |
| Protestant | | | | | | | | | | |
| Finland | .0055 | 1.58 | 4.79 | 4.78 | 3.33 | 2.96 | 2.96 | 19.5 | 17.6 | 17.7 |
| Iceland | .0075 | 4.60 | 4.04 | 4.05 | 1.67 | 2.20 | 2.20 | 15.2 | 19.3 | 19.2 |
| Sweden | .0079 | 4.04 | 3.60 | 3.60 | 4.08 | 1.97 | 1.99 | 18.7 | 18.9 | 18.9 |
| Norway | .0104 | 3.56 | 3.27 | 3.28 | 1.97 | 1.97 | 1.97 | 22.3 | 19.7 | 19.7 |
| Denmark | .0111 | 2.36 | 3.48 | 3.46 | 1.58 | 1.89 | 1.88 | 23.8 | 21.8 | 21.9 |
| Estonia | .0367 | 6.25 | 3.10 | 3.21 | 4.10 | 1.90 | 1.98 | 29.8 | 20.5 | 20.8 |
| Britain | .1606 | 3.13 | 3.27 | 3.24 | 2.43 | 2.07 | 2.12 | 25.7 | 23.3 | 23.7 |
| All Protestant countries | .0411 | 3.22 | 3.62 | 3.60 | 2.44 | 2.10 | 2.12 | 25.0 | 20.3 | 20.5 |
| 'Mixed' | | | | | | | | | | |
| E. Germany | .3081 | 2.49 | 3.27 | 3.03 | 1.73 | 1.86 | 1.82 | 18.0 | 18.6 | 18.4 |
| US | .4088 | 3.13 | 2.95 | 3.02 | 2.44 | 2.09 | 2.23 | 17.6 | 17.7 | 17.6 |
| N. Ireland | .4809 | 2.38 | 2.59 | 2.49 | 2.22 | 1.66 | 1.93 | 25.2 | 22.7 | 23.9 |
| W. Germany | .4948 | 3.89 | 4.13 | 4.01 | 2.66 | 2.73 | 2.69 | 18.8 | 19.0 | 18.8 |
| Switzerland | .5424 | 3.10 | 3.70 | 3.38 | 1.92 | 2.02 | 1.97 | n/a[3] | n/a | n/a |
| Latvia | .5436 | 3.05 | 3.32 | 3.17 | 1.85 | 1.82 | 1.83 | 23.4 | 21.8 | 22.7 |
| Canada | .5581 | 3.99 | 3.80 | 3.91 | 2.62 | 2.28 | 2.47 | 19.0 | 18.3 | 18.7 |
| Netherlands | .6089 | 5.33 | 4.86 | 5.15 | 2.58 | 2.19 | 2.43 | 23.3 | 22.1 | 22.8 |
| Hungary | .7741 | 3.52 | 3.09 | 3.43 | 3.27 | 2.82 | 3.17 | 22.5 | 22.0 | 22.4 |
| All 'mixed' countries | .5061 | 3.66 | 3.63 | 3.64 | 2.49 | 2.24 | 2.37 | 20.0 | 19.1 | 19.5 |
| Catholic | | | | | | | | | | |
| Czech Rep. | .8788 | 4.17 | 4.27 | 4.18 | 5.34 | 5.23 | 5.33 | 22.4 | 22.8 | 22.5 |
| Austria | .9251 | 3.19 | 3.64 | 3.22 | 1.84 | 1.94 | 1.85 | 17.5 | 16.9 | 17.5 |
| Mexico | .9400 | 3.64 | 3.29 | 3.62 | 4.32 | 4.16 | 4.31 | 21.6 | 21.9 | 21.6 |
| France | .9737 | 4.14 | 3.95 | 4.13 | 3.09 | 2.98 | 3.09 | 20.6 | 22.0 | 20.6 |
| Ireland | .9746 | 2.49 | 2.93 | 2.51 | 2.16 | 1.73 | 2.15 | 22.5 | 19.0 | 22.4 |
| Belgium | .9846 | 3.63 | 3.37 | 3.63 | 3.11 | 2.77 | 3.11 | 21.2 | 17.9 | 21.1 |
| Lithuania | .9864 | 2.18 | 2.81 | 2.19 | 2.02 | 3.03 | 2.03 | 23.6 | 27.7 | 23.7 |
| Italy | .9893 | 3.67 | 3.78 | 3.67 | 2.48 | 1.90 | 2.48 | 21.5 | 20.8 | 21.5 |
| Portugal | .9949 | 2.93 | 2.13 | 2.92 | 3.12 | 2.60 | 3.12 | 23.1 | 22.6 | 23.1 |
| Spain | .9953 | 3.63 | 3.34 | 3.63 | 2.69 | 2.18 | 2.69 | 23.3 | 25.7 | 23.4 |
| Slovenia | 1.0000 | 4.34 | N/a[4] | 4.34 | 2.06 | n/a | 2.06 | 18.2 | n/a | 18.2 |
| All Catholic countries | .9734 | 3.51 | 3.62 | 3.51 | 2.87 | 3.26 | 2.88 | 21.7 | 20.6 | 21.6 |
| Total | .6520 | 3.54 | 3.62 | 3.56 | 2.78 | 2.21 | 2.59 | 21.4 | 19.8 | 20.9 |

Notes:
[1] High scale score means more permissive.
[2] High scale score means more collectivist.
[3] These questions were not asked in Switzerland.
[4] The Slovenian sample included no Protestants.

Table 5.2 presents the mean[3] scores for personal and social morality for Protestants and Roman Catholics in each of the three groups of countries. Because of the large sample size, all of the main effects and interactions examined are significant beyond the 1% level. However, it is perhaps more relevant to note that the proportion of variance explained in each of the scales ($R^2$) is never as much as 4%. In other words, the effects of both individual religious identity and country religious context are substantively rather small.

**Table 5.2  Mean *log* scores on *Sexual morality* and *Honesty* and mean scores on *Collectivism*, by country type and respondent's denomination**

| Country type | log Sexual morality | | | Log Honesty | | | Collectivism | | |
|---|---|---|---|---|---|---|---|---|---|
| | RC | Prot | All | RC | Prot | All | RC | Prot | All |
| Protestant | .436 | .506 | .503 | .322 | .262 | .265 | 24.9 | 20.3 | 20.5 |
| Mixed | .482 | .488 | .485 | .319 | .280 | .300 | 20.0 | 19.2 | 19.5 |
| Catholic | .468 | .489 | .469 | .378 | .427 | .380 | 21.7 | 20.6 | 21.6 |
| All | .471 | .497 | .480 | .364 | .277 | .335 | 21.4 | 19.9 | 20.9 |
| $R^2$ | | 0.003 | | | 0.037 | | | 0.013 | |
| S | | 0.24 | | | 0.25 | | | 8.41 | |

The boxplots in Figures 5.1 and 5.2 present the logged results for sexual morality and honesty and Figure 5.3 presents the raw data for collectivism. In these charts each group of two boxes represents the difference between Catholic and Protestant respondents within a national religious context; comparison of the three dark coloured boxes within a chart indicates the variation of Protestant respondents across the three national contexts (and, correspondingly, the light coloured boxes show Catholics).

A cursory glance at the mean scores by country type indicates that, on the whole, the variations in scale scores between Catholics and Protestants, and between the three groups of countries, are not great. To the extent that this is the case, it suggests that modernization processes, to which all these countries have been subject over the past century or so, may have had a homogenizing effect on the value systems of western societies. Such findings might have been anticipated from secularization theory. On the other hand, some of the between-country differences in Table 5.1 are highly significant (p < .0001 level) but this should be interpreted in the light of the large sample size. In this light, there are some striking findings (for instance, the Czech Republic's mean Honesty permissiveness score is 1.7 standard deviations above the grand mean). Such differences point to the importance of the different historical legacies of countries which might otherwise share a similar religious context.

When we look at a range of measures of personal and social values, there do seem to be some discernible patterns. Interestingly, both the most and the next-to-least permissive countries in terms of sexual morality are religiously 'mixed'. Lithuania (99% Catholic) has the most restrictive sexual morality (though it is followed closely by Northern Ireland (mixed) and by the Irish Republic) while the Netherlands is by some way the most permissive. Both individual Catholics and Catholic societies seem to be less permissive in terms of sexual morality.

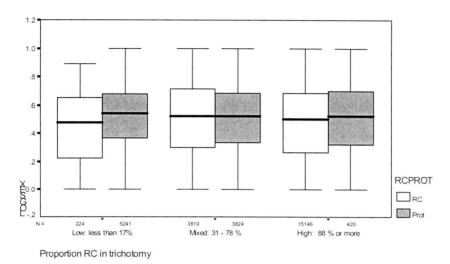

**Figure 5.1    Boxplot of log *Sexual morality*, by country type and respondent's denomination**

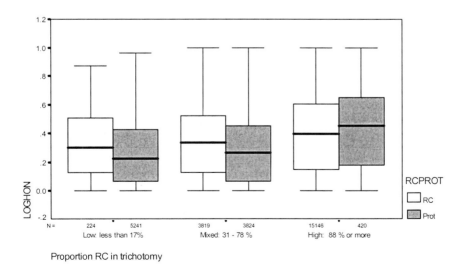

**Figure 5.2    Boxplot of log *Honesty*, by country type and respondent's denomination**

On the other hand there seems to be a greater tendency both for individual Catholics and for Catholic societies to justify dishonesty in financial and related matters. But whereas the Protestants in Protestant societies are the least permissive in these matters, the relatively small number (n = 420) of Protestants in Catholic societies appear to be the most permissive - though the picture would be very different without the Czech Republic.

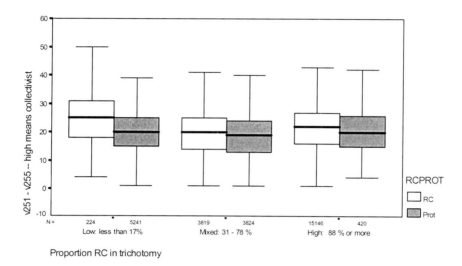

Proportion RC in trichotomy

**Figure 5.3** **Boxplot of *Collectivism*, by country type and respondent's denomination**

Overall, as one might expect, both individual Catholics and Catholic countries score highest on collectivism, though the least collectivist societies are those which are religiously 'mixed' which accords with rational choice theory and pluralism. All the same, there are some wide variations with the lowest average score on COLLECT being recorded for Catholic, social democratic Austria, by the US and by Protestant Finland, while the highest was recorded in Protestant, still Thatcherite Britain, mixed Northern Ireland and Catholic Lithuania. Other comparisons which would bear further analysis are the marked differences between Finland and the other Nordic countries, and the broad similarities among the three Baltic states, linguistically and religiously distinct though they are. Clearly, apart from some general patterns, different historical legacies are important in the interpretation of the detailed variations by country.

**4.2 Church attendance and values**

The remaining boxplots, together with Table 5.3, report on the relationship between our three value scales and the measure of church attendance, trichotomized as described above.

**Table 5.3  Mean *log* scores on *Sexual morality* and *Honesty* and mean scores on
*Collectivism*, by frequency of church attendance**

| Frequency of attendance | log Sexual morality | Log Honesty | Collectivism |
|---|---|---|---|
| Never | .61 | .41 | 21.85 |
| Sometimes | .53 | .36 | 20.73 |
| Often | .38 | .30 | 20.24 |
| All | .50 | .36 | 20.89 |
| $R^2$ | 0.13 | 0.027 | 0.006 |
| S | 0.26 | 0.26 | 8.49 |

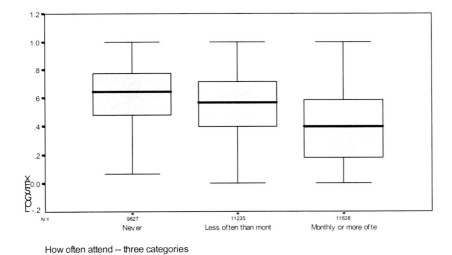

How often attend -- three categories

**Figure 5.4    Boxplot of log *Sexual morality*, by frequency of church attendance**

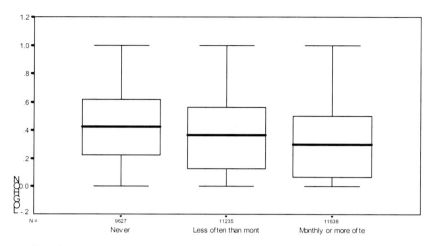

**Figure 5.5    Boxplot of log *Honesty*, by frequency of church attendance**

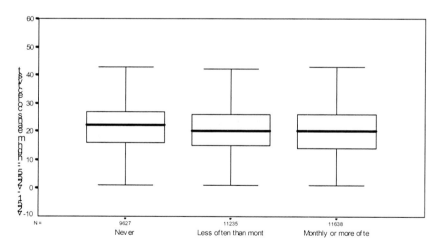

**Figure 5.6    Boxplot of log *Collectivism*, by frequency of church attendance**

As was the case in the earlier analysis, all the effects we report are statistically significant, because of the large sample size, but with one exception they are substantively small. These tiny effects remain statistically significant even when individual and national denomination are controlled, though for reasons of space we do not present these more complex results. Thus, though the more assiduous attenders are likely to be less *collectivist*, less than one percent of variance is explained. Non-attenders are more permissive on matters of personal honesty, but $R^2$ is only .027. However, sexual morality is far more strongly influenced by attendance. The difference in mean score between the two extreme groups (as we expected, the more religious are less permissive) is almost 0.9 of a standard deviation, and 13 percent of variance is explained. By survey standards this is not a spectacular level of association, but it is very much higher than the other relationships examined in this study.


## 5    DISCUSSION AND CONCLUSIONS

This chapter has explored the effects of three indicators of religiosity on three measures of personal and social values among representative samples of the populations of 27 nations in Europe and North America. We wished to see whether the major dichotomy between Catholics and Protestants in Western Christianity, either in terms of individual Catholic or Protestant identity or in terms of the religious context of the nation as a whole, was significant in terms of moral values. We also wished to see whether differences in the frequency of religious attendance was a more important predictor of values. Our hope was that our results might contribute to the current debate about rational choice theory. In the end our findings have not been as clear cut as we had hoped.

In the first place, we explored these issues using the 1990 World Values Survey data. Unfortunately, as is frequently the case with secondary data analysis, these data did not provide entirely satisfactory measures of the variables of interest to us. In particular, there were no adequate measures of biblical literalism which might have enabled us to explore more thoroughly variations between the Calvinist and Lutheran traditions of Protestantism. In the case of Catholicism there is a need to distinguish between 'progressives' and 'traditionalists', for example in terms of different theologies, views of liturgy, community emphasis, and the relationship between religion and politics (Hornsby-Smith et al., 1987). There is also a need to tease out some of the complexities in the relationships between personal and social morality and the seeming unconcern on the part of many with strict or conservative personal moralities for the issues of social justice and concern. The identification of these weaknesses may, nevertheless, be helpful in the search for better measures for use in future surveys of this sort such as the prospective cross-national *Religion and Moral Pluralism* (RAMP) surveys.

We must also recognize the usual problems associated with cross-national and, in particular, cross-lingual research. Examples of these problems include difficulties in ensuring equivalence of translated terms, and internationally varying response sets (Smith, 1988).

In spite of the limitations of the data, the findings we have reported are of some interest. They show, for example, that both individual denominational identity and the religious context of each country can have a small independent effect on the levels of personal and social morality. Catholics in Protestant countries have the most restrictive sexual morality (which supports the cultural defence hypothesis) but Protestants in Protestant societies have the most restrictive financial morality (which supports the reinforcement hypothesis). Catholics in Protestant societies are the most collectivist, which again suggests cultural defence in the case of the religious minority though Protestants in 'mixed' societies are less collectivist than those in Protestant societies. These findings give no support to the rational choice thesis in that there is no consistent evidence that either religious minorities or in situations of maximum pluralism (in 'mixed' societies) are religiously motivated values most strongly acknowledged.

But the most important conclusion which can be drawn from these data is that in the countries of Europe and North America, differences in the value orientations of both individual Catholics and Protestants, and Catholic and Protestant nations, are in general of little substantive consequence. It seems that the processes of modernization and secularization have largely dissolved the major cleavages which derived historically from the Reformation. In sum, religion does not really count for much when it comes to evaluating the consequences of Christian belief and practice on the social and political attitudes, values and behaviour of people.

Finally, though strength of religious adherence, in terms of frequency of attendance, has no more effect that our other indicators on collectivism and honesty, it has markedly greater influence on sexual morality. It seems likely that churches pay more attention to issues of sexual morality than to the other values examined. We have little direct evidence bearing on this hypothesis. However, Burns (1994) has argued persuasively that since the loss of the papal states in 1870, the Vatican has attempted to retain control over the personal morality of Catholics while accommodating pragmatically in the areas of social morality. It may also be the case that in the more individualistic culture of Protestantism there is a greater emphasis on private rather than social morality.

**Notes**

1 This chapter is a substantially revised version of a paper first given at the Annual Meeting of the Society for the Scientific Study of Religion on the theme of 'Religion and Social Justice', Albuquerque, New Mexico on 5 November, 1994. We are indebted to Loek Halman and a number of anonymous referees for their helpful suggestions.

2 World Values Study Group, World Values Survey, 1981-1984 and 1990-1993 [Computer File]. ICPSR version. Ann Arbor, MI: Institute for Social Research [producer], 1994. Ann Arbor, MI: Interuniversity Consortium for Social Research [distributor], 1994.

3 It is unfortunate that boxplots are defined in terms of the median (and quartiles), whereas the linear model methods reported elsewhere in this chapter make use of the mean (and standard deviation). However, since the distributions (transformed where necessary) are approximately symmetric, the mean and median will be very close in value, and our own checks (not reported here) have found no discrepancies.

# References

Argyle, M. & B.Beit-Hallahmi 1975. *The Social Psychology of Religion*. London and Boston: Routledge & Kegan Paul.

Berger, P.L. 1973. *The Social Reality of Religion*. Harmondsworth: Penguin (fp. in the US as *The Sacred Canopy*, 1967).

Bruce, S. 1990. *The Rise and Fall of the New Christian Right: Conservative Protestant Politics in America 1978-1988*. Oxford: Clarendon Press.

Bruce, S. 1992. 'Pluralism and Religious Vitality'. Pp. 170-194 in S. Bruce (ed.), *Religion and Modernization: Sociologists and Historians Debate the Secularization Thesis*. Oxford: Clarendon Press.

Bruce, S. 1993. 'Religion and Rational Choice: A Critique of Economic Explanations of Religious Behavior'. *Sociology of Religion* 54(2): 193-205.

Bruce, S. 1995. 'The Truth about Religion in Britain'. *Journal for the Scientific Study of Religion* 34(4): 417-430.

Buckser, A. 1995. 'Religion and the Supernatural on a Danish Island: Rewards, Compensators, and the Meaning of Religion'. *Journal for the Scientific Study of Religion* 34(1): 1-16.

Burns, G. 1994. *The Frontiers of Catholicism: The Politics of Ideology in a Liberal World*. London: University of California Press.

Campbell, R.A. & J.E. Curtis 1994. 'Religious Involvement Across Societies: Analyses for Alternative Measures in National Surveys'. *Journal for the Scientific Study of Religion* 33 (3): 215-229.

Carroll, M.P. 1996. 'Stark Realities and Eurocentric/Androcentric Bias in the Sociology of Religion'. *Sociology of Religion* 57 (3): 225-239.

Chaves, M. 1994. 'Secularization as Declining Religious Authority'. *Social Forces* 72: 749-774.

Chaves, M. 1995. 'On the Rational Choice Approach to Religion'. *Journal for the Scientific Study of Religion* 34(1): 98-104.

Cronbach, L. J. & P.E. Meehl 1955. 'Construct Validity in Psychological Tests'. *Psychological Bulletin* 52: 297-334.

Dale, A., S. Arber & M. Procter 1988. *Doing Secondary Analysis*. London: Unwin Hyman.

Durkheim, E. 1915. *The Elementary Forms of the Religious Life*. London: Allen and Unwin.

Eckberg, D.L. & T. J. Blocker 1989. 'Varieties of Religious Involvement and Environmental Concerns: Testing the Lynn White Thesis'. *Journal for the Scientific Study of Religion* 28: 509-517.

Ester, P., L. Halman & R.de Moor (eds.) 1994. *The Individualizing Society: Value Change in Europe and North America*. Tilburg: Tilburg University Press.

Finke, R. & R. Stark 1992. *The Churching of America, 1776-1990: Winners and Losers in Our Religious Economy*. New Brunswick, New Jersey: Rutgers University Press.

Greeley, A.M. 1977. *The American Catholic: A Social Portrait*. New York: Basic Books.

Greeley, A.M. 1993. 'Religion and Attitudes Toward the Environment'. *Journal for the Scientific Study of Religion* 32: 19-28.

Halman, L. & R. de Moor 1991. *Information Bulletin EVSSG 1991*. Tilburg: IVA, Institute for Social Research, Tilburg University.

Halman, L. & R. de Moor 1994a. 'Comparative Research on Values'. Pp. 21-36 in P. Ester, L. Halman & R. de Moor (eds.), *The Individualizing Society: Value Change in Europe and North America*, Tilburg: Tilburg University Press.

Halman, L. & R. de Moor 1994b. 'Religion, Churches and Moral Values'. Pp. 37-65 in P. Ester, L. Halman & R. de Moor (eds.), *The Individualizing Society*, Tilburg: Tilburg University Press.

Hamberg, E.M. & T. Pettersson 1994. 'The Religious Market: Denominational Competition and Religious Participation in Contemporary Sweden'. *Journal for the Scientific Study of Religion* 33 (3): 205-216.

Hantrais, L. 1996. 'Comparative Research Methods'. *Social Research Update 13*, Guildford: Sociology Department, University of Surrey.

Hayes, B.C. 1995. 'The Impact of Religious Identification on Political Attitudes: An International Comparison'. *Sociology of Religion* 56(2): 177-194.

Hayes, B.C. & M.P. Hornsby-Smith 1994. 'Religious Identification and Family Attitudes: An International Comparison'. Pp. 167-186 in M.L. Lynn & D.O. Moberg (eds.), *Research in the Social Scientific Study of Religion*, Vol. 6. Greenwich, Connecticut: JAI Press.

Hornsby-Smith, M.P. 1987. *Roman Catholics in England: Studies in Social Structure Since the Second World War*. Cambridge: Cambridge University Press.

Hornsby-Smith, M.P., M. Procter, L. Rajan & J. Brown 1987. 'A Typology of Progressive Catholics: A Study of the Delegates to the National Pastoral Congress'. *Journal for the Scientific Study of Religion* 26: 234-248.

Hornsby-Smith, M.P. & M. Procter 1995. 'Catholic Identity, Religious Context and Environmental Values in Western Europe: Evidence from the European Values Surveys'. *Social Compass* 42 (1): 27-34.

Iannaccone, L.R. 1990. 'Religious Participation: A Human Capital Approach'. *Journal for the Scientific Study of Religion* 29(3): 297-314.

Iannaccone, L.R. 1995. 'Voodoo Economics? Reviewing the Rational Choice Approach to Religion'. *Journal for the Scientific Study of Religion* 34(1): 76-89.

Iannaccone, L.R. 1997. 'Skewness Explained: A Rational Choice Model of Religious Giving'. *Journal for the Scientific Study of Religion* 36(2): 141-157.

Inglehart, R. 1977. *The Silent Revolution: Changing Values and Political Styles Among Western Publics*. Princeton, New Jersey: Princeton University Press.

Inglehart, R. 1990. *Culture Shift in Advanced Industrial Society*. Princeton, New Jersey: Princeton University Press.

Jelen, T.G., J. O'Donnell & C. Wilcox 1993. 'A Contextual Analysis of Catholicism and Abortion Attitudes in Western Europe'. *Sociology of Religion* 54 (4): 375-383.

Jelen, T.G. & C. Wilcox 1998. 'Context and Conscience: The Catholic Church as an Agent of Political Socialization in Western Europe'. *Journal for the Scientific Study of Religion* 37 (1): 28-40.

Johnson, S.D. 1994. 'What Relates to Vote for Three Religious Categories?'. *Sociology of Religion* 55: 263-275.

Kellstedt, L.A., J.C. Green, J.L. Guth & C.E. Smidt 1994. 'Religious Voting Blocs in the 1992 Election: The Year of the Evangelical?'. *Sociology of Religion* 55: 307-326.

Kwilecki, S. & L.S. Wilson 1998. 'Was Mother Teresa Maximizing Her Utility? An Idiographic Application of Rational Choice Theory'. *Journal for the Scientific Study of Religion.* 37 (2): 205-221.

Lechner, F. 1991. 'The Case Against Secularization: A Rebuttal'. *Social Forces* 69: 1103-1119.

Marsh, C. 1988. *Exploring Data.* Cambridge: Polity Press.

Martin, D. 1978. *A General Theory of Secularization.* Oxford: Blackwell.

Procter, M. 1993a. 'Measuring Attitudes'. Pp. 116-134 in G.N. Gilbert (ed.), *Researching Social Life.* London: Sage

Procter, M. 1993b. 'Analysing Other Researchers' Data'. Pp. 255-269 in G.N. Gilbert (ed.), *Researching Social Life.* London: Sage.

Ragin, C.C. 1989. *The Comparative Method: Moving beyond Qualitative and Quantitative Srategies.* London: University of California Press.

Ragin, C.C. (ed.) 1991. *Issues and Alternatives in Comparative Social Research,* Leiden: E.J.Brill.

Smith, T.W. 1988. 'The Ups and Downs of Cross-National Survey Research'. *IASSIST Quarterly* 12(Winter, 1989): 18-24.

Stark, R. & W.S. Bainbridge 1980. 'Toward a Theory of Religion: Religious Commitment'. *Journal for the Scientific Study of Religion* 19(2): 114-128

Stark, R. & W.S. Bainbridge 1985. *The Future of Religion: Secularization, Revival and Cult Formation.* London: University of California Press.

Stark, R. & W.S. Bainbridge 1987. *A Theory of Religion.* New York and Bern: Peter Lang.

Stark, R., R. Finke & L.R. Iannaccone 1995. 'Pluralism and Piety: England and Wales, 1851'. *Journal for the Scientific Study of Religion* 34 (4): 431-444.

Stark, R. & L.R. Iannaccone 1994. 'A Supply-Side Reinterpretation of the 'Secularization' of Europe'. *Journal for the Scientific Study of Religion* 33: 230-252.

Stark, R. & J.C. McCann 1993. 'Market Forces and Catholic Commitment: Exploring the New Paradigm'. *Journal for the Scientific Study of Religion* 32:111-124.

Swatos, W.H., P. Kivisto & S.Bruce (eds.) 1994. 'The Rapture of Politics: The Christian Right as the United States Approaches the Year 2000'. *Sociology of Religion* 55: 223-357.

Tschannen, O. 1991. 'The Secularization Paradigm: A Systematization'. *Journal for the Scientific Study of Religion* 30(4): 395-415.

Tukey, J.W. 1977. *Exploratory Data Analysis.* Reading, Mass.: Addison-Wesley.

Verweij, J., P. Ester & R. Nauta 1997. 'Secularization as an Economic and Cultural Phenomenon: A Cross-National Analysis'. *Journal for the Scientific Study of Religion* 36(2): 309-324.

Wallis, R. & S. Bruce 1984. 'The Stark-Bainbridge Theory of Religion: A Critical Analysis and Counter Proposals'. *Sociological Analysis* 45(1): 11-27.

Wallis, R. & S. Bruce 1992. 'Secularization: The Orthodox Model'. Pp. 8-30 in S. Bruce (ed.), *Religion and Modernization: Sociologists and Historians Debate the Secularization Thesis*. Oxford: Clarendon Press.

Warner, R.S. 1993. 'Work in Progress Towards a New Paradigm for the Sociological Study of Religion in the United States'. *American Journal of Sociology* 98: 1044-1093.

Wilson, B. 1982. *Religion in Sociological Perspective*. Oxford: Oxford University Press.

Wuthnow, R. 1989. *The Restructuring of American Religion*. Princeton, New Jersey: Princeton University Press.

Yamane, D. 1997. 'Secularization on Trial: In Defense of a Neosecularization Paradigm'. *Journal for the Scientific Study of Religion* 36(1): 109-122.

Chapter Six

# Integration into Catholicism and Protestantism in Europe: The Impact on Moral and Political Values

Pierre Bréchon

## 1 INTRODUCTION

According to Durkheim, 'in principle, all is religious'. Societies cannot do without religion, that is to say, without sacred things which symbolize what they are and contribute to maintaining their homogeneity. For 2000 years, European societies have been strongly influenced by Catholicism and Protestantism. Both are, in fact, at the root of European culture. In the 19th century, modernity and especially the processes of rationalization and individualization, questioned the principles and values of traditional societies, which were dominated by religious denominations. Secularization became widespread and, in many countries, criticism of religion expanded. Durkheim argued that henceforth traditional religions were obsolete and human society needed to develop new religions. The love of the nation or of the French Republic – without God – would be the new religion for the modern era.

Contrary to expectations, the main Christian denominations were in fact not entirely defeated by modernity, they evolved and adapted to the developments in society, and they still socialize people and continue to instil values and world views. Not only do they transmit religious beliefs, they also pass on a meaning of life, and moral and political values. Religion was and perhaps is an important source for the formation of a person's identity.

However, each new generation shapes its own identity as a re-composition of what parents and tradition (religion) bequeath. Socialization never stops, and people can modify, in the course of their life, the system of attitudes which they acquired during childhood and early socialization. The post-war generations have been forging new relationships to religion. Instead of adopting the legacy of past generations, they experience religion in a more individualistic and more emotional way, claiming the right to make new experiences, and turning away more from institutions (e.g., Roof, 1993).

Given this individualization of religious attitudes and beliefs, is it possible to still distinguish a Catholic and a Protestant identity? Does being brought up in one of these denominations entail long-term consequences for what and how a person is and behaves? In this chapter, we will test the hypothesis that belonging to Catholicism and Protestantism still determines the behaviours and attitudes of

Europeans.

The importance of religious identities for value systems is assumed to be diminished due to processes of secularization. It is likely that in this context of secularization, the differences between Catholics and Protestants tend to disappear. If these distinctive characteristics become blurred, it is possible that an opposition between Christian and non-religious identities is becoming more prominent. The indifference to or rejection of religions may also rest on a certain kind of socialization with potentially major consequences for the value system of those without religion. In this chapter we explore the implications for values of such non-religious identities.

## 2    RELIGION, MORALITY, AND POLITICAL ATTITUDES

The hypothesis about the differences between Catholics and Protestants is attractive and has received empirical support. In his famous work *The Protestant Ethic and the Spirit of Capitalism*, Max Weber asserted that because Protestant attitudes towards life involved a strong work ethic and asceticism, Protestant countries were more advanced economically than Catholic ones. Recently, this hypothesis was explored by Andrew Greeley (1989), who found that the links between ethics and religious denominations have remained quite strong.[1] Following David Tracy's work (1987), he defines the Catholic ethic as 'an analogical imagination', that is, a world vision in which society is analogous to God, made in His image. God is in the world, and Catholics can thus have an optimistic vision of the world; they seek to improve it and place importance on community relationships. The Protestant ethic, according to Greeley, is 'dialectic'; it is based on an opposition between society and God. Society is a world of sinners, abandoned by God. Thus, Protestants stress their individuality, which supports Weber's 'intra-world' asceticism. Greeley concludes that Catholics differ from Protestants and the differences have not diminished in those under the age of 40. The distinct ethics of Catholics and Protestants continue to work.

However, belonging to a certain denomination can have highly different meanings for different people. Jean-Marie Donegani's study on Catholic identities of the French demonstrates that although many people maintain a tenuous reference to religious institutions this does not imply a belief in the fundamental dogmas of the specific denomination (Donegani, 1993). Religious adherence is thus insufficient for determining integration into a religious system. The degree to which one is integrated into a religion must be taken into account. This can be ascertained in many ways, e.g., by practices, by beliefs, by the level of investment in religious groups. Guy Michelat (1990) has shown that such indicators of religious identity are strongly correlated. In particular, the correlation between religious practise and beliefs is strong. Religious practice without belief is rare, as is religious belief without practice.

Even if religious practice is only one aspect of religious integration, it is extremely significant. Church attendance indicates the degree of denominational integration, that is, the degree to which a denominational religious identity has been shaped. A regular church-goer is likely to approve the system of beliefs of his denomination; his religious identity clearly depends on an institutional system. The intensity of religious participation indicates the sharing of a religious culture and likely affects moral and political values.

If it is important to distinguish the level of involvement of Catholics and Protestants, we also may have to distinguish among the 'religionless', those who are just uninterested from those who have stronger anti-religious sentiments. In fact, one can distinguish those who are simply 'without religion' from the 'convinced atheists'. The former do not indicate a religious adherence, the latter do the same but they also claim to be committed atheists. In this way, anti-religious culture may be contrasted with Christian culture.

As was argued before, integration into a religious system implies internalizing the rules and the models of action which affect daily life. Since churches have a highly developed ethical discourse, it can be expected that the degree of integration into Catholicism and Protestantism has a strong impact on ethical attitudes concerning individual or collective morals, the conception of sexuality, and family. However, many churches are very careful vis-à-vis political discourse. In principle, they recognise the political realm's autonomy, and no longer seek, as they did before, to orient their members' votes. They tend more toward declarations which remind their members which evangelical values life in society should be built upon. This does not define the programmes of political action in any way. Thus, we do not expect to observe strong links between a person's religious identity and his/her political position.

Although religious or non-religious identities will be important factors in understanding a person's value system, religion is not the only explanation of differences in moral and political attitudes. The identity of an individual is, of course, also shaped by family education, social environment, institutional education, occupation, and the country where one lives. Since a well integrated European culture does not exist and each country has its own specific history and culture which will affect an individual's behaviours, attitudes, and values, national culture will be an important attribute as well.

In this chapter we explore the impact on moral and political values of:
- affiliation with Catholicism and Protestantism, or the absence of religious affiliation;
- the degree of integration into one of the two large Christian religions or atheism;
- belonging to a country.

**3    DENOMINATIONAL INTEGRATION**

We have argued that church attendance is a sensitive indicator of religious integration. For each affiliation - Catholic or Protestant - regular church-goers are defined as those who attend a religious service at least once a month; irregular church attendees are those who only go to church on special occasions; and non-church-goers attend a religious service about once a year or never go to church.[2]

**Table 6.1   Connection between denominational integration and different beliefs (Cramer's V[3])**

| Religious beliefs: | Integration into | |
| --- | --- | --- |
| | Catholicism | Protestantism |
| Believe in God (yes/no) | 0.43 | 0.42 |
| Personal God or some sort of spirit or life force | 0.29 | 0.27 |
| God is important in his life (10 positions scale) | 0.33 | 0.30 |
| Believe in life after death (yes/no) | 0.30 | 0.25 |
| Believe in soul (yes/no) | 0.31 | 0.27 |
| Believe in the Devil (yes/no) | 0.26 | 0.21 |
| Believe in hell (yes/no) | 0.29 | 0.22 |
| Believe in heaven (yes/no) | 0.33 | 0.26 |
| Believe in sin (yes/no) | 0.32 | 0.27 |
| Believe in the resurrection of the dead (yes/no) | 0.35 | 0.29 |
| Believe in reincarnation (yes/no) | 0.10 | 0.09 |
| Life is meaningful only because God exists | 0.28 | 0.25 |
| Death has a meaning only if you believe in God | 0.26 | 0.20 |
| Sorrow and suffering only have meaning if you believe in God | 0.25 | 0.20 |
| To be religious, non religious or a committed atheist | 0.61 | 0.60 |
| Religion gives comfort and strength | 0.43 | 0.37 |
| To take some moments of prayer, meditation or contemplation | 0.34 | 0.29 |
| Frequency of prayer to God | 0.30 | 0.27 |

In Table 6.1, the relationship between religious beliefs and denominational integration into Catholicism and Protestantism are presented. The stronger one's beliefs are, the more intense one's religious practice is. Of course, these connections are strong because both are part of Christianity's habitual milieu. The only exception is reincarnation, which is, of course, as could be expected. Religious beliefs which move away from the traditional Christian milieu are not strongly congruent with integration into Catholicism and Protestantism. What is striking, however, is the (weak) link between belief in reincarnation and integration into Christianity. Belief in reincarnation is least common among committed atheists while church-goers believe in reincarnation even (slightly) more than non-church-goers. To many, reincarnation is not a well-defined belief, and many church-goers claim to believe in both resurrection and reincarnation. Theologically speaking, of course, the two beliefs are considered to be antinomical.

Table 6.1 also demonstrates that church attendance is a better predictor of the belief system of Catholics than of Protestants, and finally, the bottom of the table reveals that integration into religious services is strongly linked to a feeling of being religious. The more one is integrated into Christianity, the more religious one is. Being religious while being detached is rare. Thus, we may conclude that the reconstruction of religious attitudes has not completely undermined the Christian culture in European countries. Religious feelings are still largely expressed through a Christian culture. In addition, those who attend religious services more often, pray more. Apparently, collective practises go with personalized practises.

To strengthen this conclusion, the relations between all religious beliefs have been analysed in order to create a scale of intensity, made up of ten beliefs.[4] This scale is closely linked to the two religious attendance scales (Cramer's V=0.36 with Catholicism, and 0.31 with Protestantism). However, as Table 6.2 shows, the overlap between church attendance and beliefs is not complete. There are people who regularly attend religious services and who have essentially no beliefs; there is also a small group of individuals 'without religion' who adhere to numerous religious beliefs. Grace Davie's qualification of the contemporary religious situation in terms of 'believing without belonging' is, to a certain extent, dangerous, because it underlines that religious beliefs exist and are even reconstructed independently of institutions (Davie, 1994). However, we could also say that today there is a separate 'belonging without believing' category.

**Table 6.2  Distribution of the scale of beliefs according to practise**

|  | Number of beliefs | | | |
| --- | --- | --- | --- | --- |
| Practise: | 8 to 10 | 5 to 7 | 2 to 4 | 0 or 1 |
| Regular attending Christian | 54 | 30 | 14 | 2 |
| Irregular attending Christian | 17 | 31 | 40 | 12 |
| Non-attending Christian | 11 | 21 | 40 | 28 |
| No religion | 5 | 12 | 31 | 52 |
| Mean | 24 | 23 | 29 | 24 |

Religious attendance is only one aspect of integration into a religious system. Other aspects are: membership or volunteering in 'religious or parish organisations', 'take moments of prayer, meditation or something like that', 'pray to God often'. These indicators refer to private devotion which is linked to participation in collective religious practices and thus constitute a religious identity. Those who have constructed such a religious identity expressed through certain practises and beliefs are likely to also have certain ethical, cultural, and political attitudes which distinguish them from people with a more diffuse religious identity and those who lack such an identity.

## 4 RELIGION AND ETHICAL ATTITUDES

The assumption that the degree to which Catholics and Protestants are integrated into these religions will have affected their ethical convictions has been further explored by comparing how strongly they subscribe to a number of ethical attitudes.

## 4.1 Morality of principles

There appear to be no clear differences between Catholics and Protestants as far as a morality of intangible principles is concerned.[5] Contrary to what might be expected, the former are not more in favour of such principles than the latter (see Appendix, Table 6.1). However, in each country (with the exception of Dutch Protestants), individuals from both religious groups appear more attached to the religious principles, the more integrated they are into a religious system. Those without religion and committed atheists are also less attached to a morality of principles in each country. Since, on average, individuals who are strongly integrated into religious systems are elderly, we must control for the age effect. It appears that attachment to such principles is not only stronger among older generations but also among less educated people. Yet religious integration, generation, and the level of education have independent effects. Thus, Catholic and Protestant religious cultures are accompanied by a strong enhancement of a morality of principles.

Analyses to test the impact of national cultures on the morality of principles revealed no strong logic even though countries differ considerable. Whereas traditionally Catholic countries are located on the left side of the table, and traditionally Protestant countries on the right side, the results are not organised (see 'Total' line) according to the national culture's religious origin. For example, Danes, with their Lutheran tradition, show very little support for a morality of principles, whereas at the other extreme, countries with a Catholic tradition such as Italy or Ireland, but also Britain, with an Anglican tradition, appear much more in favour of a morality of principles. A national culture is not generated solely by a religious matrix. Many other phenomena contribute to the creation of an original culture of a country.

## 4.2 Moral and civic rigourism

Respondents were asked to indicate from a long list of various behaviours, whether the behaviour is always or never justified. Two scales were constructed, tentatively indicated as moral rigourism and civic rigourism. The first scale includes behaviours having to do with sexuality and attitudes towards life (homosexuality, prostitution, abortion, divorce, euthanasia, suicide); the second scale concerns attitudes toward incivilities and cheating (claiming state benefits not entitled to, avoiding a fare on public transport, cheating on taxes, buying something you knew was stolen). In our analyses we focussed only on the rather intolerant people, those who tend not to accept such behaviours.[6]

As Table 6.2 in the Appendix shows, integration into a religious denomination has considerable impact on moral rigourism. Those without a religion as well as atheists express a high level of moral relativism (the numbers are particularly expressive for the Netherlands, Germany, and Italy). This relationship between moral rigourism and denominational integration is quite strong in each country studied. It is weak in only two countries with a strong Catholic tradition (Ireland and Portugal), and in a particularly bi-denominational country (the Netherlands). It appears that in Ireland and Portugal, moral rigourism is part of a consensus, and that even those who have no religion share - in part - a rather intransigent ethic with regard to sexuality. In the Netherlands, a situation of relative inverse consensus exists. With the exception of regular church-attending Protestants, every category shows a strong moral relativism. The differences between countries (see 'Total' line) appear to be mainly due to their degree of secularisation. Countries in which Catholicism remains strong (Ireland, Portugal, Italy, Spain) also have higher levels of moral rigourism. In countries where Christianity has lost a great deal of its strength (France, the Netherlands, Britain), rigourism has clearly weakened.

Although Catholic countries appear more rigorous than Protestant countries, it does not imply that being Catholic or Protestant affects the level of rigourism. In bi-denominational countries, the difference between Catholics and Protestants is not stable. German Catholics and Protestants appear quite similar; in Britain, there is a higher moral intransigence among Catholics; yet Dutch Protestants are morally more rigorous than Catholics.

The integration into a religious system appears to affect civic rigourism as well (see Table 6.3 in the Appendix). The more one takes part in Catholic or Protestant culture, the more rigorous one is. Those without religion and committed atheists show little concern for such principles, and they are more tolerant vis-à-vis collective norms.[7] In contrast to moral rigourism, confessional adherence has an effect on civic rigourism. At the same level of religious integration, Protestants always show a higher level of civic rigourism than Catholics. This appears to be the case in bi-confessional countries as well, despite the fact that both denominational groups share the same national culture.

Civic moralism thus appears to be a resistant trait of Protestant culture, compared to Catholic culture. Among Protestants, the deviation from the collective norms is less easily justified. The phenomenon explains why, on average, higher percentages are observed in each country with a high Protestant population.[8] Traditionally Catholic countries, however, are not homogeneous: Italy, Ireland, and Spain appear much more rigorous than Portugal, Belgium, and France. It may be attractive to attribute such differences between these Catholic countries to their national cultures, but the determining factor may simply be a more advanced secularisation in the second group of countries.

## 4.3   Family values

A scale of traditional family values has been constructed based on answers to five questions.[9] Table 6.4 (Appendix) includes only those individuals with the highest level of traditional family values (4 or 5 items). The structure of relations resembles the relationships we observed with regard to morality of principles. There is no clear difference between Protestants and Catholics. However, the more integrated one is into Protestantism or Catholicism, the more one adheres to traditional family values. Religious cultures and familial conceptions are still strongly linked. The adherence to traditional family values is lowest among people without religion and committed atheists.[10] Finally, countries vary considerably: Ireland, Denmark, Italy, and Portugal appear most in favour of traditional family values, whereas Spain, Germany, and the Netherlands are least accepting of traditional family values.

A scale of attitudes toward abortion has also been constructed using a question presenting four cases in which an individual may or may not disapprove of abortion.[11] Table 6.5 in the Appendix displays those individuals who are generally against it: at most, they agree that it is justifiable in one situation. In each country studied, Catholics and Protestants are more opposed to abortion, the more they are integrated into a religious institution. The level of hostility toward abortion is generally slightly higher among Catholics. In bi-confessional countries, Catholics tend to be more intolerant than Protestants in Germany and Britain, while in the Netherlands, Protestants appear more hostile. Once again, those without a religion, and especially committed atheists are least against abortion.[12]

## 4.4   Degree of integration: does it matter?

For all five ethical scales, it appeared integration into a confessional religious system has a strong influence. The degree of integration has been further elaborated using a question which isolates a small group of individuals who are members of a religious organisation or who work in such an organisation voluntarily. These people have a stronger religious identity than simple church-goers, and they probably will be more attentive to transferring evangelical values to the social realm.[13] This additional question provides a scale of integration into religious organisations. Table 6.3 shows that ethical variables correlate with this form of confessional integration. Like all regular church-goers, those who are highly involved in church organisations are more in favour of traditional and rigorous morals. However, in case of civic rigourism, differences appear between integration into church services and integration into church organisations. Members of Catholic organisations are not more rigorous than Catholics who do not participate in these organisations. Yet among members of Protestant organisations, the level of civic rigour is considerably higher compared to other Protestants. This confirms our earlier statement about the moral rigourism of Protestant culture.

**Table 6.3 Percentage of individuals in favour of strict ethics, according to religious affiliation and participation in religious organisations**

| | Membership and/or unpaid voluntary work in church organisations | | | |
| --- | --- | --- | --- | --- |
| | both | one* | neither | Mean |
| Morality of principles | | | | |
| Catholics | 46 | 38 | 33 | 34 |
| Protestants | 47 | 36 | 28 | 31 |
| Mean | 47 | 35 | 29 | 30 |
| Moral rigourism | | | | |
| Catholics | 76 | 65 | 56 | 58 |
| Protestants | 57 | 53 | 44 | 46 |
| Mean | 70 | 57 | 45 | 48 |
| Civic rigourism | | | | |
| Catholics | 38 | 40 | 34 | 35 |
| Protestants | 60 | 48 | 38 | 42 |
| Mean | 46 | 43 | 32 | 33 |
| Traditional family values | | | | |
| Catholics | 56 | 51 | 37 | 39 |
| Protestants | 50 | 52 | 31 | 36 |
| Mean | 55 | 51 | 30 | 33 |
| Against abortion | | | | |
| Catholics | 62 | 44 | 24 | 28 |
| Protestants | 39 | 29 | 15 | 19 |
| Mean | 55 | 36 | 20 | 23 |

Note: * either a member or doing unpaid voluntary work

Thus, with the exception of civic rigourism, the ethical values of Catholics and Protestants do not differ considerably. That is not to say, however, that religious affiliation is unimportant: Catholics and Protestants have values which differ from those without religion and committed atheists. Moreover, integration into Catholicism and Protestantism has a strong impact on how ethics are structured. Whether or not one closely shares the religious culture of one's confession has an important impact on where one stands with regards to ethics.

**5**     RELIGIOUS IDENTITIES AND POLITICAL ATTITUDES

The suggestion that religious identities no longer have a strong impact on peoples' political positions and attitudes is tested first of all by comparing the distinctive religious groups in terms of politicisation, political participation, and post-materialism. Then the impact of religious identities on confidence in institutions is examined, followed by an exploration of the relationships between religious identities and political ideologies and feelings of national identity.

## 5.1    Politicisation, political participation, and post-materialism

Politicisation is determined by the degree to which respondents are interested in politics, how often they enter into political discussions with friends, and the importance of politics in their life. Table 6.6 in the Appendix isolates the most politicised part of the sample, which is 45%. Among Europeans in general, the degree of integration into each confession does not appear to have an impact on politicisation. However, a higher politicisation is observed among church-goers as compared to non-church attendees in the Netherlands, Denmark, Belgium and especially in France (Bréchon, 1994). This suggests that certain Catholic and Protestant ecclesiastic contexts in which politicisation and presence in the world are emphasised may exist.

The table also reveals that Protestants are more politicised than Catholics. Moreover, strong differences in politicisation are observed in different countries. Traditionally Catholic countries are much less politicised than traditionally Protestant countries. A closer look at the table reveals that in the Northern European bi-confessional countries, Catholics are no less politicised than Protestants; they slip into the country's political culture. The degree of politicisation thus seems to depend most on the national cultural context. Within each country studied, regardless of its culture, being an atheist or non-religious influences politicisation considerably.[14] In almost every country, rejection of religion is accompanied by strong politicisation. Criticism of religious systems is most likely part of a symbolic world in which politics is emphasised, and, as we will see later, left-wing values are strongly supported.

Political participation is indicated by a well-known and often used question asking if the respondent has been engaged in various kinds of protest actions,[15] and forms of direct political action which are often expressed through interest groups (Barnes, Kaase et al., 1979). It was asked if one has signed a petition, or participated in a lawful demonstration, a boycott, an unofficial strike, or the occupation of offices or factories. From this question, a scale of direct political participation was created. Table 6.7 in the Appendix shows the results.[16] While Protestants appear (in the Total column) to participate more actively in politics than Catholics, this is only an indirect effect, mediated by national culture, for in bi-confessional countries, Catholics participate as much as Protestants. The differences between national cultures in the degree of participation in such protest activities appear dependent upon religious origins.[17] However, individual confessional affiliation does not have a direct effect. The analysis shows the important effect of the absence of religion and the declaration of atheism: in every country and every age group, those who reject religious systems participate more intensely in politics.

Post-materialism is measured by the well-known index proposed by Inglehart (1977; 1990; 1997). In accordance with his theoretical expectations, post-materialism is less developed in poorer European countries (Portugal, Ireland), while it is stronger in more developed countries (see Table 6.8 in the Appendix). There are considerable modulations, however: Danes, for example, have a rather low level of post-materialism. Thus, this attitude is not a mechanical adaptation to economic development. Those without religion and committed atheists appear far more post-materialist than Christians. Since young people are more post-materialist and more indifferent to religion, it is tempting to conclude that this result is merely a generation effect. This is, however, not the case. Those aged between 18 and 29 who do not belong to a denomination, as well as those who are committed atheist, appear to be more post-materialistic than other people of the same age. Post-materialism is also strongly linked to level of education: the higher one's level of education, the more post-materialist one is. Yet, at the same level of education, those without religion, and especially committed atheists, are more post-materialist than the religious categories. Thus, the absence of religion does indeed have an effect on the post-materialist attitude. However, Catholics do not differ much from Protestants in level of post-materialism, and the intensity of integration into a religious system does not have a clear effect either.

## 5.2  Confidence in institutions

A list of institutions was presented to the respondents who were asked to indicate how much confidence they had in each of them. Some of these institutions refer to the public sector (e.g., the armed forces, the police, the social security system, the education system, the legal system, Parliament, civil service), while others refer to the private sector (major companies, the press, trade unions, the church). Two sub-categories can be isolated. The first sub-category measures trust in authoritarian or hierarchical institutions (the police, the armed forces, the church). The second seems to indicate attachment to democratic institutions. It includes institutional forms typical of representative democracies (the education system, the social security system, the legal system, Parliament, civil service, the press, trade unions). In legal-rational democracies, these components mediate relationships between the citizen and political power. It is therefore possible to construct two attitude scales, one measuring trust in 'authoritarian' institutions, the other measuring trust in 'democratic' institutions.[18]

As is revealed in Table 6.9 in the Appendix, where the links between confidence in authoritarian institutions are displayed, those without religion and atheists are again a specific category. In every country studied, they do not like any of the three institutions concerned. Integration into a Christian confession also plays a role: the more one is integrated into Catholicism or Protestantism, the more confidence one has in authoritarian institutions. However, differences between Catholics and Protestants are subtle, even though Protestants are slightly more in favour of authoritarian institutions than Catholics in each bi-confessional country. Differences between countries are considerable, but show no clear logic. There is not a division between Northern and Southern Europe or traditionally Catholic and Protestant countries. The Dutch, Belgians, and Germans reject authoritarian institutions en masse, while the Irish and the British support them strongly. The specific traits of national cultures are most likely the best explanation of this phenomenon.

Confidence in democratic institutions (Table 6.10 in the Appendix) is not linked in the same way to religious values. There are only a few countries in which individuals without religion and atheists show a more critical attitude toward democratic institutions (Spain, Italy, Ireland, Germany). Integration into a religious culture has a weak impact: church-goers have only slightly more confidence in such democratic institutions than other individuals. Considerable differences exist between countries, and do not intersect with the differences observed for authoritarian institutions.

Northern European countries - whether traditionally Catholic or Protestant - appear to be most supportive of their democratic institutions (Denmark, the Netherlands, Ireland). Britain, however, is an exception: its scores are low, and very different from those of its Irish neighbour. Among Southern European countries, Italy (whose political society is in crisis) and Portugal are among the countries most critical of democratic institutions. Clearly, national culture and history play an important role in these cases.

## 5.3   Political orientation and economic options

A frequently used indicator of peoples' political orientation is the left-right scale. Although the concepts of left and right are not undisputed and their meanings are even contested,[19] they are still widely used. The respondent is asked to place him/herself on a scale from left (=1) to right (=10). Positions 6 to 10 on the scale are taken into account here to enumerate individuals with a right-wing orientation (see Table 6.11 in the Appendix).

Once again, the specificity among individuals without religion and committed atheists is demonstrated: not only are they more open to new family values, very relativist concerning ethical matters, more politicised, more active in political life and more post-materialist, they are also more left-oriented. These different features make up a symbolic system which transcends the particularities of national cultures. As for ethical values, integration into Catholicism and Protestantism has an important effect: the more religiously active the individual is, the more likely he or she is to be oriented to the right. The relationship's structure is not, however, completely the same for Catholics and Protestants. In the first group, regular Mass attendees stand out from irregular Mass attendees and Catholics who do not go to church. In the second group, regular and irregular church-goers (the most right-wing) stand out clearly from Protestants who do not go to church. This difference can be understood by the meaning of religious service in the two confessions. For Catholics, regular church attendance has a more normative meaning than for Protestants. Protestants who attend religious services irregularly are often well integrated into their community. In other words, the difference in the relationship's structure should be moderated. Further, it is known that regular church attendees are both older and more right-wing; it is thus necessary to control for the age effect. For each age group, integration into Catholicism or Protestantism has a specific impact, and people without religion as well as committed atheists are always very unlikely to be more right-wing.

Protestants are slightly more right wing than Catholics (see 'Total' column). In the bi-confessional countries, however, no considerable difference is observed between regular church-attending Catholics and Protestants.[20] Situations may have existed and probably still exist locally - especially in minority church situations - in which members of one of the two confessions are more right or left-wing than others. In fact, Catholics and Protestants do not have very different political orientations. For both confessions, integration into a religious culture is accompanied by a more frequent right-wing political orientation. There is no ontological phenomenon, no particular electoral affinity between right-wing orientations and Christian values. The evangelical message is sufficiently flexible so that electoral affinities can be found on both the right and left. This can be attributed to historical developments and circumstances. In the European context in which Catholicism was against the establishment of the modern State and Protestantism tended to be in favour of it, integration into the major churches was conducive to a right wing orientation. Historians have to explain this disturbing phenomenon. It could be argued that integration into religious services is not the only form of religious integration, and that if integration into church organisations were taken into account, the result would be that European Protestantism is, in fact, more left-wing. The data disproves this hypothesis (see Table 6.4). Catholics and Protestants who are active in ecclesiastic or parish organisations are more often right-wing than Christians who are not affiliated with these groups.

Economic conceptions constitute an important dimension of an individual's political identity. Partisans of a liberal economy tend to be oriented to the right, whereas supporters of an economy in which the state intervenes are clearly more oriented to the left. This often corresponds to considerable differences in the programmes of different European political parties. In order to measure this economic liberalism/state-interventionism dimension, a synthetic index was created from three strongly correlated scales.[21] Table 6.12 in the Appendix presents these links between economic orientations and religious attitudes which are weak (Cramer's V=0.07

with integration into Catholicism, and 0.07 with integration into Protestantism). The European average shows that those without religion are slightly less liberal than others, but the phenomenon is not confirmed in every country. Generally, Protestants are slightly more liberal than Catholics, but this is only confirmed for Germany and Britain. In any case, integration into a confession does not have an impact. This fact in itself is interesting, for in past decades, the Catholic church has often insisted upon a criticism of both liberalism and socialism in favour of a third path which calls for a social partnership. Yet this notion is hardly known among Catholics themselves, and once integrated, it will not be easy to position oneself on a polar scale without taking into account 'third paths'.

**Table 6.4  Percentage of right-wing self-placement (positions 6-10) according to religious affiliation and participation in church organisations**

| | Membership and/or unpaid voluntary work in church organisations | | | |
| | both | one* | neither | Mean |
|---|---|---|---|---|
| Catholics | 46 | 48 | 30 | 32 |
| Protestants | 48 | 49 | 38 | 40 |
| No religion | 6** | 34 | 23 | 24 |
| Atheists | - | - | 15 | 15 |
| Mean | 45 | 47 | 29 | 31 |

Notes: * either a member or doing unpaid voluntary work; ** % less than 30 respondents

Considerable differences in responses exist according to the country: Northern Europe strongly favours economic liberalism, perhaps because of its Protestant tradition (see responses to the next item). In Southern Europe, important differences are observed. The Iberian Peninsula seems unique, for its citizens have a very low level of support for economic liberalism. Is this perhaps due to the political history of these countries? Even though they are strongly rejected, Francism and Salazarism appear to have left their mark: the idea that the economy should be regulated by the public powers seems to be more firmly rooted in Spain and Portugal than in other countries.

A third indicator of ideological values, complementary to the preceding one, merits further discussion. When asked to choose between two values that many people would like to uphold together - freedom and equality[22] - a small majority chose freedom, as Table 6.13 in the Appendix shows.

The structure of these relationships is rather simple: integration into a religious system has no impact, and individuals with no religion and atheists do not have a specificity. However, differences are observed between Northern and Southern

Europe. As was the case for several variables, religion has an indirect impact. Protestantism appears to have generated this national temperament more favourably than freedom throughout history. Today, this temperament is accepted to the same extent by Protestants, Catholics and individuals without religion in these countries.[23]

## 5.4   Nationalism, national preference, and exclusion of foreigners

Individual political orientations are also linked to attitudes toward nationalism and foreigners. This section will enable us to consider the possible religious roots of these political dimensions. The Values Survey questionnaire is not very rich in indicators of nationalism, but there are essentially two: the feeling of national pride, and a statement of readiness to fight in order to defend one's country.[24] Those who are both ready to fight for their country and claim to be very or rather proud of their nationality, can be considered 'nationalists'. Fifty-two percent of the European sample are, according to these criteria, nationalist. According to the Total column in Table 6.14 in the Appendix, Protestants are slightly more nationalistic than Catholics.

This could be explained by Christianity's long history: Protestantism has been conducive to the formation of the Nation-State, whereas Catholicism opposed it. Yet this hypothesis is insufficient. Very strong differences in the level of nationalism are observed from country to country, which have more to do with national histories than national religious roots. To be sure, there is a strong nationalism in three traditionally Protestant countries. This high level of nationalism, however, has more to do with the national culture than a strictly Protestant culture, since nationalism does not differ according to one's level of religious integration. The three countries concerned are Denmark, where adherence to the national Lutheran church more often symbolises a national identity than a religious faith; and Great Britain and the Netherlands, where Protestants are as nationalistic as Catholics. While three Protestant countries have a high level of nationalism, a fourth Protestant country - Germany - has a much lower level, with no difference between Catholics and Protestants. The history of the 20th Century can only partly explain this phenomenon: certain Germans have not recovered their national pride after Nazism and the Holocaust. Another explanation can be put forth if one considers that nationalism is also quite low in two Catholic countries: Italy and Belgium. These three countries do not have a very long history of national unity; they emphasize regional identities and sometimes have strong regional conflicts. In any case, each country's culture is apparently more important than religious attitudes in explaining nationalist sentiment. The only striking impact of religious attitude which transcends national differences, concerns atheists, who are characterised in every country by a weak degree of nationalism. Their symbolic system is strongly marked by universalist values: atheists consider themselves 'citizens of the world' much more than others, and refuse to shut themselves into a nationalist identity.

It is known that individuals who are nationalistic are more likely to be hostile toward pro-immigration policies. In the questionnaire, one question allowed us to target individuals who are in favour of saving jobs for national citizens during periods of unemployment.[25] Northern European countries - where Protestants are numerous - appear least in favour of a national preference (see Table 6.15 in the Appendix). In these countries, Catholics do not differ much from Protestants.

The important religious distinction remains the same: those without religion, as well as committed atheists, are less in favour of a national preference (with the exception of Portugal). The unemployment rate does not explain differences between countries. It could help explain the high frequency of national preference assertions in Spain and Ireland, but not in Portugal (the lowest rate in the EEC in 1990 after Luxembourg). Nor does the unemployment rate explain the Danish and Dutch cases, with average unemployment rates and a low level of support for national preference. Therefore, we must conclude that each country's culture plays an important role in this type of response. And religious institutions do not seem to have a great deal of influence on public opinion, even on their members, in preventing nationalist sentiment during times of economic crisis. Indeed, integration into Catholicism or Protestantism does not lower the percentage of individuals in favour of a national preference. Among young people, and particularly among individuals with a high level of education, assertion of a national preference is less frequent. The effect of the religious variable, however, is not significantly modified when the age effect and the level of education are controlled for.

A scale of xenophobia was created from a long question in which each individual surveyed was asked to state which category of people he or she would not like to have as neighbours. The categories on the list are: 'individuals of another race', 'Muslims', 'immigrant workers', 'Jews', 'Hindus'. The scale is made up of quotes from these five groups. Table 6.16 in the Appendix lists those who rejected at least one category of foreigners.

Whereas 'national preference' is quite frequently mentioned, fear of having foreigners in their neighbourhood occurs rarely. There does not appear to be a strong logic in the table. There is no split between Northern and Southern Europe: the most xenophobic countries seem to be Belgium, Portugal, and Germany, and the least xenophobic are Spain and Ireland, followed closely by Denmark and the Netherlands. The percentage of foreigners outside the EU in each population is not very explanatory. Religious affiliation and strong integration into a religious confession do not have a clear effect, which is a result in and of itself[26]: being a church-attending Catholic or Protestant does not make one less xenophobic. Being a committed atheist appears to have a minor effect, for these individuals tend to exclude foreigners from their neighbourhoods less often. In reality, though, this is essentially due to an effect of age and education. These two variables structure the xenophobic sentiment much more strongly than religious attitude.[27] The difference between age groups is quite clear.[28] The age at which one finishes school also has an impact: the level of xenophobia is 15% among those who stayed in school until age 20 or above, and 30% among those who stayed in school until age 15. Education appears to protect against xenophobia. However, among 18- to 29-year-olds, integration into a religious system appears to have a certain protective effect against xenophobia (slightly stronger among Protestants than among Catholics). Inversely, in the group of 60+, mass-attending Catholics are slightly more xenophobic than non-mass-attending Catholics.

**Table 6.5  Percentage of individuals with a national preference, or xenophobic attitude, according to religious affiliation and participation in church organisations**

|  | Membership and/or unpaid voluntary work in church organisations | | | |
|  | both | one* | neither | Mean |
|---|---|---|---|---|
| *National Preference* | | | | |
| Catholics | 53 | 58 | 72 | 70 |
| Protestants | 35 | 45 | 57 | 54 |
| Mean | 48 | 51 | 63 | 61 |
| *Don't like outsiders* | | | | |
| Catholics | 21 | 25 | 26 | 26 |
| Protestants | 18 | 25 | 27 | 26 |
| Mean | 20 | 24 | 25 | 25 |

Notes: * either a member or doing unpaid voluntary work

The analysis of the last two variables (national preference and exclusion of foreigners) has shown that integration into a religious system does not make individuals more open toward foreigners. However, a comparison between Table 6.5 and Tables 6.15 and 6.16 in the Appendix shows that members of church organisations are quite different than simple church-attending Catholics and Protestants. The relationships are not at all like the previous ones. Participation in religious organisations appears to protect - in part - against nationalist attitudes or attitudes of social exclusion. Members of these organisations tend to be more sensitive to the institutions' discourse - which they contribute to - than simple church-goers. In almost all the European countries studied, Catholic and Protestant discourse on the importance of openness to foreigners has increased in the last few years.

## 6    CONCLUSIONS

The first important conclusion to be drawn is that, while differences between Catholics and Protestants appear in the sample's average for quite a large number of variables, a detailed analysis of the tables reveals that these differences almost always have more to do with the national context than with religious affiliation.[29] In countries with a Protestant culture, Catholics often represent a considerable percentage of the population, and are not different from Protestants, since they have adopted the country's mentality, forged throughout history. In the last few decades, the major religious confessions have lost a considerable amount of their social influence, but it should not be forgotten that they continue to mark European societies *indirectly*. Indeed, the major religious confessions formed both the matrix of Europe's cultural unity and an important source of diversity, by way of two visions of Christianity. The integration of values upheld by Catholicism and Protestantism into national cultures makes it difficult to still speak of a Catholic or Protestant life ethic. Our conclusion is thus different from Andrew Greeley's who claims that ethics linked to religious denominations remain quite strong. He admits that his model works much better for English-speaking countries than for Germany and the Netherlands. He tests more dimensions than in this chapter, and utilises other methodologies. His data are older. Above all, he does not take the degree of integration into each religious confession into account, which is questionable if one wants to emphasise the idea of a confessional ethic: individuals should correspond more to the 'confessional ethic' the more integrated they are into their religious group. It is difficult to explain why these conclusions do not converge. However, in the name of scientific deontology, it is necessary to at least mention these differences, in order to encourage new research. We should also ask ourselves if, when we discover a difference between Catholics and Protestants within a country, it is simply due to regional differences (for example in Canada where the Catholics are mainly located in the Quebec province or between the Irish Republic and Northern Ireland), or differences in ethnic origin (in the United States). What Andrew Greeley explains as a denominational ethic might simply be the product of a sub-national culture historically linked to a religious denomination.

Our thesis about an indirect effect of religions which subsists through national cultures is also supported by Ronald Inglehart who shows that Protestant and Catholic countries do not share the same value system. The former are not only richer than the latter, they are also less traditional and more post-materialist. However, the influence of the current religious institutions on attitudes and behaviours is indirect. Catholicism and Protestantism have had a great impact on national cultures: 'Although the churches themselves are now a fading influence in Western European society, religious traditions helped shape enduring national cultures that persist today' (Inglehart, 1997: 99). Several pages later he adds: 'In most countries, these cultural differences reflect the entire historical experience of given societies, and *not* the influence of the respective churches today. This point becomes vividly evident when we examine the value systems of such societies as the

Netherlands and Germany (...) Both the Netherlands and Germany manifest typically Protestant values. Moreover, the Catholics and Protestants *within* these societies do not show markedly different value systems: the Dutch Catholics today are as Calvinist as the members of the Dutch Reformed Church' (Inglehart, 1997: 99-100).

A second conclusion is that while differences between Catholics and Protestants are essentially non-existent in a secularised Europe in which religious wars are a distant memory and ecumenical processes - more efficient at the base than at the summit of institutions - contribute to the defusing of conflicts between churches, the gap between religious affiliation on the one hand, and non-religion and assertion of atheism on the other hand, appears strong. To sum up the last group's symbolic universe as it appears in our study, atheists do not like intangible principles or moral/civic rigourism; they dislike the traditional family values and support the right to abortion; they are strongly politicised and participate actively in political life; they are often post-materialist and often see themselves as 'citizens of the world'; they are very likely to be left-wing; they strongly dislike authoritarian institutions; they are not very nationalist and tend to be less xenophobic. In brief, a rejection of religion goes hand in hand with clear ethical, social, and political values that combine left-wing humanism, cultural liberalism, anti-authoritarianism and participatory will. This symbolic system transcends national borders, since it was found in every country studied, and not only in those strongly marked by traditions of anti-clericalism and strong opposition between conservative religion and a democratic political system. This system is not directed by a large unified institution, but most likely finds fulcrums in organisations that create meaning such as associative networks, press groups, etc. Sociologists have paid too little attention to this symbolic system, most likely because it is not embodied in a large institution, and because sociologists of religion have emphasised secularisation processes and religious rebirths or re-compositions, but have shown little interest in groups who refuse the religious dimension, or who do not place any importance on it.

A third conclusion is that the degree of integration into a Catholic or Protestant system has an important impact on almost every indicator having to do with the conception of ethics, family values, and attitudes concerning sexuality; it also influences right-wing orientations and confidence in authoritarian institutions. Strong integration into a religious system creates a specific identity; yet it does not create 'gaps' in every dimension. Religious identity is only one form of identity. When combined with other dimensions - in particular, belonging to a national culture, but also to a social group and an age category - religious identity gives each individual an original and unique combination. Yet even at a level as global as a European survey, which hides strong specificities of certain religious minorities, statistics allow us to pinpoint traits of the structured religious identity that are often opposed to committed atheists and people without religion. Indeed, strong integration into Catholicism and Protestantism is often accompanied by attachment to an ethic of intangible principles for daily life. It is also often accompanied by a rigourist conception of the regulation of the ethics of social relations, a strong emphasis on family and vigilance toward sexual morals, a right-wing political orientation and the defence of authoritarian institutions. These connections between ethics, social issues, and politics certainly do not exist among all Catholics and Protestants who are strongly integrated into their churches. In the same manner, the proposed model for those without religion and atheists is not shared by all members of the group, either. Here, we locate majority forms of symbolic system articulation which have a certain coherence and do not produce too much discord for individuals. This conclusion supports what factorial analyses of correspondence applied to data from the Value surveys show. The main dimension - which is supposed to influence the values systems of Europeans the most - refers to the distinction between tradition and modernity. It is defined by Olivier Galland and Yannick Lemel as: '(opposing) permissive Europeans who are a-religious, few attached to traditional institutions or values and left wing oriented, to Europeans who are sensitive to the respect of these values and traditions, and present all the traits of a greater moral rigour' (Galland & Lemel, 1995: 113-130).

Our final conclusion is that national cultural contexts have quite a strong influence on ethical, social, and political attitudes. They sometimes oppose Northern and Southern Europe, or sometimes European Protestant culture and European Catholic culture. The exception, of course, is Ireland, which has a strong Catholic culture, but belongs geographically, and in many aspects, culturally, to Northern Europe. Sometimes, too, cultural contexts only appear explainable by purely national traits, independent of any European logic.

Moreover, to speak of the influence of national cultural contexts is an oversimplification. Firstly, we would need to explain how national cultures are formed. As we have seen, religious tradition is an important matrix in these cultures; however, other phenomena certainly help define them. The level of economic development, which is often higher in traditionally Protestant countries, most likely has a specific effect on cultural values, as Inglehart's studies on post-modernism show. The degree of current secularisation in each country, that is to say, citizens' distance from religious tradition, probably also influences cultural values. This factor is not completely independent of the previous ones. Protestantism had a much more open attitude toward modernity than Catholicism, which also led to more rapid secularisation (e.g., Bruce, 1990; Willaime, 1990). It should also be emphasized that in certain Catholic countries, Catholicism's intransigence toward the modern world produced a strong anti-religious reaction, and generated differences in national cultures.

In addition, language and cultural exchange will have an impact as well. Sharing the same language probably does not have mechanical effects, as a comparison of values among 'francophones' (the French and French-Canadians, for example) might reveal. Sharing a common language may be a sign of a common origin, but it can also be linked to colonisation phenomena and opposition to the dominant population. Cultural exchanges do not have mechanical effects either. The process of globalization does not lead to a rapid homogenisation of cultures. A comparison of basic values in 1981 and 1990 shows that national differences have persisted and have not decreased (e.g., Galland & Lemel, 1995: 113-130). Still, it is clear that cosmopolitan cities and regions that have the most contact with neighbouring countries are affected by these phenomena.

The term 'national cultural context' is also an oversimplification, because certain countries exhibit considerable cultural differences from one region to another. This is clearly the case in Southern European countries (Spain, Portugal, Italy), but also to a certain extent in Belgium and France (see e.g., Chauvel, 1995). Comparing national averages is useful, but in certain realms it hides important (infra-)structural differences. No region is homogeneous; they differ markedly in class, generation, educational level and social integration. In order to study value systems, simplification is necessary. Focussing too much on particulars and specificities, will lead to the discovery of individual singularities. Each individual is unique. His or her values system is a unique synthesis, and yet this synthesis is made up of different influences, some of which come indirectly from long ago, without the individual being aware of it.

**Notes**

1    Greeley (1989) tested this hypotheses using the international data of the 1981-1983 Values Survey on five English-speaking countries (the United States, Great Britain, Ireland (both the Irish Republic and Northern Ireland), Canada, and Australia), and two European countries (Germany and the Netherlands).

2    Members of different Protestant denominations are grouped together without specifying whether the person belongs to a majority or minority church. While the questionnaire allows for this distinction, the members of minority churches are too small in number to be considered separately. For Great Britain, Anglicans are categorized with Protestants.

3    Cramer's V is an index which measures the strength of the relationship between two qualitative variables. It ranges from 0 to 1. Coefficients between 0.20 and 0.30 correspond to rather strong statistical connections for social phenomena.

4    These beliefs are: believe in God; believe that 'there is a personal God' or that 'there is some sort of spirit or life force'; importance of God in one's life (positions 7-10 on scale from 1 = not at all important to 10 = very important), believe in life after death, a soul, the devil, hell, heaven, sin, resurrection of the dead. Belief in reincarnation was omitted because it is not at all or only marginally related to other beliefs.

5    One question isolates those who claim to favour a morality of intangible principles: 'Here are two statements which people sometimes make when discussing good and evil. Which one comes closest to your own point of view?
    – There are absolutely clear guidelines about what is good and evil. These always apply to everyone, whatever the circumstances.
    – There can never be absolutely clear guidelines about what is good and evil. What is good and evil depends entirely upon the circumstances at the time'.

6    The *moral rigourism* scale includes six items. Each item ranges from 1 to 10; thus the additive scale ranges from 6 to 60. In our analyses we only included those who scored from 6 to 22, which makes up 48 % of the sample. *Civic rigourism* includes four indicators with answer categories ranging from 1 to 10. The additive scale ranges from 4 (the behaviours are never justified) to 40 (the behaviours are always justified). Our analyses are confined to those who have a score of 4.

7    As with morality of principles, civic rigourism is more frequent in the older generation (Cramer's V=0.18). The link with level of education, is rather weak (V=0.09). Generation and religious integration combined produce a high level of rigourism among elderly people strongly integrated into a Christian denomination, and a low level of rigourism among young people without a religion or committed atheists.

8    Here, the Danish specificity should be noted. Although they are highly detached from religious values, and rarely attend religious services, they are strongly attached to their national church, a symbol of their Danish identity. Since Danish society is highly secularised, the almost unanimous rejection of

a morality of principles is not at all surprising. Their level of civic rigourism, however, is surprisingly high. Denmark is a country where the morality of principles obtains the lowest score, and civic rigourism the highest score. Even among Danes who are quite detached from religious values, moral rigourism is high. This rigourism which originates from a religious culture, probably moved in part into the national culture.

9    The five items are the following:
     – Tend to agree with the statement that 'a child needs a home with both a father and a mother to grow up happily';
     – Agrees with the statement that 'a woman has to have children in order to be fulfilled' (opposed to 'not necessary');
     – Does not agree with the statement: 'Marriage is an outdated institution';
     – Disapproves 'if a woman wants to have a child as a single parent but she doesn't want to have a stable relationship with a man';
     – Tend to disagree with statement 'that individuals should have the chance to enjoy complete sexual freedom without being restricted'.
     Only the items which are most favourable to traditional conceptions of the family were taken into account.

10   Traditional family values are popular among older generations and individuals with a low level of education. However, for individuals from the same generation who have the same level of education, religious integration plays a specific role.

11   Four possible situations for abortion were presented and the respondent was asked if he/she approves or disapproves of abortion under the given circumstances. The circumstances were:
     – Where the mother's health is at risk from the pregnancy;
     – Where it is likely that the child would be born physically handicapped;
     – Where the woman is not married;
     – Where a married couple does not want to have any more children.

12   A hostile attitude toward abortion does not depend on the level of education, and its link to age is much weaker than was observed with the ethical dimensions previously examined.

13   The two measurements of integration into a religious system (church attendance and membership/volunteering in religious groups or clubs) are mutually correlated, but are not redundant (Cramer's $V=0.22$ with Catholicism; and $0.25$ with Protestantism). Those who belong to church groups/clubs, or who volunteer in them, are often regular church-goers. However, many regular church-goers do not participate at all in church organisations.

14   Those without religion, as well as committed atheists, are generally younger than the other religious categories. Their average age is 40.1 and 36.8, respectively, whereas it is 54.6 for regular church-going Protestants, 45.7 for non-church-attending Protestants, 50.6 for regular mass-attending Catholics, and 41.7 for non-mass-attending Catholics. Yet despite their young age, which should be a source of lower politicisation, those without religion and especially

committed atheists are highly politicised. Moreover, for the same level of education, committed atheists younger than 35 are always more politicised than their age group's average. Among young people, a rejection of religious systems seems to go along with a precocious political socialisation.

15  Here, the adjective 'political' should be understood in a broader sense: it applies to all forms of social and political mobilisation.

16  The link (Cramer's V) between degree of politicisation and political participation is 0.19.

17  The high level of direct political participation in Britain is noteworthy. The religious attitude does not create differences. The high level is essentially due to the important role of petitions as a form of political action in Britain.

18  For each institution, the respondent could indicate the degree of confidence: 1 = 'a great deal'; 2 = 'quite a lot'; 3 = 'not very much'; 4 = 'not at all'. Responses concerning the church, the army, and the police are added together, producing a distribution from 3 to 12. A score of 3 indicates a high level of confidence in hierarchical institutions, while 12 indicates lack of confidence. Scores up to 6 represents confidence in hierarchical institutions. The scale of confidence in democratic institutions is constructed in a similar way. It includes the education system, the social security system, the legal system, Parliament, civil service, the press, and trade unions. The observed distribution ranges from 7 to 28, and a score up to 17 indicates a high level of confidence in democratic institutions.

19  See, for instance, Kitschelt & Hellemans (1990).

20  The British situation should be noted. Protestants (especially Anglicans) who seldom go to church and those who do not attend religious services are much more right-wing than Catholics with the same degree of religious integration. This is explained by the strong institutionalisation of Anglicanism, which often made its members closer to the Conservative Party. Catholics, on the other hand, were more in favour of left-wing or centre parties.

21  Respondents were shown several opposite statements and were asked to indicate (on a ten-point scale) which statements resembled their own views most. The following opposite statements are taken into account:
   – 'Incomes should be made more equal' (=1) versus 'There should be greater incentives for individual effort' (=10);
   – 'Private ownership of business and industry should be increased' (=1) versus 'Government ownership of business and industry should be increased' (=10);
   – 'Individuals should take more responsibility for providing for themselves'(=1) versus 'The State should take more responsibility to ensure that everyone is provided for' (=10).
   The first scale was inverted in order to create a cumulative index (ranging from 3 to 30) in which the lowest scores represented the liberal options, and the highest the socialising economic options. The index was then recoded in four categories in which each represented roughly one-fourth of the sample. As expected, this index corresponds to the left/right scale (Cramer's V = 0.19).

22 The question was: 'Which of these two statements comes closest to your own opinion?' Two answers were presented:
- 'I find that both freedom and equality are important. But if I were to choose one or the other, I would consider personal freedom more important, that is, everyone can live in freedom and develop without hindrance';
- 'Certainly both freedom and equality are important. But if I were to choose one or the other, I would consider equality more important, that is, that nobody is underprivileged and that social class differences are not so strong'.

23 This indicator is not linked to age, whereas education has an effect, although not very strong: personal freedom is preferred by 46% of those who finished school at age 15, whereas it is chosen by 57% of those who finished school at age 20 or older.

24 Both indicators are correlated (Cramer's V = 0.20). Therefore we have constructed an index.

25 It was asked if the respondent agrees with the statement: 'When jobs are scarce, employers should give priority to ... (nationality of the country)'. The responses were only slightly linked to the nationalism index (Cramer's V = 0.10).

26 In fact, analyses by Jacques Billiet on Belgium and Flanders from several surveys, as well as work from the Netherlands, conclude that religious engagement has a protective effect (Billiet & Carton, 1993; Eisinga, Felling & Peters, 1993).

27 This resembles Mayer's (1990) results.

28 Nineteen percent xenophobes among 18-29 year-olds, 21% among 30-44 year-olds, 27% among 45-59 year-olds, 33% among those of 60 and older.

29 Only in the case of civic rigourism are there clear differences between Protestants and Catholics.

# References

Barnes, S., M. Kaase et al. 1979. *Political Action: Mass Participation in Five Western Democracies*. London: Sage.

Billiet, J. & A. Carton 1993. 'Contrasting Effects of Church Involvement on the Dimensions of Ethnocentrism: an Empirical Study among Flemish Catholics'. Communication to the *22nd International Society for Sociology of Religions Conference*, Budapest, 19-23 July.

Bréchon, P. 1994. 'Le rapport à la politique'. Pp. 163-200 in H. Riffault (ed.), *Les valeurs des Français*. Paris: PUF.

Bruce, S. 1990. *A House Divided. Protestantism, Schism and Secularization*. London: Routeledge.

Chauvel, L. 1995. 'Valeurs régionales et nationales en Europe'. *Futuribles* 200: 188-189.

Davie, G. 1994. *Religion in Britain Since 1945. Believing without Belonging*. London: Blackwell.

Donegani, J.M. 1993. *La liberté de choisir. Pluralisme religieux et pluralisme politique dans le catholicisme français contemporain*. Paris: Presses de la FNSP.

Eisinga, R., A. Felling & J. Peters 1993. 'Religious Belief, Church Involvement and Ethnocentrism in Netherlands'. *Journal for Scientific Study of Religion*, 29/1:54-75.

Galland, O. & Y. Lemel 1995. 'La permanence des différences. Une comparaison des systèmes de valeurs entre pays européens'. *Futuribles* 200: 113-130.

Greeley, A. 1989. 'Protestant and Catholic: Is the Analogical Imagination Extinct?'. *American Sociological Review* 54: 485-502.

Inglehart, R. 1997. *Modernization and Postmodernization*. Princeton: Princeton University Press.

Kitschelt, H. & S. Hellemans 1990. 'The Left-Right Semantics and the New Politics Cleavage'. *Comparative Political Studies* 23: 210-238.

Mayer, N. 1990. 'Ethnocentrisme, racisme et intolérance'. Pp. 17-43 in D. Boy & N. Mayer (eds.), *L'électeur français en question*. Paris: Presses de la FNSP.

Michelat G. 1990. 'L'identité catholique des Français. 1. Les dimensions de la religiosité and 2. Appartenances et socialisation religieuse'. *Revue française de sociologie* 31/3 and 31/4:355-388 and 609-633.

Roof, Wade C. 1993. *A Generation of Seekers*. New York: Harper Collins Publisher.

Tracy, D. 1987. *The Analogical Imagination. Christian Theology and the Culture of Pluralism*. New York: Seabury.

Willaime, J.P. 1990. *La précarité protestante*. Geneva: Labor et fides.

Chapter Seven

# Religion and Social Capital Revisited

**Loek Halman & Thorleif Pettersson**

## 1 INTRODUCTION

Secularization and religious change are core phenomena within the sociology of religion, while political science focuses on, for instance, political change and the possible crisis of democracy. Both political science and the sociology of religion investigate the relationships between politics and religion. Theories of secularization assume that religion's impact on political culture is decreasing, while political science finds religious cleavages to be of less importance for political behaviour. Thus, there are several issues of mutual interest to political science and the sociology of religion. Our chapter discusses one of these issues of mutual interest: the relationship between social capital and religion.

This relationship is all the more interesting, since social capital has also been found important for fields other than politics. Social capital is considered an important factor with regard to social relationships (Coleman, 1990), the family (Boisjoly et al., 1995), and economic development ( Fukuyama, 1995; Knack & Keefer, 1997). In this sense, social capital relates to several basic dimensions of social life.

Against this background, we think it of paramount interest to investigate the relationship between social capital and religion. According to Putnam, a negative association exists between the two, whereas Coleman (1990) claims the opposite. This contrast is all the more intriguing because Putnam builds on Coleman's work. However, Coleman's conclusion was based on US observations, while Putnam's conclusions were based on the Italian situation. Apparently, the association between religion and social capital might depend upon country-specific conditions and contextual factors. In this chapter, we explore to what extent this is indeed the case. Another aim of this chapter is to tentatively determine if the claims of Coleman and Putnam, which pertain to the societal level, can be generalized to the level of the individual as well. Much empirical evidence on social capital is based on macro-level analyses. Our contribution deals with comparative analyses of individual-level data.

The chapter starts with a theoretical discussion on social capital and the contrasting hypotheses on the relationships between social capital and religion. We question Putnam's assumption of a negative relationship between religion and social capital. Next we shift to the broader domain of modernization and societal change.

According to the theory of modernization, society has gradually transformed into a secular and highly individualized society. Religion in modern society is no longer regarded as a core element, shaping people's world views, their moral convictions, their private and communal lives and their politics. Instead secular values have become increasingly more important sources in modern society. One of these 'new' values is postmaterialism which is assumed to have gained prominence in the formation of social, political, and cultural life (e.g., Van Deth, 1995: 9-10). In section 3 we briefly discuss some of the issues related to these transformations. Although in a very general sense, the processes might appear similar in different countries, the degree and pace at which modernization has proceeded in Western countries is different. Therefore, the impact of religion and postmaterialism should not be expected to be exactly the same in different countries. In order to illuminate such differences, we have based our analyses on four politically and religiously very different countries: Sweden, Germany, Spain, and the US. The arguments for the selection of countries are given in section 4. In section 5 we shift to the measurements of the key concepts of our research, followed by a brief overview of the main empirical results, which seem to contradict Putnam's assumption of a negative relation between religion and social capital. In the last section, we discuss our main findings and suggest strategies for future research.

## 2    SOCIAL CAPITAL AND RELIGION

In 1993 Robert Putnam published his well known study *Making Democracy Work.* He initiated his investigation by asking the intriguing question 'Why do some democratic governments succeed and others fail?' (Putnam 1993: 3). At the end of his book, he concluded that social capital 'is the key to making democracy work' (Putnam 1993: 185). Thus, he regarded social capital, built on active memberships in voluntary associations, social trust, and generalized norms of reciprocity, an essential attribute of a pro-democratic culture and the proper functioning of political institutions. Needless to say, the importance of social capital has also been recognized by others, e.g.,with regard to social relationships (Coleman, 1990), the family (Boisjoly et al., 1995), and economic development ( Fukuyama, 1995; Knack & Keefer, 1997). In this sense, the genesis, maintenance, and workings of social capital have been important research issues in the social sciences.

In his study, Putnam investigated the effectiveness during the 1980s of the political institutions in about 20 Italian regions. He accumulated evidence that the effectiveness of the regional political institutions was strongly determined by a cultural syndrome which he termed the 'civic community', characterized by features like social trust, tolerance, solidarity, and extensive networks of secondary associations. This pro-democratic cultural syndrome he found to be more typical of the Northern Italian regions than of the Southern parts of Italy. Putnam's analyses also revealed that the regional economic development was related to the effectiveness of the regional political institutions. However, when 'civic community' was controlled for , the impact of economic development on the effectiveness of the political institutions almost disappeared. Thus, he concluded '...the predictive power of the civic community is greater than the power of economic development ... So strong is this relationship, that when we take the 'civic-ness' of a region into account, the relationship ... between economic development and institutional performance entirely vanishes' (Putnam 1993: 98).

Putnam further claimed that the regional differences in political and economic conflicts, demographic stability, urbanization, and levels of education, do not add much to the understanding and explanation of why some governments 'work' and others do not (Putnam 1993: 120). By and large, he found 'civic community' to be the crucial factor. In addition, it should be noted that Putnam found life satisfaction to be higher among regions with higher levels of the civic traditions, i.e. the northern regions. 'Happiness is living in a civic community' (Putnam 1993: 112).

In order to explain *why* the civic community is essential for making democracy work, Putnam tapped into James Coleman's theory on social capital, which assumes social relations to constitute a capital asset of the individual, that is 'a resource that, once accumulated, can be drawn on or accessed as needed.... (a resource) that make possible otherwise impossible goals' (Boisjoly et al., 1995: 609). This capital asset is termed social capital (Coleman 1990: 302). Thus, the immaterial social capital 'is embodied in the *relations* among persons' (Coleman 1990: 304). According to Coleman, social capital constitutes a basic component of a logic of action, which eases social cooperation and the attainment of collective common goods. Thus, social capital allows 'the achievement of certain ends that would not be attainable in its absence' (Coleman 1990: 302). Using such arguments, Putnam assumed the 'civic community' and social capital to be a basic prerequisite for a well functioning democracy.

Thus, Putnam regards social capital as a political moral resource, which increases when used, and decreases when not used. 'Stocks of social capital, such as trust, norms, and networks, tend to be self-reinforcing and cumulative. Virtuous circles result in social equilibria with high levels of cooperation, trust, reciprocity, civic engagement, and collective well-being. These traits define the civic community. Conversely, the absence of these traits in the *uncivic* society is also self-reinforcing' (Putnam, 1993: 177). Such virtuous and evil circles of the civic and uncivic society are said to explain the contemporary differences in levels of social capital between the regions in Northern and Southern Italy.

Few books in recent years have generated as much discussion, acclaim, and criticism as Putnam's study (Levi 1995:45). For instance, it has been suggested that all kinds of social networks do not necessarily support the common good. As examples of negative social networks, relations within criminal outlaw-culture, racist organizations, sexist environments, or extreme religious sects have been mentioned. It has also been noted that Putnam's correlational analyses do not prove the causal relations he assumes between social capital and effective political institutions and that social capital theory does not clarify by which processes social capital strengthens democracy and economic development. Furthermore, it has been emphasized that Putnam only investigated *one* dimension of the political system, e.g., the effectiveness of the political institutions, and that his conclusions may not apply to other, equally interesting dimensions of the democratic system as, for instance, its degree of legitimacy among citizens.

In this chapter, we refrain from a discussion of such general issues. As announced, our scope is more limited and of a different kind. We are primarily interested in one of the particular issues discussed by Putnam, namely the relationship between social capital and religion. This relationship has long been of prime concern in the sociology of religion. Durkheim (1915, 1965) argued that religion and social trust were positively intertwined, and religion was given a key role in the creation and maintenance of solidarity. According to Durkheim's understanding, the disappearance of religion might easily lead to autonomy, a weakened common morality and a serious decline in mutual trust. In a similar vein, Wade Clark Roof (1978) emphisized the crucial role of religion with regard to people's positive embeddedness in the local community.

At odds with such views, Putnam claims that, at least in Italy, organized religion 'is an alternative to the civic community, not a part of it' (Putnam, 1993: 107). Such a negative relationship between religion and social capital is said to exist both at the aggregated regional level and the individual level as well (Putnam 1993: 107). 'At the individual level, too, religious sentiments and civic engagement seem to be mutually incompatible' (Putnam, 1993: 107). Those who participate in religious services are said to be more interested in the 'Kingdom of God', and personal piety and church involvement are assumed to replace engagement in social issues. That church involvement is detrimental to social capital depends, according to Putnam, on the fact that the Italian Catholic organizations are hierarchical and authoritarian, and thus less adequate as frameworks for the establishment of social capital.

However, his observations of negative correlations between religion and civic traditions are hardly evidence of the causal relations he assumes (Goldberg, 1995: 8f). Furthermore, it should be noted that in this particular case, Putnam does not control for the impact of other, possibly contaminating variables such as e.g., economic differences between Southern and Northern parts of Italy. Further, the understanding of the Catholic networks as authoritarian and hierarchical has been disputed (Sabetti, 1995: 35f). However important such objections to Putnam's arguments may be, it should be noted that Coleman proposes a different view on the relation between religion and social capital than Putnam. Coleman argues that certain ideologies may create dispositions to act, which favour the establishment of social capital. 'This is clear in the effects religious ideology has in leading persons to attend the interests of others' (Coleman, 1990: 320). A religious background is assumed to establish social capital, which creates better social environments. In this regard, Coleman assumes differences between different religious traditions. 'An ideology of self-sufficiency ... or an ideology emphasizing each individual's separate relation to God, which is a basis of much Protestant doctrine, can inhibit the creation of social capital' (Coleman 1990: 321). Thus, in contrast to Putnam, Coleman suggests Protestantism and not Catholicism to be detrimental to the establishment of social capital. Similar views on the differences between Catholic and Protestant traditions have been referred to by others: 'In contrast to Catholics, Protestants are personally responsible before God in religious matters, and the church has a lesser role as mediator between the believer and God. The Catholic church, with its extensive, dogmatic, collective creed imposes a more collective identity upon its faithful' (Jagodzinski & Dobbelaere, 1995: 81).

Disregarding the possible differences between Catholicism and Protestantism, others have assumed religion in general to create social trust. Thus, social trust has been assumed to develop 'as a result of interactions among groups defined by ethnicity, religion, or some other shared value' (Levi, 1995: 48).

Since neither Putman, nor Coleman, have performed profound analyses of the relationship between religion and social capital, their assumptions call for further investigation. In such matters, a systematic study of the importance of Catholic and Protestant tradition with regard to the degree of democracy among a number of contemporary developing countries, is of interest. The study yielded evidence that *both* Protestantism *and* Catholicism had a positive impact on the level of democracy. 'Thus, the answer to the question 'does religion matter' is the affirmative. The results show that Christianity - and Protestantism in particular - has a positive effect on the level of democracy in the countries studied' (Hadenius, 1992: 121). This conclusion is closer to Coleman's views than to Putnam's.

However, it should also be noted that the general distinction between Catholicism and Protestantism might cover important variations *within* each of the two traditions. For instance, there is reason to assume liberation theology and orthodoxy within the Catholic tradition, and ecumenical and orthodox theology within Protestantism, to have a different impact on social capital. The impact of Catholic liberation theology and Protestant ecumenical theology, would likely be of a more positive kind than the impact of Catholic orthodoxy and Protestant evangelical theology.

Apart from the possible differences between various branches of Catholicism and Protestantism, other aspects of the relationship between religious involvement and social capital deserve attention as well. It is well known that the relationship between religious involvement and social and political behaviour depends upon the *kind* of religious involvement (the so-called dimensions of religious involvement: religious beliefs, membership in religious organizations, private piety, religious knowledge, ritual participation, etc.). The relationship is also known to be dependent upon the kind of *psychological motivation* of religious involvement (intrinsic vs extrinsic motivation). In other words, Putnam's view of individual religiosity as a one-motivational concept which can be measured by one dimension (church involvement) seems inappropriate (cf., Beit-Hallahmi & Argyle, 1997; Spilka et al., 1985; Wulff, 1993).

Thus, with regard to the hypotheses of Putnam and Coleman, religious studies might contribute to more differentiated hypotheses concerning the impact of religion on social capital. In analogy to recent theories on the impact of the 'religious human capital' (e.g., Gustafsson, 1994; Hamberg & Pettersson, 1994; 1995; 1997), it would for instance be of considerable interest to elaborate the analyses of the impact of the 'religious social capital'. From a discussion of the external differentiation of religious involvement, we have, in previous studies, reported two findings which are of certain interest in these matters. First, we have argued that personal religiosity is more relevant to matters belonging to the private domain as compared to the public, and secondly we have assumed that the impact of individual religiosity on both domains is stronger in Catholic than in Protestant contexts (Halman & Pettersson, 1998). The first finding suggests that religious involvement would be of less importance for social capital and political institutions (which, by definition, concern the public domain), while the second suggests that Protestant contexts ought to be especially characterized by a low impact of religious involvement on the establishment of social capital. Theoretically, we have related both findings to differentiation theory. Due to social differentiation, society has become more complex, and the different societal spheres (religion, family, politics, economy, etc.) have become increasingly autonomous and independent from each other. Family, politics, economy, etc., are no longer 'under the presidency of religion' (Wilson, 1996: 17), and the religious sector is assumed to have become differentiated from other social sectors to a large degree. This development is assumed to be more advanced in the Protestant than in Catholic societies. Seen against such a theoretical background, Putnam's as well as Coleman's views on the relationships between religion and social capital, deal with issues which are basic to religious studies.

That Putnam's and Coleman's views on the relationship between religion and social capital may benefit from further considerations, can also be substantiated by other arguments. For instance, we have shown that the degree of church involvement in Swedish contemporary municipalities is positively linked to stable social environments characterized by fewer crimes and offenses against the social order, fewer divorces and more stable family patterns (Pettersson, 1991). Similar results are reported for other countries. Since a stable social environment is a favourable condition for the establishment of social capital (Coleman, 1990: 320), such results can be used as arguments against the assumption that church involvement is detrimental to the establishment of social capital.

## 3    LONGITUDINAL CHANGES IN THE RELIGIOUS AND POLITICAL CULTURES

An important aspect of the relationship between religion and social capital concerns the ways in which the political and religious cultures have changed over time. Since both cultures are continuously changing, the relationship between them may also be changing. In the recently completed comparative project on *Beliefs in Government*, it is stated that 'the decline of religious values and the rise of postmaterialist values have transformed the cultural composition of Western democracies in recent decades' (Kaase & Newton, 1995: 63). Changes in the social structure are said to have caused value changes, which appear by intergenerational population replacements. These population replacements are in turn said to have contributed to changes in both the political and religious attitudes and behaviours. An important question is whether these changes have also affected the relationship between social capital and religion?

According to Inglehart, advanced industrial societies have witnessed a post-war value shift from materialism to postmaterialism (Inglehart, 1977; 1990; 1995; 1997). This shift is assumed to cover a wide variety of social domains. The rise of postmaterialism is regarded as 'only one aspect of a still broader process of cultural change that is reshaping the political outlook, religious orientations, gender roles, and sexual mores in advanced industrial societies' (Inglehart, 1997: 33). With respect to these values, the *Beliefs in Government* project concluded that 'both the process of value change and the content of new value priorities are more complex, and more differentiated than postmaterialist theory allows' (Scarbrough, 1995: 156). However, at the same time it is argued that 'the concept of materialist-postmaterialist value shift evidently captures some part of this process of changing value orientations' (ibid.).

The precise relation between postmaterialism, social capital, the civic community, and trust in political institutions is unclear. On the one hand, postmaterialism is assumed to be part of a pro-democratic culture: 'Interpersonal trust, subjective well-being, .... relatively high levels of political participation and organizational membership, and Postmaterialist values are all part of a highly intercorrelated syndrome that might be called a 'prodemocratic culture'' (Inglehart, 1997: 194). On the other hand, postmaterialist values tend to be negatively associated with trust in political institutions, particularly authoritarian ones, like the church. 'Thus, the properties attributed to materialists and postmaterialists can lead to contradictory expectations about their impact on trust in government' (Gabriel, 1995: 374). Postmaterialism is assumed to be positively related to social capital (social networks, social trust), but negatively correlated to what is assumed to be the fruits of such capital (trust in political institutions). From such arguments, one can even suggest a tentative hypothesis that the growth of postmaterialist values might weaken the positive relationship between social capital and a well functioning democracy, at least when it comes to trust in political institutions.

In terms of the relationship between religion and political attitudes, the pattern seems less ambiguous. The *Beliefs in Government* project concluded that religion can 'be viewed as an important integrative mechanism, and the continuing decline of religion in most West European countries may eventually lead to a more cynical view on the governing process. Moreover, the positive impact of religion on trust in government was evident regardless of various historical and socio-structural conditions - in predominantly Catholic Italy, in the religiously mixed Netherlands, and in Protestant Norway and Britain' (Gabriel, 1995: 381). These findings contradict the assumptions of differences between Catholicism and Protestantism with regard to religion as a means of social integration and a source of social capital. Of course, the results also contradict Putnam's assumption of a negative relation between religion and social capital.

## 4    THE LINK BETWEEN SOCIAL CAPITAL AND RELIGION

From the above discussion, it is obvious that a first step in the analysis of the relationship between social capital and religion should consider the comparison of societies that are as different as possible. Since different relationships are assumed for different religious and political cultures, it seems appropriate to investigate and compare countries that are as dissimilar as possible (Przeworski & Teune, 1970: 35). Since we have chosen to base our analyses on the data from the 1996 World Value Study, we can only compare countries participating in this wave of the value studies. Since we want to confine our analyses to Europe and North America, our only choice is to compare some Nordic country (Sweden, Norway, Finland), Germany, Spain, and the US. Thus, a basic question concerns the degree of variation in political and religious values between these countries. Although they all belong to the industrialized world, they differ greatly as far as economic development is concerned, degree of affluence, religious traditions and denominational cleavages, democratic legacies, political systems, etc. (Van Deth, 1995; Therborn, 1995). The Nordic countries are overwhelmingly Protestant, with Lutheran state-churches to which most people belong. Spain is a predominantly Catholic country, with most people belonging to the Catholic church. Germany and the US are religiously mixed countries. Germany is characterized by a regional division between the Protestant North and the Catholic South, while the US is marked by a religious pluralism, which by and large is fairly independent of geographical regions.

From a multidimensional analysis of the EVS data from 1990 (Ester et al., 1994: 160), it can be concluded that Sweden, (West) Germany, Spain, and the US cover a broad variation in value orientation. In contrast to the US and Spain, Sweden and Germany score comparatively low on values associated with religion, while Sweden, in contrast to the US, scores comparatively high on institutional confidence and civic morality as opposed to self-centred achievement and permissiveness. In this latter dimension, Germany and Spain form a middle group. From these analyses, Sweden, Germany, Spain, and the US, can be regarded as fairly different with regard to the general value systems of their national publics.

A very interesting question concerns whether the four cultural regions alluded to above can be related to phenomena other than aggregated individual value systems. A recently published regionalisation of the European Union countries is noteworthy in this regard. From analyses on how these countries have organized their specific blend of the three welfare systems they were divided in three groups: a) a northern group of *institutional welfare states* (Sweden, Finland, Denmark); b) a southern group of *family welfare states* (Italy, Spain, Portugal); and c) a *mediate central-European group* (Germany, France, the Netherlands, Belgium). These three groups are said to differ in terms of 'political ideologies, social security systems, gender roles, the importance of labor unions and cultural values of a religious kind' (Vogel 1997: 576; translated from the Swedish). These three groups can be related to Esping-Andersens classification of welfare regimes: liberal (US, Canada), conservative (Germany, France, Austria), and social-democratic (the Nordic countries). Many of the other typologies that have been developed based on very different criteria (e.g., Siaroff, 1994) most often reveal a similar European patterning, distinguishing Northern from Southern, and Anglo-Saxon from Germanic countries.

Thus, whether one builds on aggregated individual data on value preferences (the EVS study), or national socio-economic and political structural features, one arrives at fairly similar regions in Europe and North America. An inductive and deductive method for regionalisation yields highly similar results. From such findings, it seems logical to assume a close relationship or fit between individual value systems on the one hand, and socio-economical and political structural characteristics on the other. This relationship should, according to our view, primarily be interpreted in terms of mutual interdependence. However, since this chapter concerns the impact of religion on the political culture, it is interesting to take note of attempts to explain the structural differences between the Southern family and the Northern socio-democratic welfare states by reference to the religious factor. It has been said that 'religious differences are an important factor in determining contemporary public policy outcomes across a very range of areas and that religious doctrines, beliefs and traditions constitute the basis of a Catholic family of nations with public policies quite different from those of national groupings with other historical and cultural antecedents' (Castles 1994: 23). According to this view, the Catholic culture has given rise to the specific pattern of public policies which characterize the Southern family welfare pattern.

Thus, Sweden, Germany, Spain, and the US can be regarded as countries which cover a broad range of religious, cultural, social, political, and economic settings. To compare these countries in terms of the relationship between religion and social capital would therefore be indicative of how general or country-specific this relationship is.

# 5 MEASUREMENT OF SOCIAL CAPITAL AND ANALYTIC STRATEGY

In his book on *Making Democracies Work*, Putnam identifies social capital in a rather abstract and vague way. Social capital, he says, 'refers to features of social organization, such as trust, norms, and social networks' (Putnam, 1993: 167). To clarify the concept, he presents several examples. Following his suggestions we assume social capital to take the form of qualities of social relationships, e.g., trust, norms of reciprocity, and engagement in social networks. In this chapter we will use the 1996 WVS data to measure social capital in this sense.

The major attribute of social capital seems to be *interpersonal trust*. This component is measured by one question in the WVS: 'Generally speaking, would you say that most people can be trusted or that you can't be too careful in dealing with people?' Two replies were possible: 1. most people can be trusted; 2. Can't be too careful (have to be very careful).

Engagement in *social networks* is regarded as another component of social capital. The more socially involved people are, the greater the opportunity to build reciprocal relationships and generate trust. Here we see the mutual dependency of the different components of social capital. Not only is trust a necessary prerequisite to get involved in 'networks of civic engagement' (Putnam, 1993: 171), it is also assumed to be necessary in order to continue an existing social relationship. 'Social relationships die out if not maintained; expectations and obligations wither over time; and norms depend on regular communication' (Coleman, 1990: 321).

An indicator of the degree of people's involvement in social networks can be found in the number of organizations one is an active member of. In the questionnaire the respondent was asked whether he/she is an active member, an inactive member or not a member of a great number of organizations. The list of (formalized) organizations was: church or religious organization; sport or recreation organization; art, music or educational organization; labour union; political party; environmental organization; professional association; charitable organization; any other voluntary organization. According to Putnam, it does not matter so much what kind of organization one is active in. 'Networks of civic engagement, like the neighborhood associations, choral societies, cooperatives, sports clubs, mass-based parties, [....], represent intense horizontal interaction. Networks of civic engagement are an essential form of social capital' (Putnam, 1993: 173).

Since we intend to explore the relationship between religion and social capital, we have, for obvious reasons, not included 'religious organizations' in our measure of social networks. We have simply counted the number of organizations the respondent was an active member of. This variable thus ranges from 0 (= not an active member in any of the organizations), to 8 (= active member of all organizations mentioned).

Finally, the component of *norms of reciprocity* is indeed more difficult to measure with the WVS data. Usually a distinction is made between balanced and generalized reciprocity. Putnam argues that generalized reciprocity is conducive to social capital. 'Generalized reciprocity refers to a continuing relationship of exchange that is at any given time unrequited or imbalanced, but that involves mutual expectations that a benefit granted now should be repaid in the future' (Putnam, 1993: 172). Thus one does something for someone else not because one expects immediate repayment, but in the vague expectation that the other might do something in return in the (near) future. Here the relationship with trust is clear. One relies on the fact that the other will reciprocate at some point.

In order to investigate such norms empirically, we have chosen to follow the suggestion of Knack and Keefer that norms of reciprocity reflect 'respondents' own stated willingness to cooperate when faced with a collective action problem; it thus can be thought of as "trustworthiness"' (Knack & Keefer, 1997: 1258). Empirically, norms of reciprocity are assessed by them from questions about the justification of behaviours like: 'claiming state benefits which you are not entitled to' and 'cheating on taxes if you have the chance'. Knack and Keefer, who used the 1990 values data set, also included the degree to which 'avoiding a fare on public transport' and 'failing to report damage you've done accidentally to a parked vehicle' can be justified (Knack & Keefer, 1997: 1256). However, the latter items were not available in the WVS 1996 database. Therefore we have confined our analyses to the two issues regarding public transport and taxes. Since the degree of justification was assessed by 10-point scales ranging from 1 (= never) to 10 (= always justified), and the distributions appeared very skewed in the non acceptance direction, we calculated a score from 0 to 2, where 2 indicates that one never accepts cheating on taxes and claiming state benefits illegally (on both issues, code 1), while 1 indicates the acceptance of either of the two, and 0 indicates that both behaviours are not felt to be totally unjustified. The results of our measures of social capital are presented in Table 7.1.

According to this table, there are clear differences between the four countries. Involvement in networks, measured by active membership in various kinds of organizations is highest in the US, modest in Sweden and Germany, and low in Spain. Interpersonal trust is highest among Swedes, and lowest in Spain while what we have called 'norms of reciprocity', that is 'live up to the expectations of others' is highest in the US, and lowest in Germany. A combination of the three indices makes the US the country with the highest level of social capital, while Spain scored lowest. Sweden and Germany are in between, with Sweden higher on social capital and Germany lower.

Before analysing the results between social capital and religiosity, it is important to explore the structure of the three components of social capital, because it is far from clear in a theoretical sense how the three distinct components are mutually related. At times, Putnam argues that the components are self-reinforcing and cumulative (e.g., Putnam, 1993: 177), while on other occasions he regards them as 'other' forms of social capital, or as a 'special feature' of it (Putnam, 1993: 170). In other words, it is unclear whether or not the various components of social capital are at the same level, or if one of them is assumed to influence the others causally. For instance, social trust is occasionally said to arise from two related sources: norms of reciprocity and networks (Putnam, 1993: 170).

**Table 7.1 Responses to the three indicators of social capital and score on the combination of the three items in Sweden, Germany, Spain and the US**

|  | US | Spain | Germany | Sweden |
|---|---|---|---|---|
| Network (0-8) |  |  |  |  |
| none | 37.4% | 75.5% | 45.4% | 43.2% |
| at least one | 62.6% | 24.5% | 54.6% | 56.8% |
| *Mean* | *1.52* | *.41* | *.85* | *.89* |
| Social trust |  |  |  |  |
| no | 64.1% | 70.3% | 58.2% | 40.3% |
| yes | 35.9% | 29.7% | 41.8% | 59.7% |
| Reciprocity |  |  |  |  |
| none | 15.9% | 23.8% | 35.4% | 31.4% |
| one | 20.1% | 21.1% | 32.5% | 31.0% |
| two | 64.0% | 55.2% | 32.1% | 37.6% |
| Social capital |  |  |  |  |
| low (0) | 10.3% | 23.2% | 19.6% | 12.9% |
| middle (1) | 34.5% | 49.4% | 41.2% | 36.1% |
| high (2 3) | 55.2% | 27.4% | 39.2% | 51.0% |
| *Mean* | *1.62* | *1.08* | *1.27* | *1.51* |

Disregarding this issue, the three distinct components of social capital are assumed to be positively related in way or another. Our findings do not corroborate this assumption. The correlations between trust and social relationships are slightly positive, while the correlations between social relationships and norms of reciprocity are almost zero. However, the occasional finding in the German data of a significant negative correlation between trust and norms of reciprocity is even more challenging. At the aggregate level, the relationship is found to be positive: 'where fewer people prove to be trustworthy, fewer people will be trusting' (Hardin quoted by Knack & Keefer, 1997: 1258). Such differences once again demonstrate that aggregate level conclusions cannot automatically be generalized to the individual level and vice verse. However, at the aggregate level of our four countries, we cannot substantiate that where social trust is highest, norms of reciprocity are also highest. Sweden, for example is highest on social trust, but the US and Spain score higher on norms of reciprocity.

The unexpected low correlations between the three components of social capital, demonstrate the need to explore the relationships between social capital and religiosity in more detail, analysing each of the three components separately. However, we will also present findings for an overall measure of social capital. In this case, we have simply created an additive index from the three separate components. Those who score high on all three components of social capital, get a score of 3, while those who score low on each of them, get a score of 0.

*Religiosity* is measured by three components of traditional religion or church religion, namely belief in God, the importance of God in one's life and church attendance. Belief in God is indicated by the simple question: 'Do you believe in God?' The importance of God is tapped by the question: 'How important is God in your life?' Respondents were asked to indicate its importance on a 10-point scale ranging from 1 (= not at all) to 10 (= very). Finally, church attendance is measured in the usual way, by asking 'Apart from weddings, funerals and christenings, about how often do you attend religious services these days?' Answer categories: 1 More than once a week, 2 Once a week, 3 Once a month, 4 Only on special holy days, 5 Once a year, 6 Less often, 7 never, practically never. These three indicators have been used to create a scale, where those who believe in God, who think God is important (codes 7 - 10) and who attend religious services regularly (at least once a month) get a score of 3, while those who don't meet any of these criteria get a score of 0.

The impact of religiosity on social capital and on the separate components is then explored by applying linear regression analyses. In the case of interpersonal trust, the dependent variable is a dichotomy: trust versus no trust. Therefore, in this case we applied logistic regression analysis (Knoke & Burke, 1980).

In order to avoid spurious relationships between religion and the various components of social capital, we have included several socio-economic background variables in the analyses: age, education, income, degree of urbanization, and gender. Education is measured by age at which full-time education was completed. Although far from ideal, more exact measures of educational level are often less comparable.

Finally, we have included *postmaterialism* in the regression analyses as well. Elsewhere we have argued that the relationship between postmaterialism and religiosity is intriguing (Halman & Pettersson, 1996). Rising levels of postmaterialism are assumed to be accompanied by a corresponding decline of traditional religious orientations. But it has been noted that although traditional religious beliefs are on the decline, there is a growing concern for the meaning and purpose of life (Inglehart, 1995: 388). Since our measure mainly refers to traditional, Christian religiosity, a negative correlation between this measurement and postmaterialism is to be expected. Postmaterialists are assumed to be less religious. For the measurement of materialism-postmaterialism we relied on the extended measurement, that is, the twelve-item battery which was included in the WVS survey of 1995-1996 (Inglehart, 1990; 1995; 1997).

In order to explore the validity of the concept of social capital we have examined the relationships between social capital and issues of democracy. According to Putnam, social capital is essential for democracies to work properly. Social capital, he concludes, 'is the key to making democracy work' (Putnam, 1993: 185). The WVS questionnaire contains several items to tap various aspects of democracy. The core elements of democracy are, of course, high levels of confidence in parliament and political parties. Further, democratic attitudes are revealed in the rejection of the idea that democracy runs economic systems badly, that democracies are indecisive and have too much squabbling, and that they are not good at maintaining order. A democratic preference will also include a rejection of the idea that having a strong leader who does not have to bother with parliament and elections, and/or having experts make decisions according to what they think is best for the country, are good ways of governing a country. A democratic attitude is also revealed in a strong emphasis on work for personal and social development and a positive evaluation of gender equality. Further, democracy and ethnocentrism appear incompatible. It has also been reported that people who are richer in social capital are happier and have higher levels of satisfaction than people who lack or who have low social capital.

Based on the relationships between social capital and the indicators mentioned above, it can be concluded that indeed the correlations are as expected, although the results for Spain appear somewhat less convincing. Here some of the correlations are not in the expected direction. In the US, Sweden, and Germany nearly all of the correlations investigated are as expected (Pettersson, 1998). We believe, this demonstrates sufficiently the validity of our measure of social capital.

## 6    RESULTS

Table 7.2 reports on the relationships between religion and social capital. In general, the relationships appear modest, if significant at all. A slight tendency towards a positive relationship between religiosity and social capital, not a negative one, as was expected by Putnam, can be detected. This is the case for social capital as a compound variable, and for the three separate components as well, social trust being the exception in Sweden and the US.

Of the three components of social capital, norms of reciprocity seem to be most strongly related to religiosity. Religious people appear somewhat more trustworthy than less religious people. In a way, religious people appear more altruistic. Interpersonal trust is positively related with religiosity in West Germany, while in the US and Sweden engagement in social networks is higher among religious people than among less religious people.

**Table 7.2 The impact of religiosity, postmaterialism, age, education, income, degree of urbanization and gender on the three components of social capital separately and on social capital as a compound variable**

| Social networks | US | Spain | Germany | Sweden |
|---|---|---|---|---|
| religiosity | .11** | .05 | .06 | .07* |
| postmaterialism | .13** | .14*** | .11** | .11** |
| age | .01 | -.04 | -.08* | .01 |
| education | .11*** | .21*** | .12** | .12** |
| income | .33*** | .16*** | .14*** | .10** |
| urbanization | .00 | .04 | -.09* | -.03 |
| sex | -.02 | -.12** | -.04 | -.06 |
| $r^2$ | .17 | .14 | .07 | .05 |
| Trust | | | | |
| religiosity | -.04 | .04 | .17* | -.07 |
| postmaterialism | .07* | .06 | .30*** | .08* |
| age | -.01** | -.01 | -.01 | .01 |
| education | .02* | .00 | .04* | .03* |
| income | .19*** | .06 | .12** | .11** |
| urbanization | .05 | .02 | .02 | .04 |
| sex | .33* | -.30 | .24 | .34* |
| $r^2$ | .08 | .01 | .13 | .05 |
| Reciprocity | | | | |
| religiosity | .09* | .10* | .10** | .07* |
| postmaterialism | .05 | .04 | -.11** | -.01 |
| age | .19*** | .04 | .14*** | .22*** |
| education | -.02 | -.02 | -.15*** | .05 |
| income | .04 | -.07 | .01 | .03 |
| urbanization | -.07* | -.03 | -.03 | -.07 |
| sex | .07* | .05 | .02 | .06 |
| $r^2$ | .06 | .03 | .11 | .07 |
| Social capital | | | | |
| religiosity | .12*** | .07 | .15*** | .05 |
| postmaterialism | .10*** | .10** | .14*** | .07 |
| age | .12*** | .04 | .08* | .02 |
| education | .12*** | .08 | .05 | .14*** |
| income | .24*** | .09* | .14*** | .13*** |
| urbanization | -.01 | .02 | -.02 | -.04 |
| sex | .04 | -.08* | .02 | .02 |
| $r^2$ | .11 | .04 | .07 | .06 |

Notes: Entries are standardized regression coefficients; for trust, unstandardized $\beta$'s
* $p < .05$; ** $p < .01$; *** $p < .001$

Active membership appears related to the degree of postmaterialism and, in all countries, to income and level of education. Richer people as well as the more educated are more inclined to be actively engaged in one or more of the organizations. Both socio-demographic indices demonstrate a stronger impact than either religiosity or postmaterialism. Income, and to a lesser extent education, appear important conditions of social trust in the US, West Germany and Sweden, while trustworthiness seems to be strongly affected by age. This is particularly the case in the US, West Germany and Sweden, where older people are less likely to accept cheating on taxes and claiming state benefits illegally. Finally, the regression analyses with social capital as the compound variable reveals positive associations with religiosity, particularly in the US and in West Germany and to a lesser extent in Spain, with hardly any in Sweden. However, none of the countries showed a significant negative association as predicted by Putnam.

As discussed in the introduction, Coleman argued that the relationships between religiosity and social capital ought to be stronger among Catholics than Protestants. Table 7.3 reports the comparisons between Catholics and Protestants in Germany and the US, respectively.

**Table 7.3  Regression analysis results for Catholics and Protestants in the US and Germany**

| | US | | Germany | |
|---|---|---|---|---|
| Variables: | Catholic | Protestant | Catholic | Protestant |
| religiosity | -.01 | .12* | .21*** | .15* |
| postmaterialism | .12 | .05 | .19** | .13* |
| age | .09 | .07 | -.01 | .09 |
| education | .09 | .10 | -.02 | .03 |
| income | .16* | .31*** | .20** | .10 |
| urbanization | .04 | .01 | -.02 | .04 |
| sex | .03 | .01 | -.02 | .03 |
| $r^2$ | .05 | .14 | .11 | .07 |

Notes: * p < .05; ** p < .01; *** p < .001

At the individual level, Coleman's hypothesis is corroborated for West Germany but not for the US. Thus Catholic culture in the US does not show a stronger link between religiosity and social capital as expected by Coleman. We conclude that the hypothesis about the differential impact of religion on social capital in Catholic and Protestant contexts is not supported by our findings.

# 7   CONCLUSIONS

In this chapter we have explored whether or not Putnam's assumption of a negative relationship between religiosity and social capital can be generalized to the individual level and to different cultural contexts. Therefore, we compared a set of very different countries. Although they are all industrialized, the four societies investigated differ in important ways (e.g., Therborn, 1995; Van Deth, 1995). If the relationships between social capital and religion had been (more or less) the same in all four countries, those factors that distinguish these countries would be regarded as irrelevant. Thus, our approach resembles the strategy known as the 'most different system design' (Przeworski & Teune, 1970).

In general we conclude that at the individual level, social capital is not related to religiosity as predicted by Putnam. Religious people are not poorer in social capital than less religious people, irrespective of whether they are Catholic or Protestant. As such, Putnam's findings are not corroborated by ours at the individual level. Instead of a negative association, we observe a modest positive link. This is the case in all countries. It should be mentioned that the Italian EVS data from 1981 and 1990 yield a similar pattern. However, it should be emphasized that these positive correlations are indeed modest and that they reveal practically no substantial relationship at all. This negative overall conclusion can either be attributed to bad measurement of our key variables, or to inappropriate theory. Our findings on the validity of the measure of social capital do not support the former alternative. And the same can be said about our experiences with the several analyses in which we used our measure of religiosity. Thus, we do not believe that our results can be explained by less adequate measurements of social capital and religiosity.

However, our substantial conclusion remains tentative. In future studies we would opt for expanding the measures of interpersonal trust and the development of a better instrument for norms of reciprocity. As Coleman noted, 'a group whose members manifest trustworthiness and place extensive trust in one another will be able to accomplish much more than a comparable group lacking that trustworthiness and trust' (Coleman cited by Putnam, 1993: 167). Fukuyama has argued that without trust, 'people run into great transaction costs, such as endless meetings in order to arrive at formal, contractual arrangements and agreements, formal controls, regulations of sorts, etc. A society which lacks basic trust, one could say, is bound to become a litigating society' (Zijderveld, 1997: 16; referring to Fukuyama, 1995). Seen against such a background, we are most pleased to note that the 1999/2000 EVS/WVS study will allow for improved measurement of social capital.

Furthermore, it can be argued that social capital contains other components than those investigated here. For instance, 'access to assistance' has been mentioned as 'an important aspect of social capital' (Boisjoly et al., 1995: 630). In other words, both the concept of social capital as well as its measurement need to be carefully reconsidered. Nevertheless, our main conclusion from our analysis is that although

Putnam's hypothesis about a negative correlation between social capital and religiosity may well be valid at the societal level, we have not been able to substantiate it at the individual level. As we understand it, Putnam's arguments for the macro-level relationship explicitly and/or implicitly assume a similar relationship at the micro-level. The reasons for the different results at the macro- and micro levels therefore need further study.

# References

Beit-Halahmi, B. & M. Argyle 1997. *The Psychology of Religious Behaviour, Belief and Experience*. London: Routledge.

Boisjoly, J., G.J. Duncan & S. Hofferth 1995. 'Access to Social Capital'. *Journal of Family Issues* 16: 609-631.

Castles, F. 1994. 'On Religion and Public Policy: Does Catholicism make a Difference?', Uppsala: Scass.

Coleman, J.S. 1990. *Foundations of Social Theory*. Cambridge, Mass.: Harvard University Press.

Durkheim, E. 1915, 1965. *The Elementary Forms of the Religious Life*. New York: Free Press.

Esping-Andersen, G. 1990. *The Three Worlds of Welfare Capitalism*. Cambridge: Polity Press.

Ester, P., L. Halman & R. de Moor (eds.) 1994. *The Individualizing Society*. Tilburg: Tilburg University Press.

Fukuyama, F. 1995. *Trust. The Social Virtues and the Creation of Prosperity*. London: Penguin Books.

Gabriel, O. 1995. 'Political Efficacy and Trust'. Pp. 357-389 in J. van Deth & E. Scarbrough (eds.), *The Impact of Values*. Oxford: Oxford University Press.

Goldberg, E. 1995. 'Thinking about How Democracies Work'. *Politics & Society* 24: 7-18.

Gustafsson, G. 1994. 'En religionssociologisk teori för 1990-talet. Marknadsutbudet bestämmer den kyrkliga aktiviteten'. *Tro och tanke* 9.

Hadenius, A. 1992. *Democracy and Development*. Cambridge: Cambridge University Press.

Halman, L. & R. De Moor 1994. 'Value Patterns and Modernity'. Pp. 155-162 in P. Ester, L. Halman & R. De Moor (eds.), *The Individualizing Society*. Tilburg: Tilburg University Press.

Halman, L. & T. Pettersson 1996. 'The Shifting Sources of Morality. From Religion to Postmaterialism?'. Pp 261-284 in L. Halman & N. Nevitte (eds.), *Political Value Change in Western Democracies*. Tilburg: Tilburg University Press.

Halman, L. & T. Pettersson 1998. 'A North-South Divide in Basic Value Profiles? Comparative Analyses of Values Among the Mass Publics in Northern Protestant and Southern Catholic European Countries'. Pp. 189-209 in *Informationes Theologiae Europae. Internationales Ökomenisches Jahrbuch für Theologie*. Frankfurt/M.: Peter Lang.

Hamberg, E. & T. Pettersson 1994. 'The Religious Market: Denominational Competition and Religious Participation'. *Journal for the Scientific Journal of Religion* 33: 63-80.

Hamberg, E. & T. Pettersson 1995. 'Short Term Changes in Religious Supply and Changes in Religious Participation in Contemporary Sweden'. *Annual Yearbook of the Scientific Study of Religion* 8: 35-51.

Hamberg, E. & T. Pettersson 1997. 'Denominational Pluralism and Church Membership in Contemporary Sweden. A Longitudinal Study of the Period 1974-

1995. *Journal of Empirical theology* 10: 61-78

Inglehart, R. 1977. *The Silent Revolution*. Princeton, NJ: Princeton Universy Press.

Inglehart, R. 1990. *Culture Shift in Advanced Industrial Society*. Princeton, NJ: Princeton Universy Press.

Inglehart, R. 1995. 'Changing Values, Economic Development and Political Change'. *International Social Science Journal* XLVII: 379-404.

Inglehart, R. 1997. *Modernization and Postmodernization*. Princeton, NJ: Princeton Universy Press.

Jagodzinski, W. & K. Dobbelaere 1995. 'Secularization and Church Religiosity' Pp. 76-119 in J.W. van Deth & E. Scarbrough (eds.) *The Impact of Values*. Oxford: Oxford University Press.

Kaase, M. & K. K. Newton 1995. *Beliefs in Government*. Oxford: Oxford University Press.

Knack, S. & P. Keefer 1997. 'Does Social Capital have an Economic Payoff? A Cross-Country Investigation'. *The Quarterly Journal of Economics* 62: 1251-1288.

Knoke, D. & P.J. Burke 1980. *Loglinear Models*. Beverly Hills: Sage.

Levi, M. 1995. 'Social and Unsocial Capital: A Review Essay of Robert Putnam's Making Democracy Work'. *Politics & Society* 2: 25-53.

Listhaug, O. 1998. *Confidence in Political Institutions: Norway 1982-1996*. Trondheim: The Norwegian University of Science and Technology.

Pettersson, T. 1991. 'Religion and Criminality. Structural Relationships Between Church Involvement and Crime Rates in Contemporary Sweden'. *Journal for the Scientific Study of Religion* 30: 279-291.

Pettersson, T. 1998. *Medborgaranda och det goda samhället*. mimeo, Uppsala: Teologiska Institutionen.

Przeworski, A. & H. Teune 1970. *The Logic of Comparative Social Inquiry*. New York: Wiley-Interscience.

Putnam, R. 1993. *Making Democracy Work. Civic Traditions in Modern Italy*. Princeton: Princeton University Press.

Roof, W.C. 1978. *Community & Commitment*. New York: Elsevier.

Sabetti, F. 1996. 'Path Dependency and Civic Culture: Some Lessons from Italy About Interpreting Social Experiments'. *Politics & Society* 24: 19-43.

Scarbrough, E. 1995. 'Materialist - Postmaterialist Value Orientations'. Pp. 123-150 in J.W. van Deth & E. Scarbrough (eds.), *The Impact of Values*. Oxford: Oxford University Press.

Siaroff, A. 1994. 'Work, Welfare and Gender Equality: A New Typology'. Pp. 82-101 in D. Sainsbury (ed.), *Gendering Welfare States*. London: Sage.

Spilka, B., R. Hood & R. Gorsuch 1985. *The Psychology of Religion: An Empirical Approach*. Englewood Cliffs: Prentice-Hall.

Therborn, G. 1995. *European Modernity and Beyond*. London: Sage.

Van Deth, J.W. 1995. 'A Macro Setting for Micro Politics'. Pp. 48-75 in J.W. van Deth & E. Scarbrough (eds.), *The Impact of Values*. Oxford: Oxford University Press.

Vogel, J. 1997. 'Sverge och EU: Marknaden, välfärdsstaten och familjen'. *Välfärd och ojämlikhet i 20-årsperpektiv 1975-1995.* Stockholm: Statistika Centralbyrån.

Wilson, B. 1996. 'Religious Toleration, Pluralism and Privatization'. Pp. 11-34 in P. Repstad (ed.), *Religion and Modernity. Modes of Co-existence.* Oslo: Scandinavian University Press.

Wulff, D. 1993. *Religionspsykologi.* Lund: Studntlitteratur.

Zijderveld, A.C. 1997. 'The Democratic Triangle. The Unity of State, Society and Market'. Pp.11-24 in M.J. de Jong & A.C. Zijderveld (eds.), *The Gift of Society.* Nijkerk: Enzo Press.

Chapter Eight

# Globalization and Patterns of Religious Belief Systems

Loek Halman & Thorleif Pettersson

## 1    INTRODUCTION

Recently, a new phenomenon has entered the debate on modernization: the globalization of human society. While modernization denotes the transformation of
traditional agrarian societies into modern industrialized societies, and post-modernization refers to the shift from modern industrialized societies towards post-
modern high tech and service oriented ones, the term globalization is used to
describe more recent trends in social change. It has been argued that globalization
might become one of the main themes of the nineties. 'Just as post-modernism
was *the* concept of the 1980s, globalization may be *the* concept of the 1990s, a
key idea by which we understand the transition of human society into the third
millennium' (Waters, 1995: 1).

It is obvious that people living in contemporary society experience a wide variety
of influences from other parts of the world. People's scope is no longer limited to
their immediate surroundings but has expanded worldwide.  We have entered 'a
new world of economic giants and superpowers, of multinationals and military
blocks, of vast communications networks and international division of labour'
(Smith, 1990: 174). What is happening in one part of the globe is almost instantly
known in other parts. The Gulf war is a recent obvious example of this rapid
exchange of news. Most parts of the world witnessed the 'struggle for Kuwait',
due to the rapid broadcasting by CNN. Most sectors of societal life are influenced
by such globalization processes. They are not limited to entrepreneurs who increasingly act on a global scale; politics are no longer limited to the local or
national level. The growth of the European Union and its influence on local
politics and economies is yet another example of internationalization of trade and
growing interdependencies. One reason is simply that today's most pressing
problems cannot be solved without international collaboration. For example,
environmental problems are transboundary and thus require an international
approach and cooperative initiatives (Hughes, 1993: 79). It is more or less obvious that the world has become 'one place which must pull together to fight off
threats to world order' (Featherstone, 1990: 11). Recent phenomena like
*CocoColanisation* and *McDonaldization* may be regarded as other salient examples of an unprecedented  worldwide cultural standardization. Some interpret
both as just other expressions of the Americanization of culture; others have

argued that e.g., McDonaldization is indeed an example of a global phenomenon but that it should not be equated with globalization since 'it has all of the characteristics rejected by globalization theorists' (Ritzer, 1996: 298; for the characteristics see Ritzer).

Although this chapter focusses on religion, it will not be concerned with the impact of globalization on church policies or the relations between the established religious traditions, the churches and their leaders, but rather on the consequences of structural globalization for contemporary everyday religious beliefs and religious orientations. Due to increasing communication people are increasingly confronted with other religions. In the past, people from other religions were far away and probably perceived less as a real threat. In contemporary society however, people of different religious backgrounds are closer to each other than ever before and 's/he who used to be the unequivocal outsider is now often literally my neighbour, whether I approve it or not' (Beyer, 1990: 384). However, the ultimate consequences of such increased everyday experiences of hitherto foreign religious traditions are hard to predict. Both increasing levels of tolerance and universalism on the one hand, and rising levels of dislike and increasing emphasis on one's inherited traditional religious forms on the other, might occur. Some have argued that structural globalization will generate processes of cultural unification and homogenization, while others assume that globalization need not necessarily lead to the loss of shared national or local cultural models. Such different outcomes of globalization can be seen as the paradox of modern society, since the contradictory processes of homogenization and globalization on the one hand and regionalization or nationalization on the other seem to be occurring simultaneously (Featherstone, 1990). Thus, the possible impact of globalization on religion concerns many important but yet unsettled issues and the question on whether globalization will 'have as a great an impact on religious life as industrialization did' (Kurz, 1995: 3) does not seem unwarranted, to say the least.

In section 2, we further explore the globalization processes and advance some general hypotheses to be empirically investigated in the subsequent sections of the paper. In section 3, we develop comparative measures of structural globalization. The 'globalization debate' is mainly concerned with two dimensions of globalization: structural globalization and its cultural counterpart. Therefore, in this chapter we distinguish between the *structural* features of globalization, i.e., the material and 'hardware' issues, and the 'software' or *cultural* features and we intend to develop measures with respect to both of these dimensions of globalization.

As far as we know, comparative efforts to empirically assess the degree of cultural globalization in different countries are rare. In section 4 we introduce the comparative data we will use to empirically test our hypotheses on the cultural dimension of globalization. The data come from the European Values Studies, which were conducted in 1990 (Ester et al., 1994; Halman & Vloet, 1994). In section 5 we present the results of our analyses of the relationships between structural and cultural globalization, and in section 6 we summarize our conclusions and suggest some directions for further research.


## 2    GLOBALIZATION AND RELIGION: SOME THEORETICAL NOTIONS

Most publications on globalization discuss the issue at the aggregate level, and tend to neglect the impact of globalization at the individual level, e.g., how individual preferences and value patterns are affected by the processes of globalization. It is more or less common to describe the process of globalization in terms of structural characteristics, and most often reference is made to increased mobility and the distribution of information technology. In discussions of such structural globalization, reference is often made to the increasing numbers of 'international agencies and institutions, the increasing global forms of communication, the acceptance of unified global time, the development of global competitions and prizes, the development of standard notions of citizenship, rights and conceptions of humankind' (Featherstone, 1990: 6; see also Appadurai, 1990; Waters, 1995). All such structural changes are said to make the world smaller in the sense that it is becoming a "single place". Everything is assumed to be interrelated and people are assumed to be increasingly aware of the interconnectedness of different parts of the contemporary world. Thus, the world is assumed to be interconnected in terms of 'structure, culture and agency' (Archer quoted by Smart 1994: 152). People are said to be less isolated from each other and increasingly in contact with other cultures. Therefore Giddens argues that globalization can be defined as 'the intensification of worldwide social relations which link distant localities in such a way that local happenings are shaped by events occurring many miles away and vice versa' (Giddens, 1990: 64). In the words of Roland Robertson, a leading globalization theorist, globalization refers to 'both the compression of the world and the intensification of consciousness of the world as a whole' (Robertson, 1992: 8). In other words, globalization not only denotes structural characteristics, but also includes culture in the sense of cultural homogenization and an increasing awareness among people that they belong to a global world and that a global identity and global mentality is growing. Following Waters, globalization can be defined as: 'A social process in which the constraints of geography on social and cultural arrangements recede and in which people become increasingly aware that they are receding' (Waters, 1995: 3). From such understandings, it is obvious that scale is a key dimension. It is assumed that people no longer live in a single society isolated from the rest of the world, but in a global international society. The local or national sphere is transcended by a worldwide scope and an awareness of being a world citizen. A 'third culture' which is 'oriented beyond national boundaries' (Featherstone, 1990: 6) is said to be emerging.

Some have argued that globalization should be regarded as part of the much broader theme of modernization (e.g., Giddens, 1990). According to the theory of modernization, Western society has experienced a gradual transformation from a traditional to an industrial society, and more recently, modern, industrial society has turned into a post-modern order. 'Globalization theories add to this thesis that modernization in the West has directly resulted in the spread of certain vital institutions of Western modernization to the rest of the globe, especially the modern capitalist economy, the nation-state, and scientific rationality in the form of modern technology; and, critically, that this global spread has resulted in a new social unit which is much more than a simple expansion of Western modernity' (Beyer, 1994: 8).

The discussion on globalization has, however, been mainly theoretical and above all highly abstract. Most attention is given to the structural aspects of globalization and its impact on economy and politics, while its cultural consequences have been of less interest. 'It is strange that in a world in which the minds of individuals are so resolutely focused on mass-mediated images so much social scientific attention should have been paid to global integration by means of economics and so little to culture or consciousness' (Waters, 1995: 33). However, one of the implications of globalization theory is that people are increasingly confronted with growing numbers of opportunities and alternative options. People are assumed to be continually faced with different kinds of cultural habits, values and norms. From this point of view, it is noteworthy that comparatively little attention has been given to the impact of globalization on people's everyday religious values. In religious globalization analyses, globalization processes are mainly discussed at the institutional level. Peter Beyer, for instance, focusses on the grand religious traditions of the world and theorizes on how they might be affected by globalization processes. He describes the implications of globalization for religion as follows: 'if particular cultures are to survive in altered form in the modern global context, the religious traditions are facing the serious challenge of the relativized context. Given that religion deals with absolutes, this adjustment should result in significant crises within those traditions' (Beyer, 1994: 9). Yet another outcome is equally likely: religious traditions may orient themselves 'towards the global whole and away from the particular culture with which that tradition identified in the past' (Beyer, 1994: 10). We would add to this that whatever forms such institutional changes may take, they must in the end include common people's identities, religious beliefs, and religious practices. These are the prime focus of our analyses.

To perform such analyses, other significant processes that have been conducive to the transformation of human society must be taken into account. These processes include individualization and secularization. As a result of globalization, people 'are faced with an extending range of imaginary and information involving models of citizenship, forms of production, styles of consumption, modes of communication, principles of world order and, in addition, ways of reacting to all of these. There is enhanced capacity for reflection as a result of the exposure to globalized social processes. A main consequence of this is that the individual has tended to develop increased expectations of personal fulfilment and satisfaction. This has produced various alternative or modified lifestyles' (Spybey, 1996: 9). However, the acceptance of these various alternatives would not occur if the processes of individualization and secularization had not liberated the individual from institutional constraints. In traditional societies, people not only lived in small local communities separated from other communities, they were also strongly influenced and dominated by traditional institutions, e.g., religion. The churches in particular played an important role in these traditional settings. Economic growth, the spread of affluence, rising levels of education, increased mobilization, increased technological knowledge and its many applications, have reduced the previously dominant role of religion in human society (Berger, 1967; Luckmann, 1967; Inglehart, 1990; 1995; 1997). Due to increasing individualization, people have become freer and more autonomous in selecting their convictions, beliefs, and practices. Decisions are no longer based on what the religious institutions prescribe, but what the individual wants. In this way, the processes of individualization and secularization are important predecessors or concomitants of the globalization processes.

Assuming such processes, it is still difficult to predict people's choices of religious beliefs and moral values. It is assumed that they pick and choose what they want from the global religious and cultural marketplace. If that is indeed the situation, we hypothesize that the more globalized a society is at the structural level, the more diverse and fragmented people's beliefs will be. 'Since cultural and social diversity are the distinguishing characteristics of modern life, individuals or groups in the global village can choose their religious orientations from a variety of options rather than simply accepting the specific sacred canopy transmitted to them by their family and friends in early childhood' (Kurtz, 1995: 12). In this regard, the increased 'supply' of alternative world views and value systems, provided by the ever growing mass media and international information technologies is a crucial factor. If people are freer to choose from an enlarged pool of religious and moral options, the homogeneity in their religio-moral value systems will almost by statistical necessity decrease. Increasing numbers of individuals will demonstrate their own, personal religious patchworks and a distinguished and homogenous impact of these on other social spheres becomes less likely.

As mentioned above, some have argued that globalization ultimately will lead to a convergence of values and mentalities (e.g., Kerr, 1983). Modern mass communication means rapidly diffused knowledge about other cultures, resulting not only in an awareness of other ideas, values, and world views, but also in the possible identification with them. A salient example in this respect is the fear of Europeans that the further political and economical unification will result in a loss of the national identities, habits, and cultures. In other words, they fear a cross-cultural convergence of value orientations and the loss of national identities. On the other hand it has been argued that distinct cultures will survive, despite the globalization processes. The McDonalds formula may be an example in this respect. Although 'at face value all McDonalds outlets appear to be the same, closer examination will reveal the differences. The decor and menus are virtually identical from outlet to outlet but the actual outcome in any particular case is the result of interactions between people' (Spybey, 1996: 7). As mentioned earlier, the occurrence of both globalized unification and the trend towards more emphasis on the local or regional community has been seen as a 'paradox of modern culture' (Featherstone, 1990). As Giddens observed, 'the development of globalized social relations probably serves to diminish some aspects of nationalist feeling linked to nation-states (or some states) but may be causally involved with the intensifying of more localized nationalist sentiments [.....] At the same time as social relations become laterally stretched and as part of the same process, we see the strengthening of pressures for local autonomy and regional cultural identity' (Giddens, 1990: 65).

We shall now explore empirically, using cross-national comparisons of 16 OECD countries, the relationships between the national levels of structural globalization, and the national levels of cultural globalization on four dimensions:
a. the degree to which the citizens see themselves as belonging to a global order, i.e., the degree to which they display cosmopolitism;
b. the degree to which the citizens are heterogenous in their religious outlooks;
c. the degree to which the religious belief systems of the citizens are internally fragmented, i.e., the degree to which there is constraint and 'patchwork' among their religious belief systems;
d. the degree to which the religious belief systems of the citizens are externally fragmented, i.e. the degree to which their religious belief systems have an impact on other parts of their value systems.

Thus, our main concern is with religious cultural globalization and we expect to find differences in this regard between countries with different degrees of structural globalization. In other words, our paper deals with the relationships between structural and religious cultural globalization. With respect to these relationships it is indeed difficult to pinpoint the precise causal relations. On the one hand one could argue that structure defines culture, and thus predict that the more globalized a country is structurally, the more religiously globalized its population should be. However, it may be equally legitimate to argue the other way around. We do not intend to get involved in this 'micro-macro-' debate (Layder, 1994), but merely expect the above-mentioned relationships (a - d) to be positive, whatever the causal explanations. Thus, disregarding the causal relations, we expect countries which score higher on structural globalization will also score higher on the four dimensions of religious cultural globalization.

## 3    MEASURING STRUCTURAL GLOBALIZATION

It is obvious that globalization processes like the growth of information technology will be closely linked to economic development. Table 8.1 depicts the population sizes, the gross domestic products, and the gross domestic products per
capita of 16 OECD countries. The 16 countries demonstrate a reasonably amount
of variation with respect to these dimensions. Populationwise, they range from a
quarter of a million (Iceland) to about 1000 times that, or about 250 million (US).
In terms of GPD per capita, they range from the lowest level of about 6,000 USD
(Portugal) to the highest level of about 26,000 USD (Sweden). Thus, the country
with the highest level of GDP per capita scores about 6 times higher than the
country with the lowest. Overall, it is therefore expected that the 16 countries
should be fairly differentiated along the dimensions of structural globalization
that are related to economic development.

**Table 8.1  Population, Gross Domestic Product, and trade balance among 16
OECD countries. Data for 1990**

| Country | Population in 1000 | GDP* | GDP/capita in 1000 USD | Trade balance* |
|---|---|---|---|---|
| Austria | 7.718 | 157.157 | 20.36 | -661 |
| Belgium | 9.967 | 192.192 | 19.28 | -148 |
| Canada | 26.603 | 570.137 | 21.43 | 884 |
| Denmark | 5.141 | 129.264 | 25.14 | 278 |
| France | 56.420 | 1190.772 | 21.11 | -142 |
| West Germany | 63.232 | 1488.234 | 23.54 | 5431 |
| Iceland | 255 | 5.864 | 23.00 | -5 |
| Ireland | 3.503 | 42.612 | 12.16 | 270 |
| Italy | 56.937 | 1090.755 | 19.16 | -961 |
| Netherlands | 14.951 | 279153 | 18.67 | 462 |
| Norway | 4.241 | 105.703 | 24.92 | 594 |
| Portugal | 9.859 | 59.680 | 6.05 | -711 |
| Spain | 38.959 | 491.260 | 12.61 | -2674 |
| Sweden | 8.559 | 228.110 | 26.65 | 231 |
| Great Britain | 57.411 | 980.124 | 17.07 | -330 |
| United States | 251.523 | 5392.200 | 21.44 | -8477 |

Note: * in Million US$; Source: *United Nations Statistical Yearbook,* OECD, 1991.

To the best of our knowledge, very few attempts have been made in the social
sciences to develop comparative measures of structural globalization. However,
the understandings of globalization often refer to increasing levels of communication, interaction and integration. International (world) trade and financial flows,

international division of labour, and multinational enterprises, are all indicators of what can be called structural globalization. Modern communication technology is assumed to be rapidly spreading, giving people access to information from all over the world. As Beyer says, today's communication technology not only makes 'very rapid communication possible over almost unlimited space' but also exists 'nearly everywhere on earth, along with the will and ability to use them' (Beyer, 1994: 1). However, the situation may be somewhat more complicated and differentiated than that.

**Table 8.2  Number of Radio and TV receivers per 1,000 inhabitants, number of telephones per 10,000 inhabitants, and IT market value as percentage of GDP in 16 OECD countries. Data for 1990**

| Country | Radios | TVs | Phones | Sum: 1 -3 | Rank | IT-market |
|---|---|---|---|---|---|---|
| Austria | 617 | 478 | 418 | 1.513 | 13 | 1.87 |
| Belgium | 769 | 451 | 393 | 1.613 | 11 | 2.41 |
| Canada | 1.029 | 639 | 574 | 2.242 | 2 | |
| Denmark | 1.031 | 536 | 566 | 2.133 | 3 | 2.98 |
| France | 888 | 407 | 495 | 1.790 | 8 | 2.19 |
| W. Germany | 876 | 556 | 489 | 1.921 | 6 | 2.24 |
| Iceland | 786 | 319 | 512 | 1.617 | 10 | |
| Ireland | 630 | 76 | 281 | 987 | 15 | 1.61 |
| Italy | 791 | 421 | 388 | 1.600 | 12 | 1.49 |
| Netherlands | 907 | 485 | 464 | 1.856 | 7 | 3.01 |
| Norway | 794 | 423 | 502 | 1.719 | 9 | 2.85 |
| Portugal | 228 | 187 | 241 | 656 | 16 | 1.81 |
| Spain | 310 | 400 | 323 | 1.033 | 14 | 1.48 |
| Sweden | 877 | 468 | 683 | 2.028 | 4 | 3.00 |
| Great Britain | 1.143 | 434 | 442 | 2.019 | 5 | 2.58 |
| United States | 2.118 | 814 | 545 | 3.477 | 1 | |

Sources:  *United Nations Statistical Yearbook 1992, European Information Technology Observatory 1993*

The spread of such modern communication technology devices can be used as an indicator of the degree of structural globalization. Statistical yearbooks from UNESCO, The United Nations and OECD provide comparable measures for the national numbers of telephones, and television- and radio receivers. Similar information on the value of the IT market (computer hardware, communications hardware, office equipment, software products, IT services, pc professionals, etc.) can be found in the *European Information Technology Observatory* (1992). Unfortunately, we have not found this kind of data for the US, Canada or Iceland. Table 8.2 presents these statistics.

As can be seen in Table 8.2, the countries differ considerably with respect to the distribution of TVs, radios and telephones. Portugal and Ireland score lowest and the US and Canada highest. The US scores about three times higher than the countries with the lowest values. As for the economic value of the IT market, the country with the highest value (Sweden) scores two times higher than the country with the lowest (Spain). There is a large variation in international trade as well. The trade-balance (export - import) is highly positive in West Germany, but highly negative in the United States.

Another feature of structural globalization concerns international tourism (e.g., Hughes, 1993: 79), as well as the printed mass media. Table 8.3 presents relevant data on these issues for the 16 OECD countries. The tourism data represent the sum of national receipts and expenditures for international tourism calculated as the percentage of the national GDP, while the data on imported printed mass media represent the sum of the national costs for the import of books and newspapers calculated as the percentage of the national GDP.

In the field of international tourism, Austria ranks about 8 times higher than the US, the country with the lowest value. As for the import of books and newspapers, Ireland scores about 8 times higher than Spain, the country with the lowest level. Thus, also with respect to these aspects of structural globalization, the 16 OECD countries demonstrate a sufficient degree of variation.

Figure 8.1 demonstrates the relationships between the two sets of globalization indicators. The results from a confirmatory factor analysis of the various structural globalization indicators justify that the statistics for radios, TV sets, telephones and the value of the IT market can be combined into one scale of 'information technology' (INFTECH), while the two measures of international cultural contacts can be combined into the dimension of 'cultural import' (CULTIMP). It should be noted that the two dimensions are negatively correlated. Trade balance is a third dimension that has to be distinguished from these two dimensions. In fact, it is unrelated to the other two features of structural globalization.

**Table 8.3 International tourism receipts plus expenditures and import of books and newspapers for 14 OECD countries. Entries as share of GDP. Data for 1990**

| Country | International tourism | Rank | Books and newspaper | Rank |
|---|---|---|---|---|
| Austria | 12.24% | 1 | 3.14% | 3 |
| Belgium | 4.69% | 6 | 3.30% | 2 |
| Canada | 1.47% | 15 | - | - |
| Denmark | 5.41% | 5 | 1.00% | 10 |
| France | 2.74% | 13 | .86% | 11 |
| W. Germany | 2.72% | 14 | .47% | 12 |
| Iceland | 5.80% | 4 | 1.43% | 5 |
| Ireland | 6.12% | 3 | 3.90% | 1 |
| Italy | 3.08% | 12 | .16% | 14 |
| Netherlands | 3.92% | 10 | 1.44% | 4 |
| Norway | 4.66% | 7 | 1.19% | 6 |
| Portugal | 7.41% | 2 | 1.06% | 8 |
| Spain | 4.65% | 8 | .45% | 13 |
| Sweden | 3.93% | 9 | 1.13% | 7 |
| Great Britain | 3.22% | 11 | 1.02% | 9 |
| United States | 1.47% | 16 | - | - |

Source: *United Nations Statistical Yearbook 1990, 1992*

A confirmatory factor analysis of the measurement model yielded a CHI-square of 11.2 for 11 degrees of freedom (not significant). It can thus be concluded that the theoretical factor model is quite compatible with the empirical data.

Based on these analyses, we have developed a multidimensional measure of structural globalization. Since the two dimensions INFTECH and CULTIMP are negatively correlated, and independent of trade balance, they are expected to demonstrate different relationships to the four aspects of religious cultural globalism we are interested in. Thus, the findings demonstrated in Table 4 suggest that we should not be talking about globalization in general, but about different dimensions of globalization and their various causes and effects.

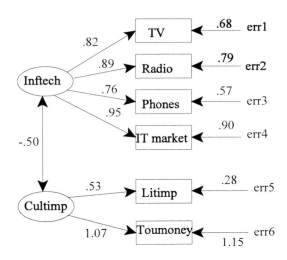

**Figure 8.1    Factor model for structural and cultural globalization**

**4    DATA AND MEASUREMENT OF CULTURAL GLOBALIZATION: COSMOPOLI-
TISM AND THE GLOBALIZATION OF RELIGIOUS BELIEF SYSTEMS**

Our analyses of cultural religious globalization are based on the survey data from
the European Values Studies of 1990 (see e.g., Ester et al., 1994; Pettersson &
Riis, 1994). One indicator of cultural globalization refers to the experiences of
global identity and cosmopolitism. In the EVS questionnaire this was measured
by two questions revealing the geographical groups one subjectively belongs to
in the first and second place, respectively. We simply counted the number of
people who chose 'the world as a whole' either first or second.

Cultural globalization can also be assessed in terms of religiosity. The EVS data
do not include direct measures for 'globalized religion', but mainly indicators to
tap traditional Christian beliefs and convictions. Thus, religious globalization can
only be established indirectly. As we have argued earlier in the paper, it can be
assumed that the more globalized a population is religiously, the more heterogeneous the population will be in religious matters. A measure of the degree of
heterogeneity can be found in the standard deviations from the mean that can be
calculated for the religious dimensions.

Another aspect of religious globalization might be found in the strength of the
mutual interconnectedness of the religious beliefs. It is often assumed that in pre-
modern traditional, religious society, religious orientations were strongly interconnected. In globalized societies these mutual connections are assumed to have
weakened, and people will increasingly select their religious orientations 'à la

carte'. Thus, it can be argued that the weaker the associations between the various religious orientations, the more religiously globalized the country will be.

Finally, it can be assumed that the more globalized the country, the more the religious factor will become disassociated from other value dimensions, e.g., the moral, political, familial dimensions, etc. In modern, globalized, secular societies, religion is no longer assumed to be the dominant overarching meaning system. In this situation, people no longer accept as given the rules and dogmas prescribed by the church. Taking the argument one step further, it can be assumed that the more globalized and secular a country is, the more people will oppose the opinion that it is proper for churches to speak out on social, ethical, and political issues.

Our analyses are based on the following four religious dimensions. *Religiosity* is measured by the answers to five items on various kinds of individual religious involvement (considers oneself a religious person, believes in a personal God, God is regarded as important, gets strength and comfort from religion, takes moments of prayer). These items can be used to construct a scale which appears to be a reliable comparative measure of individual religiosity (Halman & Vloet, 1994). By applying factor analyses, scores have been calculated for each country. *Orthodoxy* refers to traditional belief statements, like belief in God, heaven, hell, sin, the devil, and resurrection. Again, factor analysis was used to calculate scores indicating a respondent's position on this dimension. *Church adequacy* taps the idea that the churches are giving adequate answers to moral problems, family problems, spiritual needs, and social problems. These items form a strong scale and as a result of factor analysis, scores have been calculated for each country. *Church attendance* is measured by asking people how often they attend religious services and ranges from 1 = more than once a month to 8 = never.

In order to measure the degree of *religious heterogeneity* we simply calculate an average of the standard deviations among the first three measures. The higher the standard deviations, the greater the religious heterogeneity. If there is no variation at all in a country, that is if all people share the same opinion or attitude, the standard deviation is 0. If people do not share similar religious beliefs, the variety is high and thus the standard deviations will be high too. So, the more varied people's beliefs are, the higher the standard deviations, while if 'the homogeneity of a group is large, the smaller the standard deviations' (Jagodzinski & Dobbelaere, 1995: 226).

As a measure of the *internal differentiation* between the four dimensions of religious involvement we have made use of the eigenvalue for the first principal component, obtained from principal components analysis. If the first principal component explains 100% of the variances, the variables are perfectly correlated and linearly dependent upon each other (for a description of this analysis, see Dobbelaere & Jagodzinski, 1995). The lower the eigenvalue, the stronger the internal differentiation. In order to get a positive measure of internal differentiation, we have simply used the formula: Internal differentiation = eigenvalue * -1.

The degree of *external religious differentiation* can be determined from the answers to the question whether or not it is proper for churches to speak out on various issues. The items mentioned were: disarmament, abortion, third-world problems, extramarital affairs, unemployment, racial discrimination, euthanasia, homosexuality, ecology and environmental issues, and government policy. A factor analysis yielded a strong scale, enabling the calculation of a factor score for each country.

The results for the 16 OECD countries on the measures of cosmopolitism, religious heterogeneity, religious internal differentiation, and religious external differentiation are displayed in Table 8.4.

**Table 8.4 Cosmopolitism, religious heterogeneity, and internal and external religious differentiation. Data for 1990 (For entries, see text)**

| Country | Cosmo-politism | Religious heterogeneity | Internal differentiation | External differentiation |
|---|---|---|---|---|
| Austria | 6.9 | .9173 | -2.58 | -.2728 |
| Belgium | 16.0 | .9633 | -2.58 | -.4206 |
| Canada | 21.1 | .9321 | -2.42 | .0057 |
| Denmark | 7.3 | .8244 | -2.26 | -.2684 |
| France | 18.4 | .9651 | -2.69 | -.3172 |
| W. Germany | 11.9 | .9368 | -2.84 | -.1180 |
| Iceland | 15.8 | .8446 | -2.00 | .0086 |
| Ireland | 7.4 | .8515 | -2.23 | .5163 |
| Italy | 25.3 | .9798 | -2.76 | .1635 |
| Netherlands | 16.8 | .9403 | -2.53 | -.0442 |
| Norway | 8.30 | .9617 | -2.69 | .1555 |
| Portugal | 16.3 | .9679 | -2.62 | .1665 |
| Spain | 11.0 | .9991 | -2.79 | .1199 |
| Sweden | 9.8 | .8355 | -2.41 | -.0092 |
| Great Britain | 18.9 | .9709 | -2.43 | .1103 |
| United States | 27.3 | .8642 | -2.42 | .2059 |

5    RELATIONS BETWEEN STRUCTURAL GLOBALIZATION AND RELIGIOUS
     CULTURAL GLOBALIZATION

Tables 8.2 and 8.3 showed that data on the economic value of the IT market for
example, or the amount of money spent on importing books and newspapers were
missing for some of the countries. We therefore limited the number of items
included in the dimension INFTECH, and instead of CULTIMP have included
the measure of tourism, which was part of CULTIMP. IT market has been excluded from the INFTECH dimension.

Table 8.5 shows the relationships between the measures of structural globalization on the one hand, and cosmopolitism, religious heterogeneity, religious internal differentiation, and religious external differentiation on the other. Both ordinary bivariate correlations and partial correlations are presented. The partial
correlations allow the necessary controls for other variables which may affect the
relationship under study.

**Table 8.5 Relationships between structural globalization and cosmopolitan orientation, religious heterogeneity, religious internal differentiation, and religious external differentiation. Values in bold are contrary to the expectations.**

|  | Structural globalization | | |
|---|---|---|---|
|  | inftech | tourism | trade-balance |
| *Cosmopolitan orientation* | | | |
| Bivariate correlation | .39 | **-.61** | -.49 |
| Partial correlation | .51 | **-.48** | **-.49** |
| *Religious heterogeneity* | | | |
| Bivariate correlation | **-.35** | **-.10** | .17 |
| Partial correlation | **-.23** | **-.32** | .20 |
| *Internal religious differentiation* | | | |
| Bivariate correlation | .14 | .11 | **-.17** |
| Partial correlation | .13 | .24 | **-.21** |
| *External religious orientation* | | | |
| Bivariate correlation | **-.25** | **-.14** | **-.29** |
| Partial correlation | **-.05** | **-.27** | **-.23** |

Partial correlations for cosmopolitic orientation and religious heterogeneity:
    On INFTECH controlled for GDP per capita and CULTIMP
    On CULTIMP controlled for GDP per capita and INFTECH
    On GLOBALIZ controlled for GDP per capita

Partial correlations for internal and external religious differentiation:
    On INFTECH controlled for GDP per capita, CULTIMP, and percentage Catholics
    On CULTIMP controlled for GDP per capita, INFTECH, and percentage Catholics
    On GLOBALIZ controlled for GDP per capita and percentage Catholics

For analysing of the relationship between structural globalization and internal/external religious differentiation, we have introduced the percentage of Catholics as a kind of control variable since the Catholic factor still appears highly important for these two dimensions (Halman & Pettersson, 1997). Furthermore, since the degree of economic development shows a fairly strong and positive relationship to especially one of our measures of structural globalism in particular (INFTECH; cf., Tables 8.2, 8.3 and 8.4; correlation coefficient = .80), we have also introduced GDP per capita as a control variable.

The results displayed in Table 8.5 do not present strong evidence for the assumed relationships between structural and religious globalization. On the contrary, the results are multifaceted and not at all straightforward in either confirming or rejecting the expectations of globalization theory. In Table 8.5, the relationships which are contrary to our expectations are marked in bold. The associations between a cosmopolitan view and structural globalization is negative, meaning that the more global a country is culturally speaking, the less cosmopolitan the population is! A similar counter-intuitive negative relationship is found between the measures of structural globalization and religious heterogeneity, and external religious fragmentation. The more globalized a country is structurally, the less religiously heterogeneous and externally fragmented the population seems to be! At first glance, this result would imply that higher levels of structural globalization are associated with comparatively higher degrees of religious unification and homogenization. We have mentioned elsewhere in this chapter that assumptions on such a relationship have been suggested by globalization theorists.

Only with regard to religious cultural internal differentiation, are the correlations consistent with our expectations. The more globalized a country is structurally, the more the various parts of the 'religious package' seems disassociated from each other. However, the associations between religious differentiation and trade balance are in the opposite direction.

## 6   CONCLUSIONS

Although much is written about religion in a globalized world, comparative empirical investigations of the issue are, to the best of our knowledge, rare. We have investigated the relationships between two dimensions of structural globalization, and four aspects of cultural religious globalization. As for the causal chains between the structural and cultural globalization, our investigation touches the debate on the relationship between culture and structure or the micro-macro-linkage (Layder, 1994), an issue where different opinions compete. Some argue that structure affects culture, e.g., that values and attitudes are the product of specific institutional contexts (Cédora, 1994: 2), while others argue that culture determines and shapes 'the social, economic and political world' (Inglehart, 1990: 432). We have avoided the causal issue, and simply assumed that whatever the causalities, structural and cultural globalization should correlate in the theoretically expected way, e.g. that countries scoring high on structural globalization should also score comparatively high on religious cultural globalization. In this sense, 0-correlations between the two dimensions of globalization would contradict globalization theory.

Our findings indicate that structural globalization is not a one-dimensional phenomenon. The indicators for structural globalization we have selected appeared to refer to distinctive dimensions, tapping specific and negatively correlated aspects of structural globalization. However, especially those indicators we used for the measurement of 'information technology' (INFTECH) appeared to be fairly closely associated with GDP. This finding resembles some of the results of the attempts to develop a uni-dimensional measure of modernity, where most indices used appeared to be closely connected with GDP. Some have even recommended only using GDP as a measure of modernization (e.g., Van Snippenburg, 1986). Our results indicate that a similar conclusion may be appropriate for one dimension of structural globalization. If that proves to be the case, this kind of globalization may, in the end, be regarded as just another feature of modernization.

The associations we have found between structural and cultural religious globalization, do not convincingly confirm the expectations from globalization theory, especially since one dimension of structural globalization ('information technology') seems to be negatively related to another dimension of structural globalization ('cultural imports'). In other words, some of our assumptions were not corroborated, while others were, at least partly. Broadly speaking, the assumption that structural globalization should be associated with internal religious differentiation was supported by our findings, while the assumption that structural globalization should be associated with cosmopolitan orientations, religious heterogeneity, and external religious differentiation or fragmentation, was not. With respect to religious heterogeneity, our results suggest that structural globalization and religious unification and homogeneity seem to go together.

An explanation for at least some of our unexpected findings might relate to the fact that the countries we studied were not sufficiently heterogenous in terms of structural globalization. Our selection of countries was partly based on the availability of OECD and/or European statistics for structural globalization, partly on the availability of cross-culturally valid comparative measures of cultural and religious globalization. In this matter, we want to emphasize the tension between these two criteria for the selection of countries. While at least some of the statistics for structural globalization allow the inclusion of more countries, the availability and limited possibility of cross-culturally valid measures of religious globalization seem to work in the opposite direction. How to resolve this tension remains an unsettled issue.

It should be noted that our data are cross-sectional, although the theoretical framework delineates longitudinal processes. In forthcoming analyses we intend to include longitudinal data, e.g., the EVS data from 1981 and 1990 together with the World Value Study data from 1996 and possibly the forthcoming EVS data from 1999. We can then investigate whether, for example, religious cosmopolitism has developed over time as would be expected from changes in structural globalization. Similar analyses can be performed with regard to religious differentiation and heterogenization. These analyses might also shed more light on the causal linkages between structural and cultural globalization.

However, the most important result of our empirical comparative analyses is the evidence against structural globalization as a one-dimensional phenomenon and the assumption of similar patterns along the different aspects of religious cultural globalization. In fact, globalization is a multifaceted phenomenon and should be treated as such in empirical research activities. This implies, of course, complex research designs, especially since we have found that opposite outcomes can be expected for different dimensions of globalization. Thus, for those who believe that globalization is 'a key idea in order to understand the transition of human society into the third millennium' (Waters, 1995: 1), a rich variety of studies needs to be done.

# References

Appadurai, A. 1990. 'Disjuncture and Difference in the Global Cultural Economy'. Pp. 295-310 in M. Featherstone (ed.), *Global Culture*. London: Sage.

Berger, P. 1967. *The Sacred Canopy*. Garden City: Doubleday & Company.

Beyer, P. 1990. 'Privatization and the Public Influence of Religion in Global Society'. Pp. 373-398 in M. Featherstone (ed.), *Global Culture*. London: Sage.

Beyer, P. 1994. *Religion and Globalization*. London: Sage.

Cédora, J. 1994. 'The Motivational Force of Values and Attitudes on Human Behaviour in the Quest for Happiness, Well-being, and Satisfaction'. Pp. 1-30 in J. Cécora (ed.), *Changing Values and Attitudes in Family Households with Rural Peer Groups, Social Networks, and Action Spaces*. Bonn: FAA

Ester, P., L. Halman & R. de Moor (eds.) 1994. *The Individualizing Society*. Tilburg: Tilburg University Press.

*European Information Technology Observatory 93*. Frankfurt/M.: EITO.

Featherstone, M. 1990. 'Global Culture: An Introduction'. Pp. 1-14 in M. Featherstone (ed.), *Global Culture*. London: Sage.

Giddens, A. 1990. *The Consequences of Modernity*. Stanford, California: Stanford University Press.

Halman, L. & A. Vloet 1994. *Measuring and Comparing Values in 16 Countries of the Western World*. Tilburg: WORC.

Halman, L. & T. Pettersson 1997. 'A North-South Divide in Basic Value Profiles?' Paper presented at the SISR/ISSR Conference *Religion: The City and Beyond*, Toulouse, 7-11 July.

Hughes, B.B. 1993. *International Futures*. Boulder: Westview Press.

Inglehart, R. 1990. *Culture Shift in Advanced Industrial Society*. Princeton: Princeton University Press.

Inglehart, R. 1995. 'Changing Values, Economic Development and Political Change'. *International Social Science Journal* XLVII: 379-404

Inglehart, R. 1997. *Modernization and Postmodernization*. Princeton: Princeton University Press.

Jagodzinski, W. & K. Dobbelaere. 1995. 'Secularization and Church Religiosity'. Pp. 76-119 in J. van Deth & E. Scarbrough (eds.), *The Impact of Values*. Oxford: Oxford University Press.

Kerr, C. 1983. *The Future of Industrial Society: Convergence or Continuing Diversity?* Cambridge: Harvard University Press.

Kurtz, L.R. 1995. *Gods in the Global Village*. Thousand Oaks, California: Pine Forge Press.

Layder, D. 1994. *Understanding Social Theory*. London: Sage.

Luckmann, T. 1967. *The Invisible Religion*. New York: MacMillan.

OECD 1991. *Main Economic Indicators 1991*. Paris: OECD.

Pettersson, T. & O. Riis (eds.). 1994. *Scandinavian Values*, Stockholm: Almquist and Wiksell International.

Ritzer, G. 1996. 'The McDonaldization Thesis: Is Expansion Inevitable?'. *International Sociology* 11: 291-308.

Smart, B. 1994. 'Sociology, Globalisation and Postmodernity: Comments on the 'Sociology for One World' Thesis'. *International Sociology* 11: 149-160.

Smith, A.D. 1990. 'Towards a Global Culture?'. Pp. 171-192 in M. Featherstone (ed.), *Global Culture*. London: Sage.

Spybey, T. 1996. *Globalization and World Society*. Cambridge: Polity Press.

UNESCO 1992. *Statistical Yearbook 1992*. Paris: Unesco.

Van Snippenburg, L.B. 1986. *Modernisering en Sociaal Beleid* (Modernization and Social Policy). Dissertation: Nijmegen.

Waters, M. 1995. *Globalization*. London and New York: Routledge.

Chapter Nine

# Japanese Religiosity and Morals

Robert J. Kisala

## 1    INTRODUCTION

The question of the secularization of Japanese society and the content of Japanese religiosity has received much attention in Japanese religious studies (e.g., Tamaru, 1979; Swyngedouw, 1993; Reader, 1991; Ishii, 1997). What has been generally lacking in this discussion, though, is cross-cultural analysis. The differing historical and cultural contexts have made such comparison problematic. For example, whereas secularization in the West is normally seen as a bi-product of industrialization and modernization, the Japanese historian of religion Hayashi Makoto has argued that secularization is a pre-modern phenomenon in Japan, the result of the government's co-opting of the religious establishment early in the seventeen century (Hayashi, 1992). Furthermore, indicators used to measure secularization in the West, such as religious affiliation and church attendance, appear to have different meanings in the Japanese context. I have argued elsewhere that the situation in Japan regarding these indicators is the mirror-image of that in the West, since participation in religious rites is more a matter of custom and thus religious affiliation is the better indicator of religious commitment in Japan (Kisala, 1997).

While recognizing these difficulties, the Nanzan Institute for Religion and Culture has organized a group of sociologists and religious researchers to explore ways to obtain data useful for cross-cultural analysis. In light of the comprehensive nature of the European Values Study questionnaire and its broad acceptance as an instrument for cross-cultural comparisons, a decision was made to adapt the questionnaire for use in Japan and other countries in Asia. While retaining many of the same items as the European survey, questions thought to be less reflective of the religious situation in Japan and Asia were replaced with items designed to test for specifically Asian values. Thus, while the reliability of direct comparisons with regard to the complete results is compromised, the predominance of similar items should allow for meaningful analysis on the basis of a less strict understanding of comparison. A test of the survey instrument was conducted in April 1998, using a random sample of 300 respondents from the Tokyo and Osaka metropolitan areas, weighted for sex and age. As an initial experiment in cross-cultural analysis, results from that survey will be used in this chapter in order to indicate possible comparisons with religiosity and morals in the West.

## 2  INDICATORS OF SECULARIZATION

It is a common observation that although a minority of Japanese are formally affiliated with a religious group or profess belief in God, a high percentage participate in religious rites to commemorate the dead or make annual visits to a shrine or temple at the new year. This is in contrast to the situation in many Western countries, where a high percentage of the population may maintain nominal affiliation with one of the churches but a relatively small number of people participate in religious services. Interestingly enough, there seems to be an inverse correspondence in the numbers attached to these indicators in the two regions. According to a report issued by the European Values Group, four out of five Europeans identify themselves as belonging to a Christian religious denomination, while on average only 33% attend church at least once a month (Barker et al., 1992). Surveys in Japan generally indicate that about one-third of the population have some religious affiliation, while 80% participate in annual visits to shrines or temples at the new year (Swyngedouw, 1993).

Our survey reflected a rate of religious affiliation in Japan similar to that found in previous studies, with 29% of the respondents identifying themselves with a particular religious group. 2% of this total identified themselves as Christian, a rate approximately twice as high as indicated by previous studies, perhaps due to the urban bias of the sample. Significantly, only 1% identified themselves as Shinto, with the remainder divided among the Buddhist sects (20%) and the New Religions (6%). While there was no significant difference in religious affiliation according to sex, our survey also reflected previous studies in indicating a markedly decreased rate of affiliation among younger cohorts (Figure 9.1).

Specific indicators of religious participation in Japan, such as new-year shrine or temple visits, were not included in our survey. We instead opted for the general measure of religious participation found in the European survey. However, in consideration of the differing religious situation in Japan, where weekly church services are not the norm, the results must be read differently than in the European context. Only 21% of the Japanese respondents visit a shrine or temple at least once a month, a figure considerably lower than the European average, although still higher than that obtained from France and the so-called Lutheran countries (Barker et al., 1992: 42). However, an additional 36% make semiannual visits, which would reflect the cultural pattern of a visit on the feast of the dead in August and at the new year, and 18% make an annual visit, presumably on one or the other of those occasions. Nearly three-fourths of the respondents to our survey, therefore, participate fairly consistently in traditional religious rites, a figure comparable to that obtained by previous studies in Japan. A similar number of respondents felt it was important to hold religious services at death, while only 29% felt it was important at birth and 41% at marriage. This also reflects religious custom in Japan, where for centuries the Buddhist sects have been primarily engaged in the performance of funerals and memorial rites, making this the primary religious rite of passage.

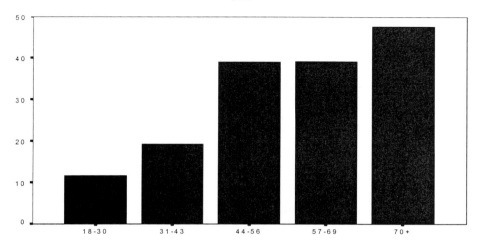

**Figure 9.1    Percent of religious affiliation, by age group**

The above considerations testify to the fact that religious affiliation and religious participation, as indicators of secularization, bear contrary meaning in European and Japanese cultures. If this is in fact so, and if we thus can transpose the indicators, it would seem that the religious situations in the two cultures are remarkably alike in indicating a high level of adherence to cultural custom (religious affiliation in Europe and religious participation in Japan) and a relatively low level personal allegiance to religion (religious participation in Europe and religious affiliation in Japan).


## 3    RELIGIOSITY

The following indicators of religiosity from the European study were included in our survey: Are you a religious person? Do you believe in a God who is either personal or some sort of spirit or life force? How important is God in your life? Do you find strength or comfort in religion? Do you take some time for prayer, meditation, or contemplation?

The responses to some of these questions indicate a level of religiosity that corresponds to the level of personal allegiance to religion found in the preceding section, one significantly lower than that apparently found in Europe. For example, only 26% of the respondents to our survey identified themselves as a religious person. On the other hand, almost 19% described themselves as atheists. Thirty percent answered affirmatively when asked if they find strength or comfort in religion, and a similar number (32%) said that they pray or meditate. The sex of the respondents had little effect on these answers, although marginally more women than men professed to draw strength or comfort from religion (34% vs 26%). The age of the respondents, however, consistently played a role in the responses, with the level of religiosity rising as we move up through the cohorts (Table 9.1).

**Table 9.1  Religiosity indicators group 1, by age group (in %)**

|  | 18-30 | 31-43 | 44-56 | 57-69 | 70+ | Total |
|---|---|---|---|---|---|---|
| religious person | 15.0 | 19.2 | 29.9 | 35.9 | 42.9 | 26.3 |
| strength/comfort | 15.0 | 17.9 | 36.4 | 40.6 | 61.9 | 30.0 |
| pray/meditate | 10.0 | 25.6 | 37.7 | 43.8 | 61.9 | 32.0 |

In contrast to the low level of religiosity reflected in the above indicators, the two questions regarding belief in God yield somewhat different results. In the European survey, belief in a personal God was taken as one indicator of a religious disposition or religiosity (Barker et al., 1992: 48). In Japan, where non-personal images of God predominate, we would expect a low level of belief in a personal God, as reflected in the 10% rate that resulted from our survey. Given the religious situation in the country, however, it would seem that images of God as a spirit or life force would also indicate a level of religiosity. Nearly two-thirds of the respondents professed such a belief, with only 22% denying any belief in God. Combining the rate of belief in personal and non-personal images of God, therefore, reveals that fully 76% of the sample profess some belief in God, a level of religiosity significantly higher than that indicated by the previous group of questions. Furthermore, the level of importance attached to God issued in a mean of 5.06 out of 10, a result that also calls into question the low level of religiosity reflected in the questions above.

**Table 9.2  Religiosity indicators group 2, by age group**

|  | 18-30 | 31-43 | 44-56 | 57-69 | 70+ | Total |
|---|---|---|---|---|---|---|
| Belief in personal/ non-personal God | 68.3% | 74.4% | 75.3% | 75.0% | 80.1% | 76.0% |
| Importance of God (mean score out of 10) | 4.00 | 4.56 | 5.31 | 5.76 | 6.45 | 5.06 |

The key to understanding these results is, I think, the associations attached to the word "religion" in Japanese society. Religion, as an institution, is poorly regarded, an issue that will be taken up in a following section. This generally low regard of religious institutions could discourage people from identifying themselves as religious or deny that they draw strength or comfort from religion. Belief in God, however, is not necessarily identified with these institutions, leading to higher levels of religiosity on these measures.

This narrower scale of religiosity reflected in the two questions regarding belief in God is likewise affected by the age of the respondent, with the level of religiosity rising with age (Table 9.2).

## 4    RELIGIOUS BELIEFS

The European survey included a question regarding belief in various religious doctrines (God, life after death, sin, heaven, hell, etc.) as a scale to measure religious orthodoxy. Given the plurality of religious traditions in Japan, orthodoxy is a less certain category than in Christian Europe. Nonetheless, the question was included in our survey, with one addition, in order to provide some measure of common religious beliefs.

Nine items were included in the question: belief in God, life after death, a spirit or soul, hell, heaven, sin, curse, resurrection, and reincarnation. As the summary of results indicates (Table 9.3), belief in the existence of God and the human soul or spirit is relatively high. Somewhat over one-third of the sample believe in some kind of existence after death. The rate of belief in resurrection is perhaps deceptively high, since fully 11% of the respondents professed belief in both reincarnation and resurrection, indicating some confusion regarding the meaning of the item. One-fourth of the respondents believe in the existence of hell, a level of belief comparable to that in Europe. Less than one-third believe is heaven, a rate somewhat lower than that seen in the European survey. Sin, however, attracts a significantly lower level of belief, perhaps because it is not a concept firmly established in the Japanese religious tradition. Indeed, we had some trouble translating the term, since the word commonly used in Japanese also refers to legal crimes. It might be more profitable in future surveys to consider other concepts that could be equivalent to sin in the West.

## Table 9.3  Religious beliefs in Japan and Europe (in %)

| Belief in: | Japan | Europe |
| --- | --- | --- |
| God | 50 | 70 |
| Life after death | 34 | 43 |
| Human spirit or soul | 59 | 60 |
| Hell | 26 | 22 |
| Heaven | 31 | 41 |
| Sin | 23 | 53 |
| Curse (*tatari*) | 36 | - |
| Resurrection | 13 | 33 |
| Reincarnation | 39 | 19 |

An item was added to this question to measure belief in curses, or *tatari*. The belief that spirits of the dead, if not properly memorialized, could produce harmful effects on the living is a traditional part of Japanese religiosity. In the modern period, this belief has been popularized by some of the New Religions and other independent spiritualists. As the above results indicate, more than one-third of the respondents believe in the existence of *tatari*. The level of belief is somewhat higher among women (40%) and those affiliated with a religious group (43%).

Three other items were added to the questionnaire to test what were hypothesized to be popular religious beliefs. A pair of questions queried the possession of charms, usually purchased at Shinto Shrines but also available at some Buddhist temples, and the level of belief in the power of those charms to ward off evil or bring good luck. The third question regarded belief in divination.

A majority of the respondents (55%) possess a charm, and 42% believe that the charms are either somewhat or very effective, indicating that for almost half of the respondents the practice of buying and displaying these charms is more than merely a matter of custom. Belief in divination is considerably less popular, with only 3% of the respondents expressing unequivocal faith in the practice and an additional 20% saying they believe somewhat. Significantly, however, 35% of people under thirty years old believe either completely or somewhat in divination, attesting to the popularity of this practice among the young.

The questions added to the survey, measuring belief in *tatari*, charms, and divination, attest to the continued popularity of items connected with popular religion. While the level of belief in divination is relatively low, the other two items score higher than our indicator of personal allegiance to religious faith, that is religious affiliation, attesting to their importance as items of Japanese religiosity.

## 5    CONFIDENCE IN RELIGION

Institutional religion in Japan suffers from a history that has bred cynicism regarding its role and purpose in society. Mention has already been made of the co-opting of the Buddhist sects by the government in the seventeenth century. At that time, Buddhist temples were appointed as agents of social control through the development of the *danka* system. Similar to the role of the 'parish' in pre-industrial Europe, where births, marriages, and deaths were registered in the village church, one had to be registered at a temple and to avail oneself of Buddhist funeral rites, and temples administered the only authorized burial grounds. To this day, most Japanese are not aware of their nominal affiliation with a certain Buddhist sect until a death occurs in the family and there is need to arrange for a funeral, often with the temple where the family grave is located. Over the centuries, the funeral business has become the main support of most Buddhist temples in the country.

This policy of state use of the Buddhist establishment was abandoned in the mid-nineteenth century, when a new state ideology was created around Shinto. Although the Western powers forced the new Japanese state to include a guarantee of religious freedom in the constitution promulgated in 1890, the argument that Shinto was a non-religious institution of the state and that participation in its rites was the patriotic duty of all Japanese justified its special position in pre-1945 Japan. In the end, defeat in the war and the renunciation of imperial divinity advanced popular disillusionment with religion as an institution that began with the co-opting of the Buddhist establishment in the seventeenth century.

New religious movements that emerged at the same time that State Shinto was being created arguably served as better vehicles for transmitting folk religious traditions to a generation caught up in the rapid modernization of the nation. However, these movements were subject to a highly critical press and varying levels of oppression from the authorities. They ultimately sought recognition from the government as sects of Shinto, willingly purveying the nationalistic creed right up through the end of the war.

The press has also played a major role in how new religious movements are perceived in the postwar period. While religious freedoms guaranteed by Occupation policy and the new constitution contributed to a proliferation of new movements, these were often dismissed by intellectuals and the press as preying on the superstitions and alienation of the lower classes, being little more than a cynical attempt to amass fortunes by bilking their believers and avoiding tax laws. Riding a wave of popular interest in the occult, the press and television began to play up the mysterious and 'odd' nature of religious groups emerging in the 1970s and 80s, and occasionally the media and some religious groups would feed off each other to boost their ratings or membership. Such coverage came to a crashing end with the Aum Shinrikyō case in 1995, with the media now focussing on the scandal-ridden and dangerous nature of these 'cults', a term popularized in the post-Aum era.

Previous surveys indicate both a widespread antipathy towards religion in contemporary Japan and that this antipathy is based primarily on the popular images of religion outlined above. For example, in a nationwide survey of university students conducted annually since 1995, almost 60% of the respondents say that they have little or no interest in religion. Significantly, only 3% of the students attribute this negative attitude to a direct experience with a religious group, with the rest presumably drawing on the media for their image of religion.[1] Results from a survey conducted by the *Yomiuri Shinbun* in 1995 also attest to the influence of the above negative popular images. Given the opportunity for multiple responses to a question on their image of religion, 40% answered that religious groups were only out to make money and 37% expressed the opinion that religions prey on people's unease in order to increase their membership. Only 6% expressed the opinion that religious groups were making a positive contribution to society (Ishii, 1997: 179-181).

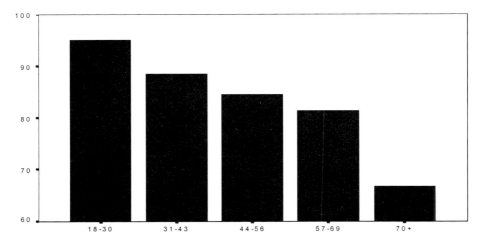

**Figure 9.2    Lack of confidence in religion, by age group**

The present survey confirms this low image of religion. 85.6% of the respondents voiced not much confidence or no confidence at all (40%) in religion, by far the lowest level recorded for any of the seventeen social institutions included in the survey. Only 13% expressed some level of confidence in religion, compared to an average of 48% in the 1990 European survey. Distrust of religion is especially high among younger cohorts, but nonetheless strong for all groups under seventy years old (Figure 9.2). Distrust also rises with education through university, but drops among those with some graduate schooling (Figure 9.3).

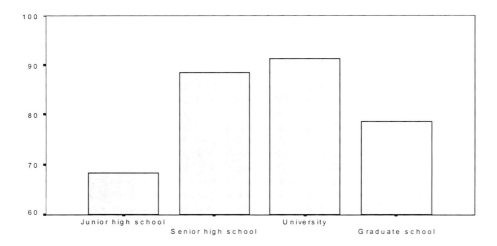

**Figure 9.3    Lack of confidence in religion, by level of education**

Queried on the adequacy of answers offered by religion to individual moral problems, problems of family life, spiritual needs, and social problems, the level of positive response, while lower than the European results, was generally comparable with those results, with the exception of religion's response to social problems (Table 9.4).

**Table 9.4  Adequacy of religion's response to problems (in %)**

| Problems: | Japan | Europe (1990) |
|---|---|---|
| Moral | 33 | 34 |
| Family | 24 | 31 |
| Spiritual | 48 | 50 |
| Social | 9 | 24 |

The highest positive response was obtained for religion's answers to spiritual needs, confirming yet another part of the popular view of religion in Japan reflected in previous surveys, that is that religion is fundamentally a 'refuge for the soul'.[2] On the other hand, it would appear that more people would like religion to be socially involved, for only 9% of the respondents felt that religion was providing adequate answers to social problems.

Religion's social involvement, however, should not extend to direct political action. A question was included in the survey asking whether religion leaders should try to exert political influence. More than three-fourths of the respondents disagreed with this proposition, an opinion that was significantly stronger among men, younger cohorts, and those with at least some university education.

## 6    RELIGIOUS PLURALISM AND THE FUTURE OF RELIGION

Two questions were added to the questionnaire to test what are assumed to be popular ideas in Japan regarding the future of religion. It has become commonplace, especially among the Japanese New Religions, to speak of the essential unity of all religious faith. In order to measure the appeal of this opinion, respondents were asked if they agree with the proposition that, in the end, all religions share the same end or goal. Just over half of the respondents answered affirmatively and less than one-quarter disagreed, with the remainder offering no opinion. Women, older respondents, and those who had not gone beyond the years of compulsory education were more likely to agree with the proposition.

The other item questioned the survival of religion. The question proposed that with the advancement of morals religion would no longer be needed. Contrary to our expectations, just 28% of the respondents felt that this would be the case. Only with respondents under the age of thirty did agreement with this proposition approach a majority, indicating that despite its present poor image many people see a continuing role for religion in society.

Responses to a question regarding the degree of attention respondents paid to the meaning and purpose of life offers the opportunity for further speculation on the image of religion in Japan and the future of this institution. We have seen that religious affiliation drops dramatically among younger cohorts. An even more dramatic falloff is seen with regard to a religious upbringing (Figure 9.4), a development that does not bode well for the future of religion in Japan.

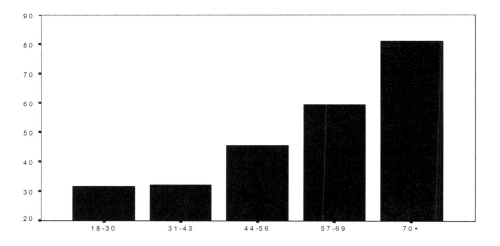

**Figure 9.4    Religious upbringing, by age group**

However, it is the cohorts younger than seventy years old, who increasingly do not belong to a religion and have not been exposed to religious belief at home, that are more inclined to think about the meaning and purpose of life (Figure 9.5). We might speculate that this high level of interest in questions of meaning and purpose, combined with a low level of interest in religion, leads to the conclusion that religion is not seen as providing answers to those questions by many contemporary Japanese.

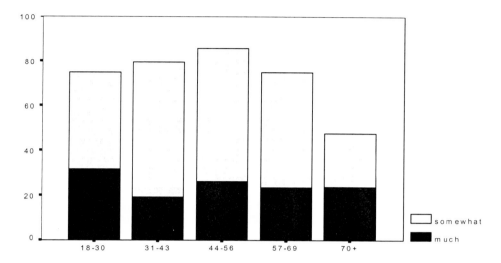

**Figure 9.5    Think about meaning and purpose of life, by age group**

## 7    PUBLIC AND PRIVATE MORALITY

Our survey used many of the same items as previous surveys by the EVS group to measure public and private morality. Private morality is defined here as matters having to do with sexual and conjugal morality (married people having affairs, sex under the age of consent, homosexuality, prostitution, divorce), the taking of drugs, and death (euthanasia, abortion, suicide). The percent of respondents saying these behaviours are never justified can be seen in Table 9.5, compared to the results from the 1990 European survey, where available. In general, the Japanese appear to be more permissive on matter of sexual and conjugal morality as well as issues pertaining to death. Japanese permissiveness is especially pronounced regarding views on euthanasia. The Japanese appear to be less accepting of drug use than the Europeans.

Although age, sex, and education appear to play a role in determining attitudes on some of these issues, the rejection of drug use seems to be across the board. Respondents over 70 years old are significantly less tolerant of marital affairs (81%), underage sex (91%), prostitution (91%), suicide (71%), and abortion (43%). Women are generally less permissive on some of the issues of sexual and conjugal morality: prostitution (64%), marital affairs (46%), and underage sex (46%). People with compulsory education (junior high school) or lower are less permissive on all of these issues except drug use.

**Table 9.5  Private morality, percent saying behaviour never justified**

|                 | Japan | Europe (1990) |
|-----------------|-------|---------------|
| Marital affairs | 41    | 53            |
| Underage sex    | 46    | 58            |
| Homosexuality   | 30    | 39            |
| Prostitution    | 54    | 48            |
| Divorce         | 11    | 15            |
| Taking drugs    | 87    | 81            |
| Euthanasia      | 10    | 28            |
| Abortion        | 16    | 21            |
| Suicide         | 42    | 50            |

While Japanese appear to be generally more permissive on issues of private morality, measures of public morality yield a mixed result. The issues involved in this measure are listed in Table 9.6, along with the percentage of those who feel these activities are never justified, from the Japanese survey and the 1990 European survey, where available. While more permissive on the issues of cheating on state benefits and fares for public transportation, the Japanese are less tolerant of tax cheats. On the one issue of private property, that of joyriding in a stolen car, the Japanese are considerably more permissive, perhaps reflecting the lower crime rate in their country. While less tolerant of lying, the Japanese survey shows a much higher tolerance of bribery. On issues of public behaviour, driving under the influence of alcohol is generally not tolerated in Japan, while littering and smoking in a no-smoking area receive the same level of censure as lying.

**Table 9.6  Public morality, percent saying behaviour never justified**

|                           | Japan | Europe (1990) |
|---------------------------|-------|---------------|
| Cheating on state benefits | 49    | 59            |
| Cheating on fares         | 54    | 58            |
| Cheating on taxes         | 68    | 49            |
| Joyriding in stolen car   | 71    | 84            |
| Lying                     | 46    | 37            |
| Taking a bribe            | 55    | 70            |
| Drunk driving             | 61    | 77            |
| Littering                 | 47    | 68            |
| Smoking                   | 47    | -             |

Age seems to play a factor in all of these issues of public morality, with younger cohorts generally more permissive. The sex of the respondent introduces a difference only on the issues of public behaviour, with women being less tolerant of driving under the influence of alcohol (65%), littering (52%), and smoking in a no-smoking area (55%). Respondents who have attended university are more permissive on two of the issues of public behaviour, littering (43%) and driving under the influence (53%), as well as the issue of bribery (46%). Permissiveness on this latter issue might be explained by the fact that it is precisely this group that would most likely find themselves in the position of being bribed.

As we might expect, affiliation with a religious group does play a role in these issues, with members of a religious group less permissive on almost all the measures of public and private morality. The are two significant exceptions worth mentioning here. Affiliation with a religious group appears to make no difference in attitudes towards drug use, testifying again to the broad censure of this activity in Japanese society. The other exception is homosexuality, indicating that this is perhaps not a religious issue in Japan.

## 8    ASIAN VALUES

Finally, a question with multiple items was added to measure the importance placed on values that are commonly identified as part of a constellation of Asian values. These items are listed in Table 9.7, along with the percentage of respondents who found these values to be either very important or somewhat important.

**Table 9.7  Percent of importance placed on Asian values**

| Value: | % |
| --- | --- |
| Authority | 24 |
| Cooperation | 95 |
| Honesty | 95 |
| Group membership | 64 |
| Diligence | 83 |
| Success at work | 66 |
| Lawfulness | 92 |
| Obedience | 60 |
| Patriotism | 69 |
| Manners | 94 |
| Helpfulness | 86 |
| Seriousness | 87 |

Cooperation, honesty, lawfulness, and manners are judged important by more than 90% of the respondents; diligence, helpfulness, and seriousness approach that level of esteem; patriotism, group membership, success at work, and obedience are held to be important by about two-thirds of the respondents; but little importance is apparently placed on authority.

The sex of the respondent appears to play little role in these results, although women were somewhat more likely to consider obedience (67%) and group membership (69) important. Age is also a factor in some of the items, with respondents under thirty years old less likely to place importance on authority (18%), lawfulness (82%), diligence (67%), and much less likely to value patriotism (37%). The cohort between thirty-one and forty-three years scored significantly lower on patriotism as well, with only 46% finding this value important. Finally, education seems to play a role in the importance attached to two of these items, with those who have attended university less likely to value obedience (50%) and patriotism (54%).

The Japanese intellectual historian Yasumaru Yoshio has argued that a 'conventional morality' was popularized by itinerant Confucian preachers in the early modern period, beginning in the urban areas in the late seventeenth century and spreading throughout the countryside by the end of the nineteenth century. These preachers emphasized the cultivation of common virtues such as honesty, filial piety, thrift, diligence, and cooperation, the virtues hypothesized here as the core of Asian values.[3] The results of our survey indicate the deep roots that the cultivation of these virtues have taken in Japanese society.

It is widely assumed that religious groups, especially the New Religions, have become the means of transmission of these values in contemporary Japan. Clearly the importance placed on these values goes beyond religious membership in Japan, but the results of our survey indicate that religion might have a role in their promotion. Affiliation with a religious group seems to affect positively the importance placed on these values, with significant correlations seen in relation to group membership, diligence, lawfulness, manners, patriotism, helpfulness, and seriousness.

## 9    CONCLUSIONS

Although only a preliminary analysis is possible at this time, the results presented here indicate that a cross-cultural comparison of the religious situation in Europe and Japan is not only possible, but might produce useful insights for further research in both regions.

The transposition of indicators used to measure the inroads of secularization, as suggested by a reading of the differing historical-cultural situation of religion in Europe and Japan, leads to the conclusion that we see a similar level of erosion in religion's influence in these societies. Roughly one-third of the population in both Europe and Japan have a fairly high degree of commitment to religious belief, while up to 80% could be called either nominally religious, or occasional participants in religious activities as a part of social custom.

Beyond the question of religious commitment, there remains in both societies a more diffuse religiosity, which takes expression as an interest in religion or God. While the Japanese express relatively less interest in items that are identified as 'religious', they would appear to have more interest in God, or a higher spiritual power, than Europeans. I would speculate that the low level of interest in items identified as religious is because of a poor image of religious institutions in Japan, an argument that is borne out by the exceedingly low level of confidence placed in institutional religion.

A higher level of religiosity is also attested to by the persistence of some folk or popular religious beliefs, such as the value placed on the possession of charms. While belief in divination remains somewhat lower than expected, due to the wide press that these practices have received in the last twenty years, the wider acceptance of this belief among the young indicates that it is a trend that must be followed.

Some initial comparisons were also made on public and private morality in Japan and Europe. Japanese seem to be generally more permissive in both of these realms, with the notable exceptions of prostitution, drugs, lying, and cheating on taxes. In planning the survey there was some concern that we would not be able to obtain honest answers to questions like these, since Japanese society is generally perceived to be more concerned with expected responses. While the theoretical issue remains, the higher level of permissiveness reflected in these results perhaps indicates that the respondents were not overly concerned with appearances.

Answers to items added to the survey tend to confirm the hypothesis that religious pluralism is widely accepted in Japanese society and that certain values identified as particularly important in Asia are, in general, highly esteemed. An important exception here is authority, which was rejected by a surprisingly large majority of the respondents. It will be important to see how these values are perceived in other Asian, and Western, societies, to test whether their codification into a 'conventional morality' in Japan in the early modern period has influenced their acceptance in contemporary Japanese society.

**Notes**

1 The survey is conducted by *The Japanese Association for the Study of Religion and Society's Religious Awareness Project*. The annual reports on the results of the survey are available from the author.
2 *Kokoro no yori dokoro* in Japanese. In a 1996 survey by Jiji Tsushin this was the second highest association with religion, surpassed only by wedding and funeral services (see Ishii, 1997: 198).
3 A concise English summary of Yasumaru's argument can be found in Shimazono, 1981.

# References

Barker, D., L. Halman & A. Vloet 1992. *The European Values Study 1981-1990.* London: Gordon Cook Foundation.

Hayashi, M. 1992. 'Nihon shukyoshi ni okeru sezokka katei' [The process of secularization in the history of Japanese religion]. In: *Gendai shukyogaku 4* [The Contemporary Study of Religion 4]. Tokyo: Tokyo University Press

Ishii, K. 1997. *Gendai nihonjin no shukyo* [Religion and the Contemporary Japanese]. Tokyo: Shinyosha

Kisala, R. 1997. 'Nihonjin no mushuko ka' [Japanese 'non-religiosity']. *Sozo* 111:8-12.

Reader, I. 1991. *Religion in Contemporary Japan.* London: Macmillan Press.

Shimazono, S. 1981. 'Religious Influences on Japan's Modernization'. *Japanese Journal of Religious Studies* 8:207-223.

Swyngedouw, J. 1993. 'Religion in Contemporary Japanese Society'. Pp.49-72 in: M. Mullins, S. Shimazono & P. Swanson (eds.), *Religion & Society in Modern Japan.* Berkeley: Asian Humanities Press.

Tamaru, N. 1979. 'The Problem of Secularization'. *Japanese Journal of Religious Studies* 6: 89-114.

**Appendix Tables Chapter 6**

**Table 6.1 Adherence to a morality of principles, according to religious attitudes and country**

| | Spain | Portugal | Belgium | Italy | Ireland | France | Great Britain | Denmark | Netherlands | West Germany | Mean |
|---|---|---|---|---|---|---|---|---|---|---|---|
| Regular attending Catholics | 33 | 32 | 43 | 53 | 43 | 43 | 50 | - | 33 | 35 | 42 |
| Irregular attending Catholics | 23 | 24 | 29 | 36 | 35 | 26 | 31* | - | 23 | 18 | 28 |
| Non-attending Catholics | 23 | 27 | 29 | 37 | 29* | 25 | 41 | 21 | 22 | 19 | 26 |
| Regular attending Protestants | - | - | - | 39* | 44* | - | 48 | 6 | 40 | 32 | 40 |
| Irregular attending Protestants | - | - | - | - | - | - | 41 | 6 | 20* | 21 | 29 |
| Non-attending Protestants | - | - | - | - | - | - | 36 | 8 | 48 | 21 | 26 |
| No religion | 18 | 29 | 24 | 26 | 17 | 15 | 28 | 10 | 20 | 15 | 22 |
| Committed atheists | 12 | 17 | 15 | 24 | - | 5 | 18 | 5* | 9 | 6 | 11 |
| Mean | 26 | 29 | 31 | 43 | 41 | 23 | 35 | 9 | 26 | 24 | 30 |

N.B. categories with less than 10 respondents are excluded from the tables. An asterisk indicates a category of 11 to 30 respondents

**Table 6.2 In favour of moral rigourism, according to religious attitudes and country**

| | Spain | Portugal | Belgium | Italy | Ireland | France | Great Britain | Denmark * | Netherlands | West Germany | Mean |
|---|---|---|---|---|---|---|---|---|---|---|---|
| Regular attending Catholics | 79 | 84 | 66 | 76 | 79 | 61 | 74 | - | 35 | 72 | 74 |
| Irregular attending Catholics | 59 | 63 | 53 | 55 | 62 | 45 | 46* | - | 22 | 28 | 48 |
| Non-attending Catholics | 43 | 53 | 46 | 40 | 52* | 34 | 49 | - | 22 | 30 | 38 |
| Regular attending Protestants | - | - | - | 70* | 67* | - | 56 | - | 56 | 69 | 60 |
| Irregular attending Protestants | - | - | - | - | - | - | 37 | - | 7* | 34 | 36 |
| Non-attending Protestants | - | - | - | - | - | - | 48 | - | 38 | 32 | 40 |
| No religion | 36 | 52 | 30 | 28 | 36 | 26 | 36 | - | 11 | 25 | 30 |
| Committed atheists | 19 | 46 | 18 | 6 | - | 14 | 18 | - | 0 | 0 | 14 |
| Mean | 59 | 66 | 47 | 59 | 75 | 36 | 44 | - | 23 | 44 | 48 |

* Moral rigourism cannot be calculated for Denmark since one of the indicators is lacking

**Table 6.3  In favour of civic rigourism, according to religious attitudes and country**

| | Spain | Portugal | Belgium | Italy | Ireland | France | Great Britain | Denmark | Netherlands | West Germany | Mean |
|---|---|---|---|---|---|---|---|---|---|---|---|
| Regular attending Catholics | 42 | 27 | 31 | 48 | 38 | 32 | 48 | - | 39 | 37 | 41 |
| Irregular attending Catholics | 34 | 23 | 15 | 34 | 26 | 27 | 23* | - | 20 | 24 | 29 |
| Non-attending Catholics | 35 | 25 | 18 | 36 | 35* | 23 | 17 | - | 33 | 24 | 28 |
| Regular attending Protestants | - | - | - | 33* | 44* | - | 60 | 58 | 50 | 47 | 53 |
| Irregular attending Protestants | - | - | - | - | - | - | 49 | 48 | 41* | 30 | 40 |
| Non-attending Protestants | - | - | - | - | - | - | 41 | 44 | 33 | 28 | 35 |
| No religion | 23 | 19 | 19 | 30 | 22 | 17 | 29 | 37 | 28 | 22 | 24 |
| Committed atheists | 16 | 18 | 14 | 38 | - | 18 | 20 | 40* | 31 | 9 | 20 |
| Mean | 36 | 24 | 22 | 41 | 37 | 23 | 39 | 46 | 34 | 31 | 33 |

**Table 6.4  Orientation toward traditional family values, according to religious attitudes and country**

| | Spain | Portugal | Belgium | Italy | Ireland | France | Great Britain | Denmark | Netherlands | West Germany | Mean |
|---|---|---|---|---|---|---|---|---|---|---|---|
| Regular attending Catholics | 40 | 56 | 52 | 55 | 55 | 56 | 48 | - | 47 | 49 | 51 |
| Irregular attending Catholics | 17 | 46 | 35 | 36 | 27 | 41 | 29* | - | 28 | 18 | 31 |
| Non-attending Catholics | 15 | 34 | 27 | 29 | 29* | 33 | 18 | - | 19 | 15 | 24 |
| Regular attending Protestants | - | - | - | 50* | 63* | - | 53 | 63 | 56 | 50 | 52 |
| Irregular attending Protestants | - | - | - | - | - | - | 38 | 46 | 18* | 20 | 29 |
| Non-attending Protestants | - | - | - | - | - | - | 36 | 41 | 53 | 18 | 28 |
| No religion | 8 | 20 | 16 | 23 | 14 | 22 | 20 | 34 | 15 | 12 | 19 |
| Committed atheists | 3 | 16 | 11 | 13 | - | 7 | 9 | 20* | 8 | 0 | 8 |
| Mean | 25 | 39 | 31 | 43 | 51 | 32 | 32 | 44 | 28 | 27 | 33 |

**Table 6.5 Against abortion, according to religious attitudes and country**

| | Spain | Portugal | Belgium | Italy | Ireland | France | Great Britain | Denmark | Netherlands | West Germany | Mean |
|---|---|---|---|---|---|---|---|---|---|---|---|
| Regular attending Catholics | 50 | 36 | 40 | 35 | 70 | 28 | 61 | - | 42 | 39 | 40 |
| Irregular attending Catholics | 24 | 9 | 27 | 13 | 52 | 18 | 35* | - | 31 | 12 | 18 |
| Non-attending Catholics | 18 | 13 | 17 | 10 | 50* | 11 | 25 | - | 37 | 14 | 14 |
| Regular attending Protestants | - | - | - | 26* | 44* | - | 25 | 26 | 63 | 28 | 29 |
| Irregular attending Protestants | - | - | - | - | - | - | 19 | 15 | 27* | 12 | 15 |
| Non-attending Protestants | - | - | - | - | - | - | 16 | 10 | 45 | 13 | 14 |
| No religion | 15 | 10 | 15 | 8 | 58 | 14 | 16 | 15 | 22 | 10 | 15 |
| Committed atheists | 7 | 14 | 10 | 0 | - | 9 | 18 | 5* | 10 | 9 | 10 |
| Mean | 32 | 21 | 24 | 23 | 67 | 16 | 21 | 13 | 33 | 20 | 23 |

**Table 6.6 Politicisation, according to religious attitudes and country**

| | Spain | Portugal | Belgium | Italy | Ireland | France | Great Britain | Denmark | Netherlands | West Germany | Mean |
|---|---|---|---|---|---|---|---|---|---|---|---|
| Regular attending Catholics | 23 | 28 | 37 | 32 | 38 | 57 | 58 | - | 66 | 67 | 41 |
| Irregular attending Catholics | 26 | 25 | 31 | 27 | 40 | 38 | 34* | - | 60 | 66 | 36 |
| Non-attending Catholics | 27 | 36 | 24 | 35 | 39* | 36 | 63 | - | 54 | 63 | 40 |
| Regular attending Protestants | - | - | - | 17* | 38* | - | 57 | 63 | 73 | 67 | 61 |
| Irregular attending Protestants | - | - | - | - | - | - | 60 | 56 | 79* | 73 | 65 |
| Non-attending Protestants | - | - | - | - | - | - | 51 | 54 | 47 | 67 | 58 |
| No religion | 30 | 42 | 29 | 39 | 50 | 35 | 42 | 64 | 65 | 71 | 44 |
| Committed atheists | 55 | 35 | 42 | 62 | - | 51 | 58 | 85* | 68 | 83 | 56 |
| Mean | 26 | 33 | 31 | 33 | 38 | 41 | 50 | 57 | 65 | 68 | 45 |

**Table 6.7 Participation in at least one political activity, according to religious attitudes and country**

|  | Spain | Portugal | Belgium | Italy | Ireland | France | Great Britain | Denmark | Netherlands | West Germany | Mean |
|---|---|---|---|---|---|---|---|---|---|---|---|
| Regular attending Catholics | 22 | 28 | 50 | 45 | 43 | 53 | 87 | - | 40 | 51 | 43 |
| Irregular attending Catholics | 22 | 30 | 50 | 53 | 54 | 53 | 64* | - | 46 | 55 | 48 |
| Non-attending Catholics | 30 | 44 | 49 | 56 | 68* | 55 | 73 | - | 36 | 57 | 49 |
| Regular attending Protestants | - | - | - | 43* | 38* | - | 76 | 55 | 54 | 55 | 64 |
| Irregular attending Protestants | - | - | - | - | - | - | 77 | 57 | 57* | 59 | 65 |
| Non-attending Protestants | - | - | - | - | - | - | 74 | 58 | 29 | 57 | 64 |
| No religion | 41 | 56 | 56 | 66 | 69 | 57 | 76 | 76 | 57 | 71 | 64 |
| Committed atheists | 62 | 53 | 61 | 94 | - | 77 | 89 | 90* | 84 | 85 | 79 |
| Mean | 28 | 40 | 52 | 52 | 45 | 57 | 76 | 59 | 53 | 57 | 55 |

**Table 6.8 Post-materialism, according to religious attitudes and country**

|  | Spain | Portugal | Belgium | Italy | Ireland | France | Great Britain | Denmark | Netherlands | West Germany | Mean |
|---|---|---|---|---|---|---|---|---|---|---|---|
| Regular attending Catholics | 23 | 12 | 37 | 26 | 21 | 32 | 32 | - | 31 | 22 | 25 |
| Irregular attending Catholics | 34 | 13 | 28 | 23 | 27 | 22 | 27* | - | 30 | 33 | 26 |
| Non-attending Catholics | 34 | 17 | 27 | 28 | 25* | 34 | 36 | - | 22 | 33 | 31 |
| Regular attending Protestants | - | - | - | 44* | 19* | - | 34 | 25 | 26 | 28 | 31 |
| Irregular attending Protestants | - | - | - | - | - | - | 20 | 20 | 40* | 33 | 28 |
| Non-attending Protestants | - | - | - | - | - | - | 23 | 28 | 14 | 33 | 28 |
| No religion | 41 | 23 | 37 | 42 | 44 | 39 | 29 | 57 | 42 | 42 | 36 |
| Committed atheists | 58 | 40 | 48 | 50 | - | 55 | 47 | 50* | 72 | 64 | 54 |
| Mean | 31 | 17 | 35 | 29 | 22 | 35 | 28 | 28 | 37 | 31 | 31 |

**Table 6.9  Confidence in authoritarian institutions, according to religious attitudes and country**

| | Spain | Portugal | Belgium | Italy | Ireland | France | Great Britain | Denmark | Netherlands | West Germany | Mean |
|---|---|---|---|---|---|---|---|---|---|---|---|
| Regular attending Catholics | 57 | 48 | 38 | 59 | 69 | 72 | 74 | - | 41 | 54 | 58 |
| Irregular attending Catholics | 34 | 45 | 33 | 38 | 27 | 56 | 57* | - | 16 | 18 | 38 |
| Non-attending Catholics | 20 | 24 | 23 | 19 | 26* | 38 | 45 | - | 14 | 11 | 24 |
| Regular attending Protestants | - | - | - | 49* | 63* | - | 74 | 72 | 49 | 55 | 64 |
| Irregular attending Protestants | - | - | - | - | - | - | 65 | 53 | 8* | 29 | 46 |
| Non-attending Protestants | - | - | - | - | - | - | 54 | 36 | 33 | 17 | 35 |
| No religion | 9 | 13 | 12 | 10 | 19 | 17 | 39 | 14 | 6 | 6 | 21 |
| Committed atheists | 0 | 7 | 4 | 0 | - | 3 | 14 | 10* | 0 | 0 | 4 |
| Mean | 35 | 31 | 24 | 42 | 63 | 37 | 52 | 41 | 19 | 28 | 38 |

**Table 6.10  Confidence in democratic institutions, according to religious attitudes and country**

| | Spain | Portugal | Belgium | Italy | Ireland | France | Great Britain | Denmark | Netherlands | West Germany | Mean |
|---|---|---|---|---|---|---|---|---|---|---|---|
| Regular attending Catholics | 50 | 36 | 54 | 35 | 58 | 45 | 36 | - | 60 | 58 | 45 |
| Irregular attending Catholics | 47 | 41 | 55 | 28 | 39 | 53 | 13* | - | 51 | 60 | 43 |
| Non-attending Catholics | 40 | 31 | 46 | 19 | 22* | 46 | 35 | - | 50 | 41 | 38 |
| Regular attending Protestants | - | - | - | 26* | 79* | - | 40 | 60 | 66 | 60 | 50 |
| Irregular attending Protestants | - | - | - | - | - | - | 32 | 63 | 39* | 61 | 47 |
| Non-attending Protestants | - | - | - | - | - | - | 30 | 63 | 43 | 48 | 42 |
| No religion | 26 | 27 | 43 | 18 | 33 | 44 | 29 | 57 | 59 | 38 | 35 |
| Committed atheists | 21 | 29 | 42 | 10 | - | 47 | 22 | 56* | 55 | 22 | 34 |
| Mean | 43 | 32 | 48 | 29 | 55 | 47 | 31 | 62 | 57 | 51 | 41 |

**Table 6.11   Right-wing self-placement, according to religious attitudes and country**

| | Spain | Portugal | Belgium | Italy | Ireland | France | Great Britain | Denmark | Netherlands | West Germany | Mean |
|---|---|---|---|---|---|---|---|---|---|---|---|
| Regular attending Catholics | 35 | 55 | 48 | 31 | 54 | 46 | 49 | - | 65 | 47 | 40 |
| Irregular attending Catholics | 18 | 45 | 38 | 22 | 44 | 34 | 21* | - | 58 | 34 | 28 |
| Non-attending Catholics | 13 | 42 | 30 | 19 | 54* | 22 | 32 | - | 46 | 29 | 23 |
| Regular attending Protestants | - | - | - | 4* | 75* | - | 43 | 60 | 71 | 40 | 43 |
| Irregular attending Protestants | - | - | - | - | - | - | 60 | 49 | 66* | 38 | 48 |
| Non-attending Protestants | - | - | - | - | - | - | 44 | 41 | 41 | 27 | 35 |
| No religion | 10 | 34 | 23 | 17 | 25 | 14 | 31 | 28 | 35 | 24 | 24 |
| Committed atheists | 9 | 28 | 23 | 10 | - | 12 | 22 | 40* | 24 | 9 | 15 |
| Mean | 22 | 45 | 34 | 25 | 52 | 24 | 39 | 43 | 47 | 34 | 31 |

**Table 6.12 In favour of economic liberalism, according to religious attitudes and country**

| | Spain | Portugal | Belgium | Italy | Ireland | France | Great Britain | Denmark | Netherlands | West Germany | Mean |
|---|---|---|---|---|---|---|---|---|---|---|---|
| Regular attending Catholics | 29 | 33 | 49 | 42 | 52 | 63 | 35 | - | 54 | 59 | 45 |
| Irregular attending Catholics | 26 | 25 | 50 | 39 | 40 | 44 | 49* | - | 57 | 58 | 42 |
| Non-attending Catholics | 25 | 32 | 46 | 40 | 64* | 45 | 35 | - | 41 | 53 | 41 |
| Regular attending Protestants | - | - | - | 14* | 21* | - | 40 | 74 | 53 | 64 | 50 |
| Irregular attending Protestants | - | - | - | - | - | - | 52 | 63 | 44* | 59 | 55 |
| Non-attending Protestants | - | - | - | - | - | - | 47 | 58 | 53 | 60 | 54 |
| No religion | 22 | 35 | 44 | 46 | 44 | 41 | 42 | 39 | 44 | 58 | 42 |
| Committed atheists | 25 | 36 | 48 | 46 | - | 34 | 36 | 47 | 37 | 56 | 37 |
| Mean | 26 | 32 | 48 | 42 | 52 | 45 | 43 | 59 | 48 | 59 | 45 |

**Table 6.13  Prefer liberty above equality, according to religious attitudes and country**

|  | Spain | Portugal | Belgium | Italy | Ireland | France | Great Britain | Denmark | Netherlands | West Germany | Mean |
|---|---|---|---|---|---|---|---|---|---|---|---|
| Regular attending Catholics | 41 | 32 | 44 | 42 | 43 | 47 | 59 | - | 53 | 53 | 45 |
| Irregular attending Catholics | 43 | 41 | 46 | 43 | 54 | 47 | 78* | - | 65 | 72 | 49 |
| Non-attending Catholics | 45 | 38 | 48 | 41 | 61* | 51 | 51 | - | 37 | 58 | 49 |
| Regular attending Protestants | - | - | - | 21* | 50* | - | 60 | 60 | 47 | 55 | 56 |
| Irregular attending Protestants | - | - | - | - | - | - | 70 | 56 | 65* | 68 | 67 |
| Non-attending Protestants | - | - | - | - | - | - | 63 | 60 | 51 | 62 | 62 |
| No religion | 50 | 42 | 51 | 45 | 44 | 47 | 62 | 40 | 58 | 57 | 54 |
| Committed atheists | 41 | 53 | 57 | 43 | - | 44 | 67 | 50* | 64 | 47 | 50 |
| Mean | 43 | 38 | 48 | 42 | 45 | 48 | 63 | 58 | 55 | 59 | 51 |

**Table 6.14  Nationalism, according to religious attitudes and country**

|  | Spain | Portugal | Belgium | Italy | Ireland | France | Great Britain | Denmark | Netherlands | West Germany | Mean |
|---|---|---|---|---|---|---|---|---|---|---|---|
| Regular attending Catholics | 59 | 62 | 38 | 33 | 61 | 64 | 67 | - | 55 | 43 | 47 |
| Irregular attending Catholics | 66 | 68 | 40 | 35 | 61 | 69 | 66* | - | 73 | 41 | 53 |
| Non-attending Catholics | 52 | 67 | 41 | 26 | 71* | 70 | 75 | - | 61 | 46 | 54 |
| Regular attending Protestants | - | - | - | 4* | 50* | - | 71 | 79 | 66 | 44 | 60 |
| Irregular attending Protestants | - | - | - | - | - | - | 84 | 83 | 61* | 45 | 67 |
| Non-attending Protestants | - | - | - | - | - | - | 74 | 80 | 57 | 34 | 59 |
| No religion | 40 | 64 | 36 | 17 | 38 | 56 | 69 | 70 | 55 | 27 | 53 |
| Committed atheists | 29 | 59 | 30 | 21 | - | 39 | 41 | 46* | 30 | 14 | 35 |
| Mean | 55 | 64 | 38 | 30 | 60 | 62 | 71 | 79 | 57 | 39 | 52 |

**Table 6.15  National preference for jobs, according to religious attitudes and country**

| | Spain | Portugal | Belgium | Italy | Ireland | France | Great Britain | Denmark | Netherlands | West Germany | Mean |
|---|---|---|---|---|---|---|---|---|---|---|---|
| Regular attending Catholics | 77 | 86 | 66 | 73 | 70 | 70 | 43 | - | 41 | 60 | 70 |
| Irregular attending Catholics | 81 | 90 | 68 | 77 | 73 | 72 | 70* | - | 40 | 65 | 73 |
| Non-attending Catholics | 76 | 87 | 68 | 72 | 68* | 66 | 25 | - | 21 | 60 | 67 |
| Regular attending Protestants | - | - | - | 65* | 63* | - | 45 | 47 | 40 | 61 | 52 |
| Irregular attending Protestants | - | - | - | - | - | - | 55 | 61 | 28* | 59 | 58 |
| Non-attending Protestants | - | - | - | - | - | - | 57 | 53 | 42 | 50 | 54 |
| No religion | 69 | 86 | 58 | 66 | 36 | 51 | 49 | 28 | 32 | 51 | 53 |
| Committed atheists | 67 | 86 | 53 | 46 | - | 49 | 27 | 30* | 15 | 34 | 45 |
| Mean | 76 | 86 | 63 | 72 | 68 | 61 | 49 | 52 | 34 | 57 | 61 |
| Unemployment in 1990 (Eurostat) | 16.1 | 4.6 | 8.1 | 9.9 | 15.6 | 9.0 | 6.4 | 8.0 | 8.1 | 5.1 | 8.4 |

**Table 6.16  Xenophobia, according to religious attitudes and country**

| | Spain | Portugal | Belgium | Italy | Ireland | France | Great Britain | Denmark | Netherlands | West Germany | Mean |
|---|---|---|---|---|---|---|---|---|---|---|---|
| Regular attending Catholics | 19 | 35 | 38 | 27 | 18 | 24 | 15 | - | 27 | 34 | 26 |
| Irregular attending Catholics | 15 | 40 | 39 | 26 | 15 | 31 | 25* | - | 27 | 33 | 27 |
| Non-attending Catholics | 16 | 25 | 34 | 26 | 25* | 26 | 18 | - | 17 | 31 | 24 |
| Regular attending Protestants | - | - | - | 5* | 13* | - | 22 | 22 | 29 | 34 | 26 |
| Irregular attending Protestants | - | - | - | - | - | - | 23 | 19 | 26* | 31 | 27 |
| Non-attending Protestants | - | - | - | - | - | - | 26 | 22 | 18 | 28 | 26 |
| No religion | 18 | 32 | 35 | 23 | 11 | 19 | 21 | 9 | 18 | 30 | 22 |
| Committed atheists | 14 | 25 | 35 | 27 | - | 19 | 23 | 20* | 11 | 23 | 21 |
| Mean | 17 | 32 | 36 | 26 | 18 | 23 | 22 | 20 | 21 | 31 | 25 |
| Foreigners outside CEE in 1989 (Eurostat) | 0.4 | 0.7 | 3.3 | 0.4 | 0.5 | 3.8 | 1.8 | 2.3 | 3.1 | 5.7 | 2.5 |

# About the Authors

*Karel Dobbelaere* (1933) is Professor Emeritus of Sociology and Sociology of Religion at the Catholic University of Leuven, Belgium. His main research interests are secularization, pillarization and religious involvement in Churches, Sects and NRMs. He is a member of the Royal Flemish Academy of Belgium for Sciences and Fine Arts, and of the Academia Europaea.

*Pierre Bréchon* (1947) is Professor of Political Science at the Institut d'Etudes Politiques and researcher at CIDSP, the Centre d'Informatisation des Données socio-politiques in Grenoble (France). He has conducted research on political and religious values, electoral sociology, political parties, and European attitudes. He is member of the teams which carried out the European Values Survey in France and the annual survey of the International Social Survey Programme (ISSP). His most recent publications include *Les partis politiques* (Paris: Montchrestien, 1999), and *Les enquêtes Eurobaromètres. Analyse comparée des données socio-politiques* (with Bruno Cautrès. Paris: L'Harmattan, 1998).

*Josette Gevers* is currently a PhD student at Eindhoven University where she is involved in a collaborative project between the Department of Technology & Work of Eindhoven University of Technology, and the Department of Work & Organizational Psychology at the Faculty of Social Sciences of Tilburg University. At the time of writing she was a junior researcher and database-manager at WORC, the Work & Organization Research Centre of Tilburg University.

*Loek Halman* (1956) is a senior Research Fellow at WORC, the Work & Organization Research Centre of Tilburg University, the Netherlands. His main interests are comparative research on values and value change. He is currently involved in the European Values Study and the international project on Religious and Moral pluralism. He is secretary to the Steering Committee of the European Values Study and the Board of the EVS Foundation, and Program Director of the 1999 EVS study.

*Michael P. Hornsby-Smith* is Professor Emeritus of Sociology at the University of Surrey, England. His publications include *Catholic Education* (1978), *Roman Catholic Opinion* (with R.M.Lee, 1979), *The Changing Parish* (1989), *Roman Catholic Beliefs in England* (1991), *The Politics of Spirituality* (with John Fulton and margaret Norris, 1995), and the edited volume *Catholics in England 1950-2000* (1999).

*Robert Kisala* (1957) is a research fellow at the Nanzan Institute for Religion and Culture and Associate Professor at Nanzan University in Nagoya, Japan. His field is the sociology of religion, and his research has focussed on the social ethics of

Japanese new religious movements. He is currently involved in a study of Japanese and Asian values. His most recent book is *Prophets of Peace: Pacifism and Cultural Identity in Japan's New Religions*, University of Hawaii Press (1999).

*Thorleif Pettersson* (1940) studied Sociology of Religion at the University of Uppsala, Sweden. Since 1988 he has been Professor in Sociology of Religion on the Faculty of Theology at the University of Uppsala. His main research interests are comparative research on values and church sociology. He is currently involved in the European Values Study, the World Values Study and the International Project on Religious and Moral pluralism. He is the principal investigator of the Swedish EVS survey of 1990 and the 1995/1996 World Values Study survey. He is coordinator of the 1999 EVS for Sweden.

*Michael Procter* is Lecturer in Sociology at the University of Surrey, Guildford, England. He has specialized in the secondary data analysis of large data sets and has collaborated in a number of analyses of the European Values Surveys data. He is co-author of *Doing Secondary Analysis* (1988), contributed three chapters to *Researching Social Life* (1993), and has contributed to the *Journal for the Scientific Study of Religion*.

*Ole Riis* (1944) has been Associate Professor of Sociology at University of Århus (Denmark) since 1985, though he is temporarily teaching methodology at the University of Aalborg (Denmark). His long list of publications covers a wide range of topics, including a book on Danish values, *Danskernes Værdier* (1992, with Peter Gundelach). He is presently involved in an international survey project on Religious and Moral Pluralism (RAMP), a Nordic project on state churches vs religious pluralism, and the Danish project group studying the 1999 round of the European Value Study.